Filing & Winning Small Claims

FOR

DUMMIES®

A Wiley Brand

by Hon. Philip S. Straniere

FOR

DUMMIES®

A Wiley Brand

Filing & Winning Small Claims For Dummies®

Published by
John Wiley & Sons, Inc.
111 River St.
Hoboken, NJ 07030-5774
www.wiley.com

Copyright © 2013 by John Wiley & Sons, Inc., Indianapolis, Indiana

Published by John Wiley & Sons, Inc., Indianapolis, Indiana

Published simultaneously in Canada

For general information on our other products and services, please contact our Customer Care Department within the U.S. at 877-762-2974, outside the U.S. at 317-572-3993, or fax 317-572-4002.

For technical support, please visit www.wiley.com/techsupport.

Wiley also publishes its books in a variety of electronic formats and by print-on-demand. Not all content that is available in standard print versions of this book may appear or be packaged in all book formats. If you have purchased a version of this book that did not include media that is referenced by or accompanies a standard print version, you may request this media by visiting http://booksupport.wiley.com. For more information about Wiley products, visit us at www.wiley.com.

Library of Congress Control Number: 2013932109

ISBN 978-1-118-42444-5 (pbk); ISBN 978-1-118-46104-4 (ebk); ISBN 978-1-118-46101-3 (ebk); ISBN 978-1-118-46100-6 (ebk)

Manufactured in the United States of America

10 9 8 7 6 5 4 3 2 1

About the Author

Hon. Philip S. Straniere was elected to the New York City Civil Court in November 1996 from the Second Civil Court District on Staten Island, and was reelected in 2006. In 2004 he was named an Acting Justice of the New York State Supreme Court and Supervising Judge of Civil Court, Richmond County.

Straniere received his JD from New York University School of Law and his BA (Magna Cum Laude) and MA in history from Wagner College on Staten Island. Prior to going on the bench he was in private practice for more than 20 years.

He is currently an adjunct assistant professor at St. John's University, where he has taught undergraduate law for over 30 years. He also taught at St. John's University in the College of Business Administration before becoming a judge, and served as an administrative law judge for the New York City Board of Education Impartial Hearing Office, the Taxi and Limousine Commission, the Parking Violations Bureau, and the Environmental Control Board.

Known for using humor as well as references to popular culture in his decisions, Judge Straniere has been the subject of articles in the *New York Times* and *The Wall Street Journal*. In addition, his writing style has been the subject of an academic paper presented to the Mid-Atlantic Popular/ American Culture Association in 2011.

He is married to Jennifer and has three children — Gregory, Amanda, and Nicholas.

Dedication

This book is dedicated to all the court clerks across the United States who every day answer the same questions over and over in an effort to make litigants' encounters with the court system as easy as possible; to all attorneys who volunteer their time to serve as arbitrators and in other roles so that small claims courts can handle the volume of cases they deal with on a regular basis; and to all of the judges who are committed to ensuring that every litigant gets his or her day in court and who, after sitting in small claims court, will turn to colleagues, staff, family, and friends and say, "You won't believe the case I just heard; you can't make this stuff up."

Author's Acknowledgments

First I have to acknowledge my family. My wife, Jennifer, and my children, Gregory, Amanda, and Nicholas, who kept suggesting that I should write a book. Well, here it is. I was hoping it would be *101 Moose Jokes*, but I guess a book that helps people understand small claims court will be just as good (and humorous).

Next on the list are Maria Colonna Emanuel and Helene Donlan Sacco, my current and my original court attorneys. Helene graduated from the world of small claims court to become a Family Court Judge and, like Maria, quickly gave up trying to eliminate the references to popular culture, theatre, and sports from my decisions.

To my secretaries, Traci Batiancela and Collette Curry, who come to me after reading a decision and let me know when something doesn't make sense.

I also have to thank the gang I work with at 927 Castleton Avenue, Staten Island. They're all dedicated public servants who spend their days trying to help people navigate the legal system so that the process is less intimidating.

I should also mention my law student intern, Tara Pistilli, who, after spending a summer checking out every state's small claims law, has apparently decided to focus on patent law.

Also deserving mention are the individuals who have led the court system in New York during my time on the bench: Hon. Judith Kaye, Hon. Jonathan Lippman, Hon. Ann Pfau, Hon. Gail Prudenti, and my direct supervisor, Hon. Fern Fisher. Their commitment to making the legal process understandable to the general public, to simplifying forms, and to providing much-needed services to the unrepresented litigants who dominate my court has made New York a leader in ensuring that people, through the access to justice program, get both their day and their say in court.

Special mention has to be made of Joe Gebbia. Max Bialystock may be the "King of Broadway," but Joe is the "King of Small Claims Court" in New York City. He established a training program for judges and arbitrators, in addition to getting a manual published that serves as a handy reference to arbitrators in New York City small claims court.

I really have to thank the people at Wiley who, even though they work for a company named after a coyote who gets hit in the head with Acme Anvils on a regular basis, helped me navigate the *For Dummies* process to completion: Sharon Perkins, Erin Mooney, Tracy Brown Hamilton, and Kathleen Dobie. And thanks also to my technical editor, Kari Race.

Finally, I want to thank my agent, Bookends, and my friend Dan Marotta, who mentioned one day that he had a friend who was looking for someone to write a book on small claims court.

Publisher's Acknowledgments

We're proud of this book; please send us your comments at http://dummies.custhelp.com. For other comments, please contact our Customer Care Department within the U.S. at 877-762-2974, outside the U.S. at 317-572-3993, or fax 317-572-4002.

Some of the people who helped bring this book to market include the following:

Acquisitions, Editorial, and Media Development

Project Editor: Tracy Brown Hamilton

Acquisitions Editor: Erin Mooney

Assistant Editor: David Lutton

Editorial Program Coordinator: Joe Niesen

Technical Editor: Kari Race

Senior Editorial Manager: Jennifer Ehrlich

Editorial Manager: Carmen Krikorian

Editorial Assistant: Alexa Koschier

Art Coordinator: Alicia B. South

Cover Photos: © Ricky Corey / iStockphoto.com

Composition Services

Project Coordinator: Patrick Redmond

Layout and Graphics: Carrie A. Cesavice, Jennifer Creasey, Joyce Haughey

Proofreaders: Glenn L. McMullen, Dwight Ramsey

Indexer: Infodex Indexing Services, Inc.

Special Help: Sharon Perkins

Publishing and Editorial for Consumer Dummies

    Kathleen Nebenhaus, Vice President and Executive Publisher

    Kristin Ferguson-Wagstaffe, Product Development Director

    Ensley Eikenburg, Associate Publisher, Travel

    Kelly Regan, Editorial Director, Travel

Publishing for Technology Dummies

    Andy Cummings, Vice President and Publisher

Composition Services

    Debbie Stailey, Director of Composition Services

Contents at a Glance

Table of Contents

Introduction

. . . .

*I*f you're reading this book, it's a fair bet that you're interested in suing somebody — or that somebody has decided to sue you. If you're getting ready for your day in court, reading this book can dramatically increase your chances of winning by helping you prepare and avoid the pitfalls that derail so many small claims cases. Because I'm a judge, I approach your courtroom education from the other side of the bench, so I can tell you what you're likely to do wrong — after all, I see it every day.

Going to small claims court isn't like going to traffic court — you're going to need to be better prepared than you would to fight a $100 speeding ticket. But it's not rocket science, either. You don't have to be the cousin of a lawyer or a part-time brain surgeon to find out how to gather information, present it in a logical way, and avoid irritating the court so much that your case gets thrown out because the judge doesn't like you.

Be forewarned: I'm not giving you legal advice and I'm not guaranteeing that you'll win your case. In some cases, I may even convince you to resolve your dispute outside of the courts. I'm simply trying to point out common errors parties on both sides of the litigation process make that prevent them from presenting their case in the best possible light. The task is further complicated by the fact that each state has slightly different rules for their small claims court, so it's important that you check your local court and not just plunge ahead blindly like the proverbial bull in a china shop.

About This Book

This book will discuss everything you need to know about small claims court. Much of the information centers around the plaintiff — the person bringing the suit against someone else — but I also address issues that interest the defendant. Much of the information in this book applies to both parties.

You may be avoiding reading a book on this topic, even though you desperately need the information it contains, because you're afraid it's going to be

- ✔ Too dry and difficult to plow through in an afternoon
- ✔ Full of confusing jargon and information
- ✔ Boring beyond belief

I've tried to ensure that this book is none of these things, because I wouldn't want to read it if it were, either. The court system is sometimes dry and dull enough on its own; my job in this book is to make the information both easily accessible and easily understandable — as well as a bit funny where possible. And believe me, court is often quite funny, whether intentionally or unintentionally so.

Conventions Used in This Book

It's too cumbersome to use the term "he or she" all the time when talking about judges, defendants, and plaintiffs, so I alternate them with each chapter, using male pronouns in odd-numbered chapters and female pronouns in even-numbered chapters. Please note that throughout this book, the word *guy* is used in its most common meaning and refers to both men and women — sort of like *actor* in the movie industry.

New terms that may be unfamiliar to you are italicized the first time I use them; you can look them up in the glossary at the back of the book.

(Not So) Foolish Assumptions

I'm going out on a limb here and making some brazen assumptions about you. These are

- ✔ You're either suing someone or being sued in small claims court.
- ✔ You have already been to small claims court and want to know what you did wrong so you can do it right next time.
- ✔ You have a secret interest in becoming a judge and trying small claims court cases.

If none of these describe you, you're still more than welcome to read this book.

How This Book Is Organized

Books must be organized, or you'll never find the information you need. This one is well organized into sensible parts, because I'm a judge and have a logical mind.

Part I: Making Your Big Problem a Small Claim

Going to small claims court always involves an issue you consider a big problem, or you wouldn't go through all the trouble to do it. In this part, I help you determine whether your case belongs in small claims court in the first place. I also assist with the big decisions — such as how much money you'd like to get and whether you need a lawyer to help you get it — before you take the next step and file.

Part II: Getting Ready to Go to Court

Preparing to go to court can take a lot of prep work. If you don't have all the paperwork and information you need, or if you don't properly identify your opponent in court, you have no chance of winning. This part tells you what to do ahead of your court date.

Part III: Presenting Your Case in Court

Even if your notes and paperwork are in pristine order, you can blow your case by not presenting to the right person at the right time in the right way. In this part, I explain how to avoid making any missteps that will compromise your case.

Part IV: Dealing with Specific Problems

You may be hungry for more information about cases similar to yours. In this part, I describe some of the most common types of small claims cases and how to prepare specifically for them.

Part V: Handling Post-Trial Issues

When the verdict comes in, you may not like it. This part tells you what to do if you're not happy with the judge's decision. I also talk about what to do if you're ecstatic with the decision but the defendant has disappeared into the sunset without paying you a dime of what she owes.

Part VI: The Part of Tens

If you're into short sound bites, the Part of Tens chapters will appeal to you. They're short, pithy, and they address two of the most important aspects of small claims court: ways to increase your chances of winning and common mistakes to avoid.

Icons Used in This Book

Obviously, I think every word in the book is essential to someone, or I wouldn't include it. But some bits of information are more important than others, so I mark them with an icon that identifies them as something you should pay extra attention to.

The "Remember" icon sits next to information I hope stays in your head long enough for you to get to the courtroom and use it.

The "Tip" icon gives insider info it would take years to discover on your own. Because you probably don't have time to become a judge before your case goes to court, I give you the tips I've gleaned.

I'm only going to warn you if I think the information I'm giving is essential to not messing up your case.

Because law can be a little complex, I use it occasionally to point out particularly technical details.

Where to Go from Here

For Dummies books are designed to be modular, which means you don't have to read them cover-to-cover from the first page to the last . The information in each chapter is complete on its own, so if you're going to court in an hour and just want to know what to wear, turn to Chapter 11 where I explain how your appearance can affect your case. If you've get a few weeks to prepare, take the time to read through a chapter, digest what's in it, and then move on to the next, if you want. Or if you find the book so fascinating that you just can't put it down, feel free to read through the entire thing in one sitting.

Part I

Making Your Big Problem a Small Claim

getting started with **Small Claims**

For additional guidance understanding legalese, check out www.dummies.com/extras/filingandwinningsmallclaims.

In this part . . .

✔ Get to know the specific rules of small claims court, how the system works and how to navigate it, and the key ways in which small claims court differs from other courts.

✔ Gain insight from a practicing judge on what types of complaints are best suited to be resolved in small claims court, and what alternatives exist outside of the court system.

✔ Get ready to represent yourself in small claims court by knowing how to select, work with, and pay for a lawyer to consult with you on preparing your case, should you choose to work with one.

✔ Recognize the various classifications of cases, from contract breaches to personal injuries, and know which kind of case you are dealing with and what you hope to gain from your day in court.

✔ Understand how to arrive at and justify monetary amounts when requesting compensation from a defendant, and familiarize yourself with the monetary rules of the court to better your chances of getting what is fair.

✔ Check out `www.dummies.com/extras/filingand winningsmallclaims` online for free information on important things to do before filing for court.

Chapter 1

Understanding the Ins and Outs of Small Claims Court

Most people don't really want to court. It's stressful, it can be expensive, and it takes a big chunk of time out of what I assume for most of you is a busy enough schedule. Of course, there are exceptions: Lawyers go there because that's their job, and people who love drama — and create lots of it in their daily lives — may find going to court to get people to listen to them somewhat addicting.

If you're an average Joe or Jane, staying out of court probably seems like a better idea to you, until something happens that seems so unfair that you start considering going to court to get it resolved. If that happens, then this book can help you figure out the best way to go forward with the greatest shot of getting what you want out of small claims court.

In this chapter, I give you a quick overview of small claims court, why it exists, and a quick analysis of whether it's where you should be to resolve your problem. The information here gives you an overview of the kinds of topics covered in greater detail throughout the book.

Starting Down the Road to Small Claims Court

Why are you going, or considering going, to small claims court? Everyone has different reasons, but usually frustration, aggravation, and a sense of outrage at the way a business or personal transaction has turned out is the impetus.

If you could solve things in another way, you probably would. Many litigants say they end up in small claims court because the person they're having a problem with doesn't seem to be listening to them or responding to what's an important issue to them. Some of these situations may be better resolved outside of the court system through mediation or conciliation.

Let's say you threw a garden party in an effort to spiff up your social standing in your neighborhood — you know, tea, crumpets, watercress sandwiches, and the like. You decked yourself out in your white linen suit. You were strolling your garden, greeting neighbors, when the dog next door, Tiny, greeted you by putting his muddy paws on your suit and licking your face.

Although everyone had a good laugh at your expense and the incident won first prize in a funniest video contest, your neighbor refused your request that he pay for the dry cleaning bill for your suit. Not only did he refuse, but he insists you pay the veterinarian's bill because his dog is allergic to linen.

Rather than challenge your neighbor to a duel, you decide to take a more civilized approach and call your lawyer, who tells you that the legal fees involved would be more than any money you may recover. You call several other lawyers and get the same response.

Well, don't despair. Throw your shoulders back, lift your head up high, and put a smile on your face. There is hope. You have a remedy tailor-made (pardon the expression) that suits situations like yours. It's called small claims court.

Small claims court is part of the court system available in every state. It's a court where you don't need a lawyer, where the rules of evidence are not strictly applied, and where the goal is to obtain "substantial justice" for the parties in an expeditious manner. Substantial justice is explained in Chapter 2.

But don't run out and file just yet. Because there are 51 different small claims courts in the United States — the 50 states and the District of Columbia — it's important that you check with your local court system before you start your lawsuit, because not every state permits the same kind of case to be brought in small claims court.

Doing It Without a Net — Or a Lawyer

A book such as this one is very handy to the average citizen who has not passed the bar, because small claims court is a court where lawyers are not only not required but in some places actually prohibited. Yes, you read that correctly: Some courts actually prohibit lawyers in small claims court, which makes it a unique place ripe for human error.

Did you ever hear the saying, "A person who represents himself has a fool for an attorney?" Or is it, "A person who represents himself has a fool for a client?" The point is that someone going to court without legal representation is the sort of thing you've always heard is a really bad idea. The people who get most upset about self-representation are called lawyers or attorneys or counselors.

Small claims courts operate on the assumption that you don't need a lawyer in order to have your case presented easily and decided fairly. Because lawyers have chosen the law as a profession, they generally don't like programs where legal services are available to just anyone — and at no cost or very little. You have a job, right? And you wouldn't be happy if someone found a method of doing your job without having to pay you for it, so too lawyers are often skeptical of ideas that reduce potential income sources.

Well, if lawyers control state legislatures — which may actually be a myth — how did we end up with small claims courts all over the country? It's really very simple. It's called *small* claims court for a reason. The amount of money you can sue for is limited; In fact, in most places, it's downright puny. Each state has set a limit as to what is the most money you can sue for in small claims court.

The cost of using a lawyer to represent you on your small claims court case in all likelihood would exceed the amount of money you potentially can recover, making it really hard to hire counsel. This makes the lawyers feel much better about letting you represent yourself.

Don't think that my intent here is to bash lawyers. Small claims court can't function without the thousands of attorneys who volunteer their time to serve as arbitrators in small claims courts throughout the United States. The court system couldn't handle all of the cases brought in small claims court each year in a timely manner if every lawsuit had to be heard by a judge. It would be remiss of me not to recognize the contribution of members of the bar in every jurisdiction who help make the American court system function.

That being the case, if at times throughout this book, it seems as if I'm throwing lawyers under the bus, I ask forgiveness and I promise not to shift into reverse after they're on the ground. To find out more about how lawyers fit into the small claims court system, check out Chapter 3.

To broadcast or not to broadcast? That is the question

For those of you who are not currently starring on your own reality show, small claims court may be you opportunity to obtain your 15 minutes of fame. The producers of courtroom television shows and their offspring — both legitimate and illegitimate — often send staff members to small claims court to sift through the filings and identify potential cases to be heard before all of America on one of these television programs.

If the staff members think the case you filed with the small claims court clerk sounds interesting, the producers send you and your opponent a letter asking if you want to have your dispute heard on television. If you both agree to do this, you sign a contract with the television show producers and the case is decided under the rules established by the production company and not in your local small claims court. The production company's rules determine how the case will proceed and whether you have any recourse after the television judge decides the case in the event you're dissatisfied.

The advantage of having your case heard on television is that everyone is a winner in that they're compensated by the producers. If you're bringing the case and you win, the producers pay you the amount of the judgment awarded by the television judge. The person you're suing doesn't lay out a cent. That person is also paid a fee for agreeing to have the case heard on television and appearing on the program. If you don't prove your case, and the television judge rules against you, both you and the person you are suing are compensated by the production company.

You may be thinking, fame and/or fortune, what's the downside? Well, as I mention, the entire proceeding is subject to the terms of the contract you sign with the producers. This means you may be sacrificing any rights you would have under the laws of the state in which you live and agreeing to be bound by the rules of the television show. Should there be a dispute between you and the producers, you may be subjecting yourself to the law of a different state, such as the state where the television show is filmed. You may be limiting your monetary compensation should the show not be broadcast on television for any reason. You'll also be subject to the editing discretion of the production company. This means you can end up looking like the complete incompetent your mother-in-law always thought you were.

If you and your opponent both decide that television is me, you can close this book and save yourself the trouble of reading it, because nothing that happens on television is even remotely like going to real court.

Understanding Why Small Claims Court Rules Seem So Confusing

Although you may not need a lawyer to use small claims court, you may need one to ferret out your state's various rules and regulations.

The information you need about the procedures of small claims court are contained in your state's statutes. You may not be able to find it conveniently located in just one section of your state's law — you may have to skip around to various statutes to figure out what court to file in, what procedures to follow, and what rules of evidence are used in small claims court. Sometimes the rules may also be contained in some local regulation as well as in the state law.

Even after you find the information, understanding the statutes may require a lawyer or at least a reference to a legal dictionary, as many states still use terms that have been applied since colonial times from *common law* rather than plain language to describe the process and your rights.

Check whether your court system or the state bar association has some user-friendly pamphlets or websites that explain how small claims court operates in your area.

Getting the go signal for small claims court

Because every state is different, I can only generalize about your state's rules about small claims court. But generally, small claims court maybe an option for you if you meet three criteria:

✔ You're looking for a limited amount of money.

✔ The transaction arose locally rather than across county or state lines.

✔ The potential defendant is a readily identifiable individual or business.

See Chapter 2 for all the details about determining whether you belong in small claims court, or whether just knocking on your neighbor's door and apologizing for all the scenes you caused in the last month may be more appropriate.

Being rejected by the small claims system

Sometimes it's evident from the start that you and small claims court aren't a match made in heaven. For example, you don't belong in small claims court if:

✔ You want a remedy or result other than money, such as forcing someone to meet the terms of a contract or stopping your neighbor from doing something that really annoys you.

✔ You're looking to win enough money from the defendant to retire to a tropical paradise and never have to handle money again in your life.

✔ You want to sue so many people that you need a sports arena to seat them all and interpreters from every member nation of the UN.

Preparing for Your Big Day

One thing that becomes apparent as you read this book, which I'm assuming that you find it so informative and entertaining that you read it from cover to cover and give as a holiday gift to all your friends and some of your enemies, is that preparation is the key to success.

Preparation for small claims court means:

- Knowing what kind of claim you have. Do you have a contract claim, property damage claim, or something else? (Chapter 4 can help you figure it out.)

- Figuring out how much money to seek and properly classifying your damage claim. (Chapter 5 explains money matters.)

- Determining who you're planning to sue: Is it a person or a business? If the defendant is a business, you need to know whether it's a sole proprietorship, a partnership, or a corporation. Chapter 6 tells you how to ferret out this information.

- Discovering the procedures used in your local court. (The clerk has all the answers; find out how to work with the clerk in Chapter 7.)

- Planning what you intend to do when you get to court. (Chapter 11 can help you avoid making a fool of yourself in court.)

- Deciding how to present your case. (Turn to Chapter 12 for tips on this.)

Finding specifics on your type of case

Because small claims cases tend to fit into certain general categories, I've picked out some of the more typical situations I've seen in court to give a more detailed treatment as to what to expect and how to better prepare your case.

Chapter 16 talks about contract cases that involve where you live; landlord and condominium disputes both fit into this category.

If you're doing battle with a business, turn to Chapter 17 for details on what this entails. Chapters 18 and 19 discuss all the things that go wrong in daily living, such as arguments associated with weddings in Chapter 18 and irritating situations with the neighbors in Chapter 19. If you're struggling with issues rising from Internet transactions, Chapter 20 can help you succeed in court.

Showing Up in Court

Woody Allen once said something to the effect that 80 percent of success is just showing up. That may be good in some situations, but in small claims court, just showing up will be a disaster for you — although not showing up is worse.

Even if you're prepared for your case, you still have to be prepared for court. This means being dressed for the occasion and treating it as an important event. You also have to be prepared to deal with the clerks of the court, the courtroom staff, your opponent, and the judge.

A confrontational attitude with everyone you meet along the way in your quest for justice is a good way to undo all of the preparation you did for your day in court. Let Chapters 11 and 14 help you win your case by not losing your case through your own incorrect actions.

Living Through the Aftermath

One thing that people who aren't familiar with the legal process discover quickly is that there is a difference between winning a case and collecting your money. I hope this book sets you on the path to victory. But even if you win your case, you still have to figure out how to collect a money judgment in your favor.

Historical aspects of small claims court

Because I have a master's degree in American history, I'm forced to place some historical information in this book. Lots of significant events occurred 100 years ago in 1912. The *Titanic* sank. Fenway Park opened in Boston. Teddy Roosevelt and William Howard Taft split the Republican vote, leading to the election of Woodrow Wilson. And more germane to this book, some sources say that the first small claims court was started in Kansas.

Before long it became apparent that you didn't have to be in Kansas anymore to find a small claims court, as every state created one for its citizens. Some other sources have concluded that the first small claims court started in Cleveland, Ohio, in 1913. It really doesn't matter for the purposes of this book, but by going with 1912 and Kansas, I get to refer to some events that just about everyone knows about and to make a reference to *The Wizard of Oz* that just doesn't work with 1913 and Cleveland.

Deciding to settle your case for less than you want in order to insure prompt payment is an option to explore. Chapter 21 helps you figure out how to get what you have coming to you. It also explains options for what you can do if you're not paid and who can help you enforce your judgment using the legal process.

In every small claims trial, someone wins and someone loses. What to do if you're not satisfied with the court's determination is something to think about almost before you start your case. Chapter 22 helps you make decisions about what to do if the verdict doesn't go your way. It helps you prepare for the possibility of losing and tells you how to proceed to either appeal a decision or to respond to an appeal.

Chapter 2

Deciding if Your Case Belongs in Small Claims Court

*N*ot every case is suitable for small claims court. Before you begin your quest for justice, you need to determine whether the facts and circumstances of your particular situation are right for a civil suit.

In this chapter, I look at the factors that help you decide whether you have a small claims case, including the limitations of small claims court. I also help you decide what you hope to achieve by going to small claims court, whether it be monetary compensation or some other form of satisfaction.

Why Small Claims and Not Regular Court

Many cases that end up in court do not, in my opinion, really belong there. But some disputes truly are best resolved in the small claims court system. After you decide you have a case worth suing over (look to the next section for help making that decision), small claims court may seem like a viable option because it's less intimidating than regular court. Small claims courts are more user-friendly, for the following reasons:

> ✔ **You aren't required to have a lawyer,** which saves money but also allows you to present the facts in the way that you choose. This isn't always the best option for winning your case, however.

✔ **Filing fees are less**, so not only do you save on lawyer's fees, but you also pay less in court fees.

✔ **The rules of evidence and procedure tend to be relaxed**, so you don't feel like you have to memorize a year's worth of current legal television show scripts just to walk through the doors.

✔ **Cases move quickly and are often tried at night or, in some states, on weekends.** The expanded hours make small claims court appealing if you still have a regular life to live while bringing your lawsuit.

Evaluating Your Decision to Go to Court

One of the first things to do before heading for the courthouse is to decide whether you really belong there: Do you really have a legal problem that requires you to go to court? You may have very valid reasons to go to court to resolve a dispute, but the decision to take a case to court should not be made lightly.

Not everything that happens in your life results in harm that a court of law can fix, so the first consideration really is whether there is a better way to resolve your issue, including just letting it go.

Judging from some of the lawsuits you read about in the news or see on popular court programs like *The People's Court* and *Judge Judy,* it's obvious many people feel justified in bringing all kinds of problems to the courts to fix. You see claims being brought for things most people would assume are part of the hassles of everyday living rather than an excuse to go to court.

For example, you have, after massive effort and six years in school, graduated from your local college with a degree in accounting. In spite of your efforts, you can't get a job anywhere.

It can't be because you have shown up late for every interview, have typos in your resume, or arrive to appointments with conservative companies sporting a purple Mohawk and wearing ripped clothing that shows off your plentiful tattoos. It must be the fault of the college for not educating you properly. You decide to sue the college for "negligent education."

The clerk of the court, after nearly passing out from laughing at the ridiculousness of your claim, cannot reject the papers just because no one ever brought such a suit before. Only a court can decide whether you have a viable claim. In fact, some courts may even let the case proceed to a full trial, preferring to err on the side of giving you your day in court rather than closing the courthouse door in your face.

Potential backlashes of small claims suits

Suing isn't always the most prudent action. It may result in outcomes that don't better your situation, and in fact make it much worse. For example, say you're looking for a new job and the prospective employer does a background check, which shows that you sued several prior employers for discrimination or filed wages claims against them. A background check may show that you have filed a number of suits against neighbors and merchants in the community. The prospective employer may conclude that, even though you're qualified on paper, you have difficulty getting along with people and are a lawsuit waiting to happen.

Or, say you're looking for a new apartment and the prospective landlord discovers that not only have you been evicted from your last three apartments for failing to pay rent, but you then sued the landlord in small claims court for the return of your security deposit. Would you blame the new landlord for not wanting to have you as a tenant?

Just because you can, doesn't mean you should. In small claims court, you don't need a lawyer to represent you. And because you, the potential plaintiff of a small claims case, are not bound to the same ethical prohibitions as a lawyer, you can in theory bring any case you want. (In "regular" court, ethical rules require lawyers only to bring lawsuits that they reasonably believe have a legal basis.).

Generally speaking, the clerk of the court can't look at your papers and proclaim you a blithering idiot and refuse to accept the filing, even though she may want to. Only a judge has the ability to do that. She can, however, refuse to file if you've screwed up the paperwork in some way.

So you have to decide whether you have a valid argument that can be satisfactorily settled in court.

Consider these factors before gathering up your legal-size notepad and studying the latest episodes of all the current law shows:

- ✔ **Who are you going to sue?** Are you planning to sue a relative, your next-door neighbor, or a merchant you've dealt with for years? If you bring a lawsuit against someone you know, you must be willing to forgo any further relationship with them. Maybe you should just tell them what the problem is and hope you can work it out. Or contact a third party such as a mediation service to see if the problem can be resolved in a friendly way.

- ✔ **Do you have proof to support what you're saying?** Having something happen to you is a completely different issue from being able to prove it happened, that the defendant did it, and that you suffered some harm. Sometimes discretion is a better part of valor, and treating the incident as a life lesson rather than a lawsuit is the best course.

✔ **What do you really want the outcome to be?** Many small claims cases are brought because people don't communicate. One person feels that the other person did something wrong and either won't take responsibility for her action or won't acknowledge causing bad feelings. In these cases, perhaps some counseling service makes more sense than coming to court. Judges aren't therapists.

✔ **Do you really want to air your dirty linen in public?** Your case will be brought in front of other people, many of whom may be your neighbors and friends. Sometimes local newspapers run stories about interesting small claims cases. Consider whether your case is something you want people to read about in the paper. On the other hand, if you're a businessperson, do you want people to know either that you sue or refuse to settle disputes with customers?

Keep in mind that a record will be made by the court for posterity. In some states, the information is readily available online. Do you work someplace or are you applying for a job where a background check is going to bring out the fact that you are a litigious person? Such information may adversely affect your position.

✔ **Are you willing to commit the time and money necessary to bring the suit?** You may have to take time off from work to file the claim with the court or to try the case if there are no night or weekend sessions in your area. You may have to ask witnesses to do the same, and they may be willing to do so only if you pay them for their time.

Keep It Civil: Civil Suits versus Criminal Cases

The word *civil* has a specific meaning in the law. It's not used in the context of civil versus uncivil behavior. In a legal sense, *civil* refers to a category of law different from *criminal* litigation, which differ in the following ways:

✔ **Civil litigation refers to disputes between individuals and/or businesses where a party is seeking money damages or some other relief from the court.** It differs from criminal litigation where society, not the individual harmed, brings the suit and punishes the wrongdoer.

✔ **Civil litigation doesn't seek to put the other person in prison or subject them to a fine.** As much as you may like to send someone who's harmed you to jail, you can't achieve that goal in civil court. Only courts established to enforce criminal law have that power. With civil litigation, justice comes in the form of getting money from the person who wronged you.

✔ **Civil litigation is brought to court by the injured party.** A criminal case is brought to court by the district attorney or county prosecutor, not the person harmed.

In the next section, I look at the factors that determine whether you have a case worth pursuing.

Knowing what a civil suit covers

Although you can bring any case you want to the court, there's no point in wasting time filing a civil suit that the judge will likely throw out. Civil suits, like those handled by small claims courts, cover only specific problems and can only be filed if you're limiting the amount of money you want to recover. In civil court, you can only sue for amounts set by the state and no more, no matter what your actual damages were.

Civil litigation covers many of the disagreements that arise between people and includes:

✔ **Breach of contract claims,** which are acts where the other person failed to live up to the terms of a legal agreement.

✔ **Intentionally wrongful acts, called intentional torts.** *Intentional torts* are wrongful acts done deliberately to cause harm, such as assault, trespassing, and defamation.

✔ **Negligence actions** are things done deliberately that were not intended to cause harm but still did. Car accidents, repairs that weren't done properly, or a tree branch falling on your house from your neighbor's tree all fit into this category.

Examples of the difference between an intentional tort and negligence can make the difference clearer:

✔ **Negligence:** You get in your car to go to your local fast food chain for a snack because your goal is consume enough calories to qualify for your local sumo wrestling team. You're driving along and are in an accident when someone steps out from the curb in front of you. In this case, you intended the act, driving your car, but you didn't intend to cause any harm because you didn't purposefully want to run someone over.

✔ **Intentional tort:** In the same situation, however, you see your archenemy — the person who makes your life miserable — standing on the sidewalk with her back to you. You decide to take advantage of the situation and drive on the sidewalk intending to run your nemesis over. In this case you intended the act — driving— and intended the harm — running her over.

Civil suits and criminal liability aren't mutually exclusive. In some cases, you may want to file both a civil lawsuit to recover money damages and a separate and distinct criminal complaint with the authorities. If your case has merit, it would be pursued in both civil and criminal court, with you bringing the civil case and the district attorney or county prosecutor pursuing the criminal case on behalf of society.

For example, I go to a baseball game in a New England city known for its beans and having a tea party 200 years ago. I'm decked out in the pinstriped colors of the opposing team, which has in fact won 27 world titles. I make sure I sit in the cheap seats, where the price of the tickets is less than the cost of the beer. I then proceed to yell at the top of my voice my opinion of the parentage of all the players on the home team as well as their general lack of playing skills.

After I am released from the emergency room at the nearest hospital, I want to sue the perpetrators of my injuries in a civil court for money damage. I also ask the local authorities to arrest those individuals and prosecute them criminally for the attack.

In this example, my suit for money damages would be a case I can pursue in a civil court, such as small claims court. The criminal prosecution would not be in small claims court.

Knowing what is not a civil suit

The same regulations that make small claims court appealing for many people also limit the kind of cases you can bring there. There's a long list of cases that can't be heard in small claims courts, including the following:

- ✔ Adoptions
- ✔ Enforcement of trust agreements
- ✔ Matrimonial actions
- ✔ Mortgage foreclosures
- ✔ Name change applications
- ✔ Pension problems
- ✔ Probating of wills
- ✔ Support and custody litigation
- ✔ Union disputes

Almost all these types of civil dispute require special expertise of the judge and the court personnel. Most suits of these types also involve complex issues beyond the monetary aspect of the case.

It's not uncommon for a former spouse to bring a small claims action to collect money owed under a divorce decree or property settlement agreement. And even though technically the case may fall within the monetary range of small claims court jurisdiction and is based on a contract — the property settlement agreement — the better place to handle the matter is the court where the divorce or property settlement agreement was first dealt with.

In fact, many divorce decrees and settlement agreements limit the courts where disputes can be brought, and small claims court is generally not on that list. Invariably, in marital cases, the issues go beyond the money owed. Visitation rights or other side issues are often triggering the non-payment of support.

Understanding the laws of your state

The rules that stipulate what types of cases can be brought in small claims court differ from state to state. The legislature of each state decides what type of case may be tried.

The legislature of each state determines what types of cases are tried in every type of court, including small claims courts. Because of this, what can be done in small claims court in your state may not be the same as in a neighboring state. This can be frustrating if you live near a border and spend time in both states. Your case may be allowed in the state you live in but not in the neighboring state where the damage actually occurred.

Small claims courts have certain similarities in every state, but just because you saw a case like yours on a popular legal television show doesn't mean you'll be able to bring a similar case in your small claims court. Take the following steps to find out if you have a case in your state:

- ✔ Check out the small claims court limitations for your state.

- ✔ Write down a concise statement of why you're thinking of going to court. What's the basic problem you want solved? What do you want the court to do?

- ✔ Contact the clerk of the small claims court in your area and ask if your case fits your state's criteria.

  Giving the clerk an inaccurate description of your case is the first step on the road to disaster.

Even though your case may fit into the rules for bringing a case in small claims court, you still may not want to bring your lawsuit there; another court may be better able to handle your issue.

Limiting your options: Subject matter jurisdiction

The legal term for the kinds of cases that can be tried in small claims court is _subject matter jurisdiction._ This wordy term is really simple to understand if you break it down:

- ✔ The word _jurisdiction_ generally means _power_ or _authority._
- ✔ _Subject matter_ means just what it sounds like — it's what a case is about.
- ✔ _Subject matter jurisdiction,_ then, means that the court has the power or authority to hear a particular kind of case.

The legislature of each state establishes the subject matter jurisdiction of all courts in that particular state. Courts such as small claims court are called courts of _special_ or _limited_ jurisdiction.

Because they have limited jurisdiction, small claims courts are restricted to hearing lawsuits that fit into the category of cases the legislature gave that court. A court that can hear all cases is often referred to as a court of _general_ or _original_ jurisdiction.

The goal of substantial justice

One of the goals of your suit is to achieve justice for yourself. Most people are familiar with the statue of Lady Justice standing blindfolded with scales in her hand. _Substantial justice_ is the idea that Lady Justice may be peeking out of the blindfold just to make sure the scale is even. It's actually a benefit to both plaintiffs and defendants who represent themselves in court.

Just about every state law creating small claims court states that the purpose of the court is to provide "substantial justice" to the litigants. You may be asking yourself _substantial_ as opposed to what, _insubstantial?_ Not exactly.

Substantial justice in small claims court means:

- ✔ The judge or person hearing the case is not bound to follow the strict rules of procedure and evidence.

    ✔ The judge can ignore certain defects in a party's proof so as to reach a just result.

    ✔ The judge is not locked into formal pleading and proof requirements expected in other parts of the court.

In other words, certain rules may be bent so as to do justice in a particular situation. Remember, I said bent, not broken.

The fact that the rules of small claims courts aren't as rigid as in other courts doesn't excuse either you or your opponent from having at least some semblance of a claim or defense. It means that if something wasn't presented according to the rules of evidence, a judge can still consider the material in making a decision.

All too frequently a plaintiff comes in, claiming the defendant home improvement contractor didn't install the new kitchen properly. I ask, "Assuming what you're telling me is correct, what are your damages; that is, what will it cost to fix the problem?"

The usual response is "I have pictures" and "Isn't that what you do, judge?" To which I say, "If I knew what it cost to install kitchens, I'd be doing that for a living and making some real money instead of waiting 13 years for the legislature to raise my pay." In other words, the fact that you didn't realize that as the plaintiff you have to prove your case is something the judge can't magically fix — no judge can consider evidence that doesn't exist.

Small claims court is designed to insure that the *substantive law* — that is, the legal rights of the parties — isn't lost by following strictly procedural rules.

Take another example: Say you're suing your landlord to get back your security deposit on the apartment you vacated six months ago. You can't find an original signed copy of the lease or a copy of a receipt, but you have an unsigned photocopy of the lease and a bank statement showing the withdrawal of cash on the same date as the lease and in the same amount as the security deposit. If the strict rules of evidence were applied, your case may have to dismissed because you lack all original documents. But under the rule of substantial justice, the judge can accept the evidence you offer as adequate proof and can rule in your favor even if the defendant denied everything.

Law versus Equity Compensation

When you sue someone, you're looking for one of two things: monetary compensation or some other result. If you're suing a mechanic who took your money and didn't fix your car, for example, you may want your car fixed and not your money back, or you may want the money you paid returned so you can go to someone else for the repairs. Before you go to small claims court, you need to determine what it is you want the court to do for you.

The two classes of cases are both based on English common law:

- ✔ **Law** or **legal cases** are generally settled for money.
- ✔ **Equity cases** involve some other type of relief — a repair made or damaged property replaced, for example.

Generally speaking, small claims cases are about money and not other types of relief.

Years ago, you had to go to one court for legal claims and another court for equitable relief. Each had different rules of practice. If you brought your case in the wrong court, for instance seeking equitable relief in a law court, your case would be dismissed. For the most part, that's no longer the situation. Almost all courts grant both legal and equitable relief, and you can ask for both types of relief in the same lawsuit.

When it's all about the money: Law cases

Money can't buy happiness, but it certainly helps in some cases. In most situations, small claims court cases are brought for money, not other relief. If you want justice in the form of cold, hard cash, and you're willing to stick to the limits the courts allow, small claims court is probably a good place to be: If you're injured in an accident, the court gives you money; if you're damaged because of a breach of contract, the court gives you money; if you suffer discrimination, the court gives you money. Are you sensing the trend here?

Because there's a limit on the amount of money you can sue for in small claims court, one of the things you have to consider is how much money you plan to seek from the defendant.

The amount you can sue for is called the *monetary jurisdiction of the court.* (You've probably noticed that the word "jurisdiction" shows up frequently in the legal world.) The *monetary jurisdiction* is the maximum amount that can be sued for in small claims court. As this is a limit set by the legislature of each individual state, check with the clerk of the court in your area to determine the maximum amount you can seek. Suing for less than the limit is rarely a problem, but suing for more can cause you some grief.

States have been raising the monetary limit of small claims in recent years, so checking with your local clerk of the court is important. A case you couldn't bring in small claims court a few years ago because you were suing for too much money may now be allowed.

Currently, most states set $5,000 as the maximum amount you can sue for. The state with the highest monetary jurisdiction is Tennessee where, in some counties, you can sue for as much as $25,000. In other Tennessee counties, the maximum suit amount is $15,000.

Ironically, the state with the lowest monetary jurisdiction is Tennessee's neighbor, Kentucky. Kentucky has a $1,500 limit. Other states also have a limit, which varies by county or by the nature of the claim.

When money isn't everything: Equity cases

Believe it or not, sometimes you don't want money as a remedy. Shocking, I know. But hard as it is to believe, money doesn't solve every problem. Equity courts developed in England to enforce claims in which money isn't an adequate remedy.

Types of equity claims and examples of each are explained in the following list:

- ✔ **Specific performance:** Historically, specific performance is used in cases where the subject matter of the lawsuit is something unique such as real estate, antiques, art work, heirlooms, collectibles, and the like where you want the item itself and not the dollar value. If you want to compel someone to abide by the terms of a contract to transfer ownership of land or personal property to you, you would sue for specific performance.

- ✔ **Injunction:** You use an injunction to make someone stop doing something. Injunctions often involve neighbors: If your neighbor is creating a nuisance by using her land in a manner that causes flooding or other damage to your land, you would seek an injunction to make her stop. Likewise, you may seek an injunction to stop your neighbor from trimming your tree or prevent her son's band from practicing at 3 a.m.

- ✔ **Replevin:** If you want personal property returned to you by the defendant, you use replevin as a basis for your lawsuit. Replevin claims are one of the few types of equity cases heard in small claims court. Some states allow a direct replevin action permitting the plaintiff to sue just to get the property returned and not ask for money damages.

  Most states don't permit direct replevin actions. But they will let you sue the defendant for the cost of the personal property being held and not for the return of the item.

Replevin cases often result in countersuits, with the defendant alleging that she hasn't returned the property because you owe her money. A small claims court in this situation may rule that after you pay all or part of the bill the defendant must return the property. The replevin would be granted only as a part of or as a condition of the money damage claim.

Say you loan your neighbor your lawn mower and, in spite of numerous requests, she never returns it. All you want is your lawn mower back. If your state permits direct replevin actions, you can sue to get it back. If your state doesn't allow direct replevin actions, you would have to sue in small claims court for the value of the lawn mower on the date of loss.

Or say you sue your wedding photographer because she never delivered your wedding album as agreed. You want your pictures. You can either sue for the album — a replevin action — or sue to get your money back — a money damage claim. The photographer can file a counterclaim saying she didn't deliver the album because you didn't make the final payment. If that is correct, the court would order you to make the final payment and order the photographer to deliver the album after receiving the payment.

Generally speaking, small claims courts don't grant equitable relief. There are a few exceptions, so if you do have an equitable claim for specific performance or for an injunction, check with the clerk of the court to make sure you can bring such an action in small claims court.

When Small Claims Court Is Not For You

Not all cases are appropriate for small claims court. In some situations, what you hope to gain or who you're trying to sue makes it unlikely that a judge will hear your case in small claims court.

When you want too much money

If you want more money from the defendant than your state regulations allow, you have several options open to you. One that isn't generally available is splitting your claim into smaller amounts so as to fit the monetary jurisdiction of the court.

Logs, bananas, and infinities can be split, but not small claims court cases, although there are exceptions and ways to get around this rule in some cases.

Bringing your case to regular court

The first option if you're over the money limit is to bring your case in the regular civil part of your local court.

This requires that you bring a lawsuit, which is subject to the normal civil procedure rules as well as the rules of evidence. This may seem more complicated, but it really isn't. Most courts now have procedures that allow you to represent yourself in regular civil actions.

The explosion of consumer debt collection litigation, where defendants often are not represented due to a lack of money to pay a lawyer, has triggered courts to provide more resources to unrepresented defendants. Also, as more and more people are unable or unwilling to pay for legal representation, many court systems have either established or expanded the advisory services provided for unrepresented litigants in civil matters. The court systems realize that if you can't get a lawyer for a small claims court suit, usually a $5,000 claim, raising the amount of the claim to $6,000 won't magically attract a lawyer to your case or help you find the money to pay for one.

Your local court may call representing yourself in civil court a *pro se* or a *self-represented part*. This just means that one of the parties — either the plaintiff or the defendant — doesn't have legal counsel. In fact, more and more cases have both sides without counsel. These cases are often heard in the self-represented part of the civil court.

You cannot be barred from bringing a lawsuit just because you don't have a lawyer. Every individual has the right to represent herself if she so chooses. The difference between civil courts and small claims court is that small claims procedures are not as strict, the filing fees are generally less, and the cases tend to move faster.

In many courts, such as the Civil Court of the City of New York, attorneys employed by the court system are assigned to the courthouse at a Help Center. These attorneys can't give legal advice, but they can help explain court procedures and legal terminology.

If your court system has a help service available, it can't hurt to go there first with any questions you have even before you file your suit. Taking advantage of available resources before you sue is the legal equivalent of the sign in my 8th grade wood shop class — "measure twice, saw once." Being prepared before you go to court can save you time and possible problems down the road.

Reducing your claims amount

If your case is worth more than you're allowed to sue for, you can bring a small claims action but limit your claim to the monetary jurisdiction of the court. That is, you voluntarily reduce your claim to the dollar limit of the small claims court.

Sticking to small claims court isn't always smart

As a judge, sometimes I'm amazed at how many people are willing to walk away from their cases and abandon the chance for getting all the money they deserve from the defendant simply because they want to file in small claims court and only small claims court. I'm always puzzled by the number of people who abandon claims for monies owed in excess of the $5,000 jurisdictional amount either because they think that bringing a regular civil case is too complicated or simply because they find the hours of small claims court, which are usually at night, more convenient.

It really isn't all that difficult to sue in the regular civil courts, especially if the alternative is losing a large chunk of your hard-earned money. Even when I offer plaintiffs the opportunity to re-file the case so that they can try and collect all the money due to them, most of these litigants decline the offer and elect to remain in small claims court, even if it means collecting less money.

Say you claim you're owed $6,000 and can prove you're owed that amount. If the monetary jurisdiction of the court is $5,000, you can only recover $5,000 — not the full amount of your claim. By using the simplified procedure of the small claims court rather than the regular civil court, you forfeit the right to collect any money due to you beyond the monetary jurisdiction of the small claims court. So, you voluntarily wave goodbye to $1,000 in the strong hope of being awarded $5,000.

Check with the clerk of the court as to what the rules are in your state. In some small claims courts, you aren't allowed to file the case if you're claiming more than the monetary jurisdiction is owed. You'll be required to proceed in regular civil court.

Splitting your claim into smaller amounts

Although it may seem like a good way to collect everything you deserve, you can't circumvent the monetary limits of small claims court by splitting your claim into two cases.

If all of the money you're suing for comes from the same contract or event, the claim cannot be split solely to qualify for the small claims court monetary jurisdiction.

For example, a house painter is owed $6,000 from a homeowner to fulfill a contract. In a state where the small claims limit is $5,000, the painter cannot bring two separate lawsuits for $3,000, alleging that there was one contract for $3,000 to paint the first floor of the house and a second contract for $3,000 to paint the second floor.

Similarly, most courts won't let a landlord split a claim for rent due from a tenant by claiming that each month's rent is a separate cause of action. If the total amount due exceeds the monetary jurisdiction at the time you file your case, the claim cannot be split so as to meet the small claims criterion.

Say your tenant hasn't paid any rent this year. If you wait until April to sue for rent for January, February, and March, when the unpaid rent totals $6,000, the small claims court wouldn't be able to hear the case because your claim exceeds the monetary jurisdiction of $5,000. So, unless you're willing to limit your recovery to $5,000, you can't file in small claims court. You can't file three separate $2,000 claims in April to be able to stay in small claims court.

In some cases, you can work around this rule. If the defendant owes rent of $2,000 for January, as the landlord, you can sue in February, then bring a separate suit when February's rent isn't paid, and a third suit when March's rent is delinquent. So you file three separate $2,000 claims and they're all within the court's monetary jurisdiction. In this example, you're only looking for the money owed and not to evict the tenant — which may be the better course of action if your tenant isn't paying any rent.

Another hypothetical scenario involves you suing the defendant for damages from a car accident. The repairs cost $4,500 and a rental car for the period yours was in the shop was $750. You can't bring two separate claims — one for the repair and a second one for the car rental — because both claims arose from the same accident. To keep your case in small claims court, you would have to sue for the $5,000 limit and forfeit the additional $250 you spent.

If you realize that you have more damages than the court limit, you can always ask to have your case discontinued *without prejudice* so you can start over in the regular civil part. In some courts, you can ask the judge to transfer the case to the regular civil part so you won't have to re-serve the defendant with the complaint. But you may have to pay a new filing fee. If you do this, make sure the transfer is without prejudice because if it is *with prejudice,* your case is over.

When you want to sue the government

As a general rule, an individual can't sue the government. Doesn't sound very democratic, does it? That's because it's not. The idea that you can't sue the government is part of the English common law that came across the ocean with the first soon-to-be Americans.

Granting government bodies sovereign immunity

English common law developed the idea of *sovereign immunity,* the concept that the king or queen can do no wrong. Which is why, as the saying goes, "It's great to be king" — or queen, as the case may be. For its own benefit, every level of government in the United States has decided it has equal rights to royalty as far as being sued goes.

Although republican (with a small "R") forms of government were established in the former colonies on the state and national levels, the concepts of the English court systems continued after the United States of America won freedom from sovereign rule. Americans got rid of the sovereign but not some of the rights that title possessed. The doctrine of sovereign immunity was replaced with the idea of governmental immunity.

This means that the citizens of a particular city or state cannot sue the city or state government nor can that citizen of the United States sue the federal government. If you sue any level of government, in all likelihood your case would be dismissed because of the doctrine of governmental immunity.

Noting an exception

Although the government generally considers itself immune from being sued, there is an exception to the rule. The government can waive its right of sovereign immunity and can, by statute, permit itself to be sued. Most cities, states, and the federal government have waived this right in certain situations. However, in doing so, they put into place procedures that must be strictly adhered to in order to bring a lawsuit against them. This applies not only to the government but also to all governmental agencies.

The most common restriction is to require that you give notice to the government before you use the court system to enforce your rights. Many states and cities call this a notice of claim. A *notice of claim* sets out the details of the events that you claim the government did or failed to do that caused you harm.

The idea is that if the government is given notice before it is sued, it has the opportunity to properly investigate the incident and resolve the dispute prior to incurring the cost and expense of defending litigation.

In addition to filing a notice of claim, you may have a shortened time period in which to bring the lawsuit against a government body. In other words, the statute of limitations to sue the government may be much shorter than it is for a suit against a private person. (I explain what a statute of limitations is and how it affects your case in Chapter 4.)

If you fail to file a required notice of claim or similar document and fail to comply with any other requirements in the statute in which governmental immunity was waived, your case would in all likelihood be dismissed because you failed to comply with the rules the government sets to protect itself. In other words, the government wins without ever setting foot in the courtroom. The law considers compliance with all of these requirements a *condition precedent* to bringing suit, which means that all of these things must be done before you can sue.

If you do comply with all of the statutory conditions and the government does not resolve the dispute, you may then bring the lawsuit in a civil proceeding.

In all likelihood, a case against a government would not be permitted in small claims court unless a particular state statute allows it in that court. Some states require all lawsuits to be in a particular court just of that purpose; in New York, for example, the State of New York must be sued in the Court of Claims. In other states, such cases are heard in a special part of the court of general jurisdiction dedicated to lawsuits against the state.

Just to keep it interesting, in New York, you sue the City of New York in the regular court system, which makes for some interesting problems, if, for example, you damage your car on a pothole on a state highway in the city.

In any case, in situations where the federal government has waived governmental immunity, those cases may be brought only in a federal court. They cannot be heard in a local small claims court, and there is no federal small claims court.

The idea of governmental immunity is applied primarily to negligence and intentional tort actions. (I discuss both in "Knowing what a civil suit covers" earlier in this chapter.) Suits for breach of contract against the government generally are permitted, provided you comply with any rules for bringing the suit set out in the contract. These cases may be brought in small claims court if all the conditions are met.

However, suits to compel the government to do something or not to do something are generally limited to special parts of regular civil courts because they involve issues far beyond that of small claims court. Small claims court is concerned primarily with relatively straightforward money claims.

When you want to sue a charity

Under English common law, charities were immune from lawsuits. The theory was that charities do good deeds and benefit the public. If they could be sued, then the money that was going to the charitable purpose would be spent defending lawsuits and paying out damage awards. Most states have abolished charitable immunity because of the advent of insurance. Charities like everyone else can purchase insurance coverage to protect themselves against having to pay out large sums in a lawsuit.

However, some states still have exceptions for suits against charities such as limiting the amount of any recovery. In other words, the law may permit the suit to be brought, but it cap the amount that can be awarded as damages. The odds are that if your state permits such suits, the amount you're permitted to seek in small claims court would be less than the damage amount set by statute.

For example, you're in a car accident caused by Sister Geraldine from the Church of What's Happenin' Now. If there is complete charitable immunity in your state, you are out of luck. You can't sue. If your state allows suits but has a cap on the amount of money you can recover from the charity, such as $10,000, you can sue up to that amount. In that case, you can sue for the damage to your car of $5,000 and your out-of-pocket medical bills up to $5,000. But if you had serious personal injuries giving you a pain and suffering claim, you would be precluded from recovering anything above that $10,000 amount.

When you want to bring a suit against bankrupt defendants

Suppose you're all set to sue the defendant and you learn that she has filed for bankruptcy. The first thing filing for bankruptcy does is stops all legal proceedings against the defendant, so your case comes to a screeching halt. The legal term for this is a *stay* of the litigation. If you want to pursue your claim, you probably have to go to the bankruptcy court and file a claim there, behind a long line of creditors.

Bankruptcy courts are part of the federal court system, so you may have to travel some distance to file your claim. How you find out about the bankruptcy determines your next actions.

- ✔ If you learned of the bankruptcy because you got a notice from the bankruptcy court, the defendant listed you as a *creditor* — someone she owes money to — in the bankruptcy court. If the bankruptcy court collects any money, you may get paid without having to go to court. You have to file a proof of claim to collect.

- ✔ If you find out about the bankruptcy some other way, such as in the newspaper, you aren't listed as a creditor in the bankruptcy action. You have to contact the bankruptcy court to see whether you can still file a claim.

If you aren't listed in the bankruptcy court filing by the debtor, in theory, your case may not be stayed or could be pursued against the defendant after the defendant is discharged in bankruptcy. Of course, there may not be any assets to pay you at that point because the defendant is out of business.

Some debtors are very skilled at using the legal system. They file bankruptcy as a means of stopping all collection efforts against them by creditors. This stays all actions. But they never complete the bankruptcy and are never discharged. This means all of the original claims may still be viable. If you never did anything, the statute of limitations on your claim may run down and it may be too late to file a suit by the time you realize the bankruptcy action never went through.

The better procedure is to sue in small claims court or some other civil court and let the matter be stayed. After the bankruptcy is withdrawn, you can then pursue the defendant — again assuming she has any money.

The following scenario can also occur: You think the defendant-debtor owes you money, but she lists you in the bankruptcy as someone who owes her. You are then contacted by the bankruptcy court and have to participate in the process. You may be able to file proof of your claim to counter what the defendant-debtor told the bankruptcy court.

When you want to sue the deceased

Death is never pleasant; if the person you're thinking of suing dies, you can end up in a tangled legal mess. If the defendant owed you money, you're still owed the money but your ability to collect it may be substantially reduced. Her spouse or family aren't responsible for it, unless they specifically acknowledged the debt in some manner, generally in writing.

You have to sue the dead defendant's estate to get your money. Check with the probate or surrogates court to see if the estate is being probated. If it is, you may be allowed to submit a claim only in that court, and you may not be able to sue in small claims court. Ironically, if the defendant dies, and no one else takes steps to probate the estate, you may have to do so if you want to be paid. When someone dies, she ceases to exist as a legal entity and are replaced by the legal entity of the "estate of."

If you do sue, you name the "Estate of Doris Dirteater" or the "Estate of Doris Dirteater by her Executor or Administrator Berry L. Service." If you just sue Doris Dirteater, the case will be dismissed as there is no legal entity by that name.

If you already started the case and the defendant dies, the case will be stayed until these issues are resolved.

You can't sue the dead person directly because you can't serve her with the summons and complaint. And if there's no probate proceeding, there's no representative of the estate to serve, either.

In all likelihood, you'll probably end up making a business decision to abandon your lawsuit after weighing the small amount of money involved in a small claims case against the large amount of work involved in pursuing your claim. Because unless you belong to the select group of individuals who see dead people, negotiating a settlement with a deceased defendant is often more trouble than it's worth.

If you die, as the plaintiff, the same problems arise and your family will have to take steps to continue the suit, which can be difficult if your personal knowledge is needed to prove the case.

Chapter 3

Evaluating Whether You Need a Lawyer

In This Chapter

▶ Determining whether you need — or want — a lawyer

▶ Going about finding the right lawyer

▶ Figuring out how to pay a lawyer

*O*ne of the appealing features of small claims court is that you don't usually need a lawyer. In fact, in many states, you can't have a lawyer for a small claims court case. But if your state allows it, and if you have a complicated case, getting a lawyer may be the best thing for you to do. After all, you wouldn't remove your own appendix, would you? (If you had to stop and think about this, you'd probably be better off spending your time trying to straighten a spoon using only brain waves.)

There are advantages and disadvantages to using a lawyer if it's an option in your state. In this chapter, I help you figure out whether you can take on the Perry Mason role alone or whether you'll do better in court if someone else does the talking — commonly referred to as a "mouthpiece" in 1930s crime films.

Going It Alone: Heading to Court Lawyer-Free

In all likelihood, among the reasons you decided to pursue your case in small claims court is because you don't want to have to or can't afford to pay a lawyer. Before looking at instances when hiring a lawyer is probably a good idea, take look at situations in which you can probably do without the extra expense.

Handling your own case is a good idea if

✔ **You have a simple case.** The more legwork you have to do to collect information, track down witnesses, or review complex laws crucial to your case, the less logical it is to handle your case on your own.

✔ **You're organized.** If you can put your hands on every receipt, note, slip of paper, and phone record pertinent to your case, can keep things organized without losing them before your trial, and can organize your thoughts well enough to present your case in court, representing your-self will probably go well.

✔ **You can keep your cool in court.** If you're a hothead who will alienate the judge every time you open your mouth, having someone else do the talking is probably good idea. (See Chapter 11 for more information on behaving yourself in court.)

In some instances, however, you may want to hire a lawyer and yet be unable to find one who will take your case. Two main reasons lawyers won't agree to fight your battle are:

✔ **You don't have a good case.** You don't have a good case if the law doesn't recognize your problem as a legal claim, or your evidence is flimsy, or the damage is difficult to prove.

If you're making a mountain out of a molehill, you'll have trouble finding a good lawyer. You may be interested in the "principle" of the matter but a lawyer will be interested in the "principal."

✔ **Lawyers don't see any opportunity to make any money on your case.** Either the damages don't add up to enough cash to make it worth their while, or the case would require too much work on their part. Lawyers, like most people who work for a living, like to make money, so they may turn your case down even if it's a valid case.

Understanding What a Lawyer Can Do for You

A lawyer can be a real asset if you're not comfortable navigating the legal maze without one or because your case is complex, but hiring a lawyer isn't a one-size-fits-all proposition. You have several options for which services you want a lawyer to provide. You can hire a lawyer to guide you through the entire process or hire one just to help you with the tricky parts of the process. For example:

✔ You can consult with a lawyer before you even file the case in court and pay him just for his time. A lawyer can help you to decide whether you even have a legitimate case and can give you tips on how to proceed.

✔ You can consult with a lawyer before trial to help you acquire all the documents you need and to review your evidence to make sure it's complete.

✔ You can hire a lawyer just for the trial if your state allows lawyers to represent clients in small claims court.

Many people retain an attorney when they show up for their trial by hiring one of the lawyers they see in the courtroom. Although this may seem a little late, if you ask for a lawyer even at that late date, a judge often will give you a short adjournment for that purpose — especially if the lawyer asks the judge for time to prepare the case. Judges generally would rather deal with a lawyer than you as a self-represented litigant. Plus, denying someone a reasonable adjournment to get legal help is a sure way to have the case appealed.

✔ You can hire a lawyer post-trial to help you with an appeal or to help you collect your judgment.

Many states have adopted *unbundled legal services,* which allow clients to hire a lawyer for just one particular purpose. The lawyers like this because they are not stuck in a case and don't have to remain counsel through the entire proceeding. The idea of unbundled legal services is an effort to allow people to have some legal representation at various points in the process when they may need some advice without having to retain an attorney for the entire case.

Hiring a lawyer after you've started your case

What if you proceed with your case and realize at some point that you're in over your head? Can you hire a lawyer after you've started your case? The not-so-straightforward lawyer-type answer to this question is maybe:

✔ In states that allow lawyers in small claims court the answer is yes, you can hire a lawyer to help with any part of your case.

✔ In states where the small claims rules prohibit the participation of a lawyer, the answer is no.

But if the defendant shows up with an attorney, it must be legal in your state, except in specific circumstances. For example, in some states businesses are required to have representation in court. (See the upcoming section, "When you sue a corporation or business," for more information on this.)

If you realize that your case is beyond your ability to handle in a state where legal representation isn't allowed, bringing the lawsuit in the regular civil part of the court with a lawyer is probably your best bet. You'd do this by asking the court to discontinue the case without prejudice.

Most states have rules governing attorney's activities that require a lawyer to stay with a case from start to finish unless discharged by the client or relieved of representation with the consent of the court.

Although not all states allow lawyers in the small claims courtroom, no state has rules against consulting with a lawyer to help you prepare your case. Lawyers are just prohibited from participating in the actual filing and litigating in certain states.

Recognizing When You May Need a Lawyer

In most cases, it's better to determine whether you need a lawyer upfront rather than waiting until you're embroiled in the middle of the case and asking someone else to sort out the mess. You may want to check with your local county bar association to see if it has lawyers who will provide free consultations.

When the defendant has a lawyer

If you find out that the person you're suing is using a lawyer and you aren't, your first thought will probably be that you need a lawyer, too. After all, you don't want the defendant having what seems like the unfair advantage of professional help.

If you start your small claims case without an attorney, and the defendant hires counsel, generally the court will give you the right to get an attorney if you want. For example:

✔ You sue the defendant for damage to your car in a fender-bender accident. The defendant shows up with a lawyer because under his automobile insurance policy, the insurance company has to defend its insured on all claims. You may then decide to hire a lawyer as well.

✔ In a fender-bender accident, the defendant files a counterclaim, asserting you damaged his car. In this case, you should contact your insurance company to defend you on the counterclaim.

You may end up with a situation in which you have no lawyer on your claim against the defendant, but the defendant has a lawyer defending your claim. The defendant has no lawyer on his counterclaim against you, but you have a lawyer defending you on the defendant's counterclaim. Simple, right? No wonder people are afraid to navigate the legal waters without legal help.

If you want to delay the case because you're not ready to do battle by your court date, saying that you now want a lawyer isn't a good tactic. The judge may take the position that you had ample opportunity to get an attorney ahead of the trial date and deny your request. The court can decide to give you options: going forward without a lawyer; discontinuing your case *without prejudice,* meaning you can bring it again later; or discontinuing it *with prejudice,* which means the case is over and you can't bring it again. It's important to think about the whole small claims process when you start and be prepared from day one.

When you sue a corporation or business

If you're suing a corporation or business, it's prudent to hire a lawyer if possible. Because businesses entities are not living, breathing individuals, but legal entities, many states mandate that they have a lawyer present in all court proceedings.

Even if you're not using a lawyer for court, speaking to one can be helpful if you need guidance on finding the real name of your defendant, because the name on the door may not be the legal name of the business. (I describe the ways to find out who you're really suing in Chapter 6.)

If you're suing a corporation, be prepared to encounter a lawyer — or team of lawyers — on the other side because of the general requirement that corporations be represented. The fact that a corporate defendant may be required to have counsel may prompt you to consider whether you should have an attorney when you start the litigation.

Some states waive this requirement of counsel for small claims court and permit all corporations to represent themselves just like individuals. Other states limit the waiver only to small "mom and pop" businesses who are corporations only for liability or tax purposes.

If you're the representative or head of a corporation or a similar entity, and either bringing a lawsuit or forced to defend one, check the specific rule of the small claims court in your state as to whether or not you need to be represented by an attorney.

Even if a business is prohibited from bringing a case in small claims court, most states permit individuals to sue businesses there.

In some states, the small claims rules prohibit you from having an attorney as the plaintiff but require the defendant as a corporation to have a lawyer. This probably doesn't seem all that fair to you. However, as the person bringing the suit who selected small claims court, you have to abide by the rules limiting the use of attorneys, unfair or not. After all, you could've brought your case in regular civil court and had a lawyer.

The court has different rules for different parties and different circumstances, such as:

- If you're a business required to be represented by counsel in litigation, and you didn't know that when you answered the complaint, in all likelihood the court would advise you of that requirement and give you a short adjournment. You will not be permitted to defend the suit yourself; if you choose not to use a lawyer, the person bringing the suit will automatically win the judgment against you. This is because the law required the business to have counsel and if it doesn't it is as if the business is not present in court.

- If you're the person bringing the case to court and don't get an attorney when you're required to have one, your case will be dismissed.

When you sue a government agency

An attorney may have to appear in court to defend a lawsuit involving a branch of the government or a governmental agency. If you sue an official entity, the government or the governmental agency may be required to be represented by counsel.

Because of the *governmental immunity* doctrine, you may not be able to sue the government at all, especially in a place like small claims court. Some states require lawsuits against the government or one of its agencies to be brought in specific courts or parts of the court. (See Chapter 2 for information about governmental immunity.) So your first encounter with the defendant in court will probably be an application to dismiss your case for that reason or transfer it to another court.

It's unlikely that the government can bring its own case in small claims court as a plaintiff because the court is designed primarily for individual litigants.

Choosing the Right Lawyer for Your Situation

Choosing a lawyer who you like isn't essential, but it will make the process more pleasant. Working with a lawyer who is competent, trustworthy, and will do a good job for you is more important than personality or looks.

If you have no idea about how to find a lawyer, the best way is to contact your local county bar associations. Bar associations often also maintain a referral list just for these purposes. This is a list of local lawyers who have expertise in a particular area of the law and who can help you with your particular problem. These referral services are usually free, but you will have to make your own deal with the lawyer if you decide to hire one.

Smart ways to find good lawyers

There are several bad ways to find a lawyer: Jotting down a phone number as it flashes by on the bottom of the television screen during a 30-second commercial; responding to a pop-up ad on the Internet; and picking a lawyer out of the Yellow Pages based on a really eye-catching ad are all methods not to use.

Although a personal recommendation from a person you trust or firsthand experience is the best way to choose a lawyer, the Internet has made it easier to research legal firms to find the ones that may meet your needs. Check the following as you peruse lawyer's websites:

- **Location:** You want a lawyer who practices in your general area, not only for your own convenience but also because a lawyer who lives far away is less likely to take your case. Using the Internet or television referrals may start you with an attorney somewhere else in the state or the country and then refer you to a totally different local lawyer affiliated with the one who advertised.

- **Legal degrees:** Most lawyers list their credentials, professional organizations, and other experience on their website. You want your lawyer to be licensed and a graduate of something besides a mail-order school. However, for small claims court, you probably don't need someone who was on law review at a top-five law school; you'll be better served by an experienced practitioner from a local school who knows the people and procedures in your area and is on first-name basis with everyone in the courthouse.

- **Areas of expertise:** Many lawyers specialize to some degree. You want a lawyer familiar with and experienced in handling your type of case. Most lawyers never go to court — they're *transactional lawyers,* which means that they don't do litigation and are more at home preparing wills, handling real estate matters, or incorporating businesses — so make sure the attorney's area of expertise is what you need. Someone who prepares briefs for the U.S. Supreme Court, wrote a book on interpreting the Internal Revenue Code, or teaches law full-time is probably not going to be well versed at getting a police accident report into evidence.

After you narrow the pool of potential attorneys, call the office of each and set up an appointment for a consultation. If you like one better than the other or one has an office in an area you prefer, your choice is made. Always ask if there's any charge for a consultation so you're not surprised if the lawyer actually wants to be paid for his advice. Some lawyers may offer a "free" consultation, but remember that sometimes you get what you pay for. Obviously, if you've already gathered any documents or other evidence, bring it with you. The attorney can then hone in on your particular problem and not give a generalized answer to your generalized question.

A bad start to the conversation is "I have a friend who has this problem." This will result in a response such as "Why don't you have your friend schedule an appointment" as you're ushered out the door.

Make sure you feel comfortable with the person and are willing to accept his advice and guidance. Sometimes the job of the lawyer is to tell you things you really don't want to hear — including the fact that you have an unwinnable case.

Put it in writing: Protecting yourself with a retainer

Whenever you engage an attorney to represent you, get a written retainer. A *retainer* is a document that spells out every single detail regarding the rights and obligations of both you and your attorney. This document reduces any disputes in the future concerning the lawyer's fee and the service he provides you. A written retainer prevents surprises and misunderstandings, mostly on your part. In some states, the lawyer is required to provide you with a written retainer.

Three ironclad rules apply to retainers:

- ✔ **Rule #1:** Always have a written retainer with your lawyer.
- ✔ **Rule #2:** When you think a handshake is enough, re-read Rule #1.
- ✔ **Rule #3:** Read the retainer before you sign it!

Paying Up: Dealing with Lawyer Fees

Allow me to open this discussion on paying your lawyer with a joke:

> Lawyer to client: I charge $500, and for that $500 you can ask me two questions.
>
> Client: Isn't that a lot of money for two questions?
>
> Lawyer: Yes, it is. What's your second question?

Although lawyers and billable hours have become somewhat of a point of scorn over the years, lawyers need to be paid for their services like everyone else.

The next sections describe the three main methods of paying a lawyer after you hire one; some have advantages for you, others favor your lawyer.

Taking your case on a contingency agreement

If a lawyer takes a case on a *contingency basis,* it means the lawyer gets paid only if he's successful in getting you money. The lawyer usually doesn't receive any fee in advance, but instead receives a percentage of the monies you receive. The most common fee is one-third of the recovery whether by suit, settlement, or otherwise.

Contingency fees are most common in personal injury actions, malpractice actions, and any other lawsuit where the potential dollar recovery is substantial. It's unlikely that a lawyer would take a small claims case on a contingency basis because the potential recovery is so small.

When you see television ads with a lawyer touting his expertise in a certain type of case and saying, "We don't get paid unless we recover money for you," you can be sure that the lawyer only takes a case if he's fairly certain he will win it. The reason he says that in the ad is because that's the law when a case is taken on a contingency basis. Lawyers can't underwrite litigation.

The idea behind contingency fees is that you hire the best lawyer available irrespective of your ability to pay him as opposed to selecting the lawyer who's willing to bankroll the lawsuit. The lawyer has an interest in getting you the best recovery possible because he's getting a piece of the recovery

Check out these two examples on the extreme ends of contingency settlements:

- ✔ **Big bucks for little work:** You hire an attorney on a contingency basis to represent you for injuries you received in a car accident. After you leave the office, he calls the insurance company and settles the case for $100,000. If the contingency agreement provided for the lawyer's compensation as one-third whether by suit, settlement, or otherwise, the lawyer gets $33,333.33 for the phone call.

- ✔ **Lots of work and no pay:** That same attorney spends four years preparing the case and representing you vigorously all the way through a six-week trial. The jury brings in a verdict in favor of the defendant. The lawyer gets nothing because you got nothing.

In every case, as the client you're responsible for all fees and expenses incurred. Some typical fees other than those related to filing the case may be for medical records, expert reports, or witness fees. Ethics rules prohibit a lawyer from subsidizing the cost of litigation. This may mean that the lawyer will ask you to pay expenses as they are incurred or, what is more likely and most common in contingency cases, the lawyer pays the expenses upfront and those costs are paid first from any recovery. If there is no recovery, your retainer has a clause mandating that you reimburse the lawyer for these costs.

Make sure your retainer provides for the lawyer to inform you about any costs and disbursements being incurred as you go along, so you don't end up with a surprise at the end. In fact, a discussion of what are some likely anticipated expenses before you start the case is essential. You wouldn't want to go home at the end with a recovery that is less than what you paid for litigation expenses, a result always possible if you lose and sometimes the result when you're fighting for principle only.

Paying by the hour

Hourly agreements are what have given billable hours a bad name. You pay an attorney hired on an hourly basis as services are rendered based on the number of hours he says he's worked for you. Most contract and matrimonial litigation is done on an hourly basis.

You pay the lawyer an initial retainer, like a down payment, and the lawyer performs services calculated and billed on an hourly basis. As the retainer money is used up, the lawyer sends a monthly bill and you advance some more money. The amount of the retainer is no guarantee as to what the total cost may be. No lawyer can know in advance how much litigation will cost on an hourly basis. A lawyer almost never caps the cost at a certain amount.

The lawyer will make a good faith estimate as to what your problem will cost to solve based on prior experience, but if the other side decides to contest every issue and has unlimited financial resources, you can be in for a long and expensive ride.

This kind of litigation can get very expensive for a client, especially if it is a difficult case, and you're going against parties who have the financial ability to keep paying the lawyers.

If you don't keep up with the payments, the lawyer may be able to stop performing services for you. If the case is in litigation and you don't pay, the lawyer can go to court, make an application to the judge, and get an order allowing him to be removed as your counsel.

You may then find yourself going it alone or trying to find another lawyer to take your case. Finding another lawyer will be time-consuming in the best-case scenario and totally frustrating in the worst case scenario because the new lawyer will want to know why your old one bailed on you. He will want to be paid to review the file to determine whether he even wants to take the case, and you probably will be spending more money for his time to get back to the same place in the litigation that your former lawyer was at when that relationship ended.

Hourly payment agreements can provide an impetus for convincing you or the defendant that the only people making money are the lawyers and that perhaps you should resolve your dispute on your own before neither of you has any money left.

No one likes to work for free, so it is important that you understand the extent of your financial commitment when you hire an attorney on an hourly basis. You should also understand that you will be billed for everything the lawyer does for you, no matter how small. You'll be billed for every phone call, letter, meeting, photocopy, and other action.

Agreeing to a flat fee

Most lawyers realize that compensation based on an hourly rate would not be feasible in small claims court because the amount being sued for is so small and the amount of time spent on the case can quickly exceed any recovery. In a *flat-fee agreement,* the lawyer is paid a set amount of money unrelated to the potential recovery or the amount of time involved.

Flat-free agreements are common for simple small claims cases. The lawyer anticipates having the matter disposed of quickly and without providing too many hours of service. Another instance where flat-fee retainers are commonly used is in the buying and selling of real estate, making a will, and some other relatively simple transactions.

The flat-fee applies only to that transaction, so if the deal blows up and there is litigation, you'll have to pay the lawyer for those new services as well. If you have a flat-fee retainer, make sure you understand what exactly is included in the fee. Your small claims lawyer may only be appearing for that one court appearance. If the case gets adjourned or appealed, he may expect and be entitled to another fee.

Getting free legal services

If you don't have enough money to pay a lawyer but would still like to talk to one, you can look into getting free legal services. Unfortunately, it's extremely rare for the government or third-party agencies to provide free legal services for civil lawsuits like those found in small claims court.

Legal services for people who cannot afford them are provided in criminal cases because the United States Constitution guarantees the right to effective counsel in all criminal proceedings. No such constitutional guarantee is provided for civil cases.

Some states and private agencies provide free legal services in housing matters or in domestic disputes, but these resources are very limited in the type of cases they take on. Generally, if money is the primary object of the litigation, free legal services are not available.

Many lawyers who frequently appear in small claims court work for less than they charge for work in other forums because they anticipate that they will be done quickly, and — believe it or not — they consider helping people in small claims court part of their obligation to the profession to provide legal services for the public. If you hire a local lawyer, he may also feel that by helping you in small claims court, you will come back as a client for more significant legal work.

One of the best ways to get an attorney is by a personal reference from someone you trust. This is one of the ways lawyers develop a client base. Your lawyer hopes you'll spread the word for him being a good lawyer.

There's an adage in the legal profession that you always hire local counsel so you don't get "Hey Zeke'd." What's "Hey Zeke," you ask? It's when you show up in court and the judge says "Morn' Zeke, how are the fish bitin' today?" And the judge isn't talking to your lawyer — he's talking to your opposition's attorney. Go for the home court advantage!

Chapter 4

Classifying Your Claim: Figuring Out What Kind of Case You Have

You probably wouldn't be reading this book unless you'd already considered the facts and your evidence and decided that you have a case appropriate for small claims court. But you need to know what kind of case you have, or how to classify your claim.

One of the first questions that comes up when you fill out your claim form with the clerk of the court is what type of case you're pursuing. The facts of your case must fit into one of the accepted classes of cases that make it to small claims court: a breach of contract, an intentional tort or negligence, or something else.

This chapter helps you classify your claim, define the type of damages you may be able to get, and get up to speed on legalese — a language you need to be familiar with if you hope to navigate small claims court.

Classifying Your Case

Correctly classifying your case is very important right from the beginning. You need to make a short statement of the nature of your complaint when you file the claim with the clerk of the court. That statement is placed in the papers sent to the defendant (called the *summons and complaint*) and tells the defendant why you're suing her. How the case is classified also determines whether the *statute of limitations* has run out on your complaint, meaning whether you brought the case in a timely manner or you waited too long to file.

The most common areas of civil dispute, each of which has its own peculiarities, are:

- ✔ Contract actions
- ✔ Intentional torts
- ✔ Negligence

In the following sections, I look at each of these case types in more detail.

Breaking promises: Contract agreements

One of the most common types of case heard in small claims court involves the claim by one party that the other party breached a contract. The simplest definition of *contract* is an agreement that a court of law will enforce. Not every agreement, however, is a contract, as you see as you read through this section.

A *breach* of contract occurs when one or both parties fails to do what they agreed to do in the contract. Not every breach of an agreement can be resolved in a court, because certain agreements never grow up to be contracts and other agreements lack the basic essentials to be called a contract.

Talking the talk: Oral contracts

A contract may be either written or oral; courts enforce rights created under both types of agreement.

The main legal problem with an oral contract is obvious — it's very difficult to prove unless you habitually carry a tape recorder or one of those snazzy new phones that records every moment of your life and immediately transmits it to your friends so as to bore them to death in your pocket. Proving the terms of an oral agreement is difficult, unless you have witnesses.

As Sam Goldwyn, a famous movie producer, once said, "Verbal contracts aren't worth the paper they're written on." Disputes over verbal contracts often deteriorate into "He said, she said" arguments. It becomes your word against the defendant with the judge deciding whose story is more believable.

Because small claims courts by their very nature encourage and allow a more liberal interpretation of the rules of evidence, it's sometimes a better place to bring a lawsuit based on an oral contract as opposed to bringing the same lawsuit in a non–small claims part of the court.

Putting it in writing: Written contracts

Some contracts must be in writing to be enforceable. These contracts are subject to what is referred to as the *statute of frauds*. (Not to be confused with the monument to Albert Ponzi, the creator of Ponzi schemes — that's the *statue* of frauds.)

The types of contracts required to be in writing include

- ✔ Contracts that affect real property, such as buying and selling real estate, mortgages, and leases longer than a year
- ✔ Contracts to answer for the debt of another, for instance, when the car dealer asks the "Bank of Mom & Dad" to guarantee in writing the loan to "sonny boy" or "princess"
- ✔ Contracts that cannot be performed in less than one year

Pop quiz: Does a lifetime contract have to be in writing to be enforceable? Time's up. The answer is no. A contract for a lifetime may take less than a year to perform because you may not live a full year. The criteria applied is: Is it possible for the contract to be completed in less than a year? If the answer is yes, it doesn't have to be in writing.

Understanding the statute of frauds is easier when you realize it refers to statutes — laws, in other words — designed to prevent one party from taking advantage of the other by some means, especially fraud or lying.

Perhaps it's easier to understand if you know that the technical and complete name is the "statute of frauds and perjuries." Laws dealing with contracts that must be in writing developed in common law to prevent one party from lying through her teeth to steal the real property or other valuable items from another party. All this means is that legislatures took some common contract situations and created laws to deal with them to prevent fraudulent transactions. A statute helps prevent inconsistent rulings by courts dealing with similar fact situations and gets the judge out of the business of having to determine which party is lying in a contract suit.

Perhaps an example everyone is familiar with will point out how the law developed. Remember, in whatever Robin Hood movie you're familiar with, how the sheriff of Nottingham comes and takes some peasant's land for King John or one of his henchman, claiming the peasant agreed to give him the property? The sheriff has a handful of his cronies swear that the peasant agreed to the transfer. If the peasant went to court, the sheriff would win because he had more people falsely swearing to the occurrence and there was nothing in writing. The statute of frauds was designed to prevent this by requiring the peasant to sign an agreement to transfer his land.

Each state puts its own rules into statutory form and classifies them as being subject to "the statute of frauds."

Because each state has its own statute of frauds, you need to find out if the agreement in your lawsuit is covered by your state's law. This information will help you determine whether you have a provable case and if you do, what evidence you need to establish your case.

If the contract has to be in writing to be enforceable, and it isn't, the court will dismiss the case. This is the rule in all courts, not just small claims.

You can pursue all types of contract actions in small claims courts as long as you're seeking money damages as relief.

Examples of some common contract actions in small claims court include

- ✔ A tenant seeking the return of a security deposit
- ✔ A home improvement contractor or other service provider trying to get paid for work performed
- ✔ A condominium or homeowners' association claiming dues are owed

Some states allow their small claims court to handle landlord-tenant disputes where the landlord is suing to collect rent or recover the property from the tenant. (Hop over to Chapter 16 to read about specific types of landlord-tenant disputes.) Because each state has its own rules as to what cases can be brought in small claims court, if you're contemplating a lawsuit, the first place to stop is the clerk's office to see if small claims is an option.

Understanding why not all agreements are contracts

Some agreements aren't enforceable in court and therefore aren't recognized as contracts:

- ✔ **Social agreements:** For example, if you tell a friend to meet you for dinner at your favorite restaurant and then you don't show up, that friend cannot successfully sue you for the inconvenience she suffered by waiting for you at the restaurant. The law does not recognize that your friend suffered any real compensable damages.

In some situations involving a social agreement, a court may award your friend money, but those are not common situations.

Say I tell my friends to meet me for dinner as my guest at my favorite restaurant. I tell them that I may be late and to order without me, which they do. I never arrive. My guests are presented with a bill they cannot pay and this results in my friends having to wash dishes to pay for the check (if this ever really happens outside the comics and the movies). Because they relied on my promise to their detriment, a court may award them compensation for my failure to show up even though it started out as a social agreement.

✔ **A contract to commit a crime:** Suppose you've done something fairly stupid, like sitting on the opposing team's side in your team's colors and making derogatory remarks throughout a critical ballgame. Your actions led to physical damages, for which you sued the people who ripped the opposing colors off your back.

Both your civil suit and the criminal prosecution against the perpetrators were thrown out in the local court on the grounds that the defendants were justified in their actions. Not wanting to let the incident go, you take out the kind of contract you sign in a dark alley with some guy whose voice is akin to gravel being driven over by a Sherman tank and who can break a mirror by looking at it to extract some extra-legal justice from the perpetrators of your injuries.

If you contract with someone to do a dirty deed and then refuse to pay, she can't resort to the court system to enforce the written agreement, because the underlying purpose was illegal. No court will enforce an illegal agreement. Of course, you may have to leave town and change your name, but you're safe from any legal action.

Some agreements may technically be legal but are said to violate public policy. This means the court won't enforce them because the agreement is morally reprehensible or in some other manner shocks the public conscience.

Including exculpatory clauses

Businesses often put clauses into contracts that say they're not responsible for damage to your property or personal injuries you experience. These contract terms are called *exculpatory clauses,* and businesses use them to relieve themselves of liability for their own wrongful acts.

In other words, an exculpatory clause in a contract enables the defendant to say that even though she's responsible for the harm you suffered, you can't sue.

Courts don't like to enforce exculpatory clauses. They're usually held to be unenforceable because they're against public policy. People in general and courts in particular don't like to reward other people for their wrongful acts, especially if someone has been harmed by them. Exculpatory clauses are found in contracts but cross over to negligence and tort law, where one of the parties to the contract is trying to be relieved from responsibility for her own wrongful acts.

So say you, an experienced skater, go to the ice skating rink where posted signs say that the rink owners are not responsible if you fall on the ice. In addition, before you skate you sign an agreement, called a *release,* which says the rink is not responsible if you fall on the ice.

You're skating properly and you fall because, well, ice is slippery and skate blades are narrow. In this situation the exculpatory clause is enforceable because you assumed the risk involved in the activity and the owner of the rink didn't do anything to cause you harm.

But now say you go to the same rink with the signs and the release agreement, and you're skating properly but are injured because the ice making machinery malfunctions in a part of the rink causing the ice to turn to slush. Your skate catches in the slush, and you fall and are injured. The exculpatory clause does not relieve the rink of its liability in this case because the rink didn't provide a safe skating surface.

In another instance, you're skating properly on the same night the local college fraternities are having their 25th annual "Broad Street Bullies" contest, and a bunch of intoxicated college students cause you to fall and be injured. The rink can't use the exculpatory clause to escape liability because it didn't provide a safe environment and enforce the rules of the rink concerning such behavior.

Think of it this way in regard to exculpatory clauses: Can you put a big sign on your car saying "NOT RESPONSIBLE FOR HOW I DRIVE" and then proceed to rack up points running down pedestrians without being responsible for their injuries? Certainly not, but that's what businesses try to do with these clauses.

Another example of an exculpatory clause is a mail order company that charges for packing and shipping your order, but indicates in the agreement, "Not responsible for the condition in which the product arrives." When it arrives, it's no longer the Tiffany glass Faberge egg scene of the Oompa-Loompas from *Willy Wonka and the Chocolate Factory* but a several- thousand-piece jigsaw puzzle. The mail-order company can't escape responsibility for the damage just by asserting the existence of the exculpatory clause, because it undertook to ship and pack the product.

Perhaps an even more common exculpatory clause is when you go to a sporting event. Ever read the back of a ticket to a baseball game? If you take a line drive off the noggin or an errant pickoff throw conks you in the old bean, you're out of luck. You can't sue. The small print on the back of the ticket warns you of that possibility and relieves the teams and the players of liability. In fact, there is even case law that pretty much says that all Americans are charged with knowledge of how baseball is played and the awareness that batted balls and errant throws can go in the stands, so if you're hurt, you can't sue, irrespective of what's on the ticket.

Causing harm: The law of torts

The other area of law that is litigated in small claims court involves tort law. A *tort* is a civil wrong other than breach of contract. A *civil wrong* is a wrong against an individual committed by another individual, a business, or the government.

Torts can be intentional or unintentional, with the difference being:

- An **intentional tort** is a situation in which a person intends an act and intends the result of that act or intends the act and should have reasonably foreseen the result.

- **Negligence** is acting in an unreasonable matter in a given set of circumstances, although no harm was intended.

Intentional torts: Causing harm on purpose

Many intentional torts have a criminal law equivalent. Just remember that you're in small claims court, a civil arena, and are looking for money from the defendant. One major downside of suing for an intentional tort is that insurance usually doesn't cover the defendant who commits an intentional tort. This means that if you win your case, you'll be trying to collect directly from the defendant and her assets. And if there is also a criminal case filed by the district attorney against the defendant and she gets jail time, collecting for your injuries may be an even more difficult task.

Intentional torts include

- **Assault** is the apprehension or perceived threat of unauthorized touching of one person by another person.
- **Battery** is the actual touching.

  Assault and battery are often linked together in tort law. In criminal law in many states, the term battery is no longer used and the tort of battery is part of the crime of assault. Perhaps some examples will help explain the difference:

- You're a student in my law class at 7 a.m. I notice you sleeping; to get your attention, I pick up my textbook and throw it at you, hitting you in the head and causing you injury. Your claim against me would be a battery because of the unauthorized touching. I intended the act (throwing the book) and intended the result (hitting you). There would be no assault because you didn't see the book coming so you had no apprehension of being touched.

- On the other hand, if you're awake, see the book being thrown at you, and duck so the book misses you completely, there would only be an assault — the apprehension of being touched — but no battery because there was no contact. In this instance I intended the act — throwing — and although I didn't intend to miss you, the law presumes that by throwing the book at you I should have reasonably foreseen that you would have the apprehension of being hit, which means I committed the tort of assault.

- Finally, I get lucky, and you see the book coming, and because I just completed reading *Throwing Fastballs For Dummies,* you're unable to get out of the way. I committed both torts — the assault because you saw the book before it hit you and the battery because it hit you.

One of the theories of medical malpractice is battery. This is when you consent to have the doctor do surgery on your right knee and because the X-ray was flipped, she operates on your left knee. The battery exists because you didn't consent to the left knee surgery and you could get a recovery even if it turned out that you would have needed the surgery on that knee in another six months anyway. The issue is the unauthorized touching. This is why when you go for surgery they sometimes write, "This one" on one leg and "Wrong leg" on the other.

✔ **Defamation** is the intentional making of a false statement about a person that injures her reputation. Libel and slander are the most common examples of defamation. If the statement is in writing, it's *libel.* If the statement is made orally, it's *slander.*

Pop quiz: You're watching a newscast on television. Your picture appears while the talking head reports that you're chairperson of the John Wilkes Booth Fan Club and other allegations that are untrue. You want to sue the television station. Is it libel or slander? If you said slander, you're wrong. Even though you're hearing the telecast, the reporter is reading the news from a script. The fact that the false statement was written down and then read aloud makes it libel because the false statement first appeared in written form.

✔ **False imprisonment** is sometimes called false arrest. Ironically, there is no need for you to be taken into custody by the police for the tort to exist — although a wrongful arrest by the police can lead to the tort being committed. False imprisonment arises when you reasonably believe you can't leave the location you're in. Most of these claims arise when persons are wrongfully stopped at a store and accused of shoplifting. Whether the store calls the police is not necessarily important; the issue is whether you think you can't leave the store. Obviously if you're shoplifting, you can't sue for false imprisonment. Also most states now have anti-shoplifting statutes that permit store owners who have a reasonable belief that a person was shoplifting to stop that person, and make an inquiry in a reasonable manner without the store being liable for the tort of false imprisonment.

For example, you're shopping in your favorite department store. A clerk yells, "Stop, thief." The next thing you know you're tackled by two former football linebackers and subdued in front of just about everyone in your town who owns a cellphone with a camera. It turns out you have a receipt for everything you purchased, the "stop, thief" cry wasn't from a clerk but from a parrot in the pet department who used to watch the crime channel on cable, and you're released. There's a good chance you can succeed on a false imprisonment claim.

On the other hand, as you and a dozen other people are about to exit the store, the security buzzer goes off. The security staff politely asks you and the other people by the exit if they can inspect your purchases. In doing so they find that one of the people in the area failed to have the security tag on a sweater removed by the sales clerk and that person has a proper receipt. Because the store had a reasonable cause to stop everyone in the area when the buzzer went off and acted in a reasonable manner conducting an inquiry, there would not be any viable claim for false arrest.

✔ **Trespass** is one kind of intentional tort that does appears frequently in small claims court. *Trespass* is intentional interference with someone's property. Trespass cases are often brought in small claims court because the monetary damages usually aren't very high.

Most people think of trespassing only as walking on your neighbor's property without permission, but that's just one example. The tort of trespass also applies to personal property, such as borrowing a friend's car without permission.

There is a difference between *trespass to personal property* — the unauthorized use of someone's personal property that you eventually return — and *conversion,* the taking of someone's personal property with the intent not to return it or the inability to return it. These two types of intentional torts are illustrated in these examples:

- **Trespass to personal property:** You leave your car keys on your desk at work. I have some errands to run at lunchtime. Being inherently cheap and not wanting to use the gasoline in my car, I take your keys and "borrow" your car without telling you what I'm doing. I return an hour later, put your keys back, and you're none the wiser. I committed the tort of trespass to personal property. I used your property without your permission, denying you the use of the car for the one hour.

- **Conversion:** Same set of facts, but while out using your car, I drive off the road trying to avoid a gecko crossing the street and total your car. I have now committed the tort of conversion, because I can no longer return your property.

Cases arising from intentional torts aren't usually brought in small claims court because the person bringing the suit would more than likely be suing for amounts of money far in excess of the limits of small claims court. This is also the type of litigation that requires the expertise of an attorney because an intentional tort usually requires that the defendant prove specific facts that, if not established, would defeat the claim.

Many states specifically bar this category of litigation from small claims court. Check your local court rules.

In assault and battery cases, there is the concept of *transferred intent.* What this means is that if I intend the act and some other person is harmed, I'm responsible. As an example, we're back in the classroom with you as the sleeping student and me as the book-throwing professor; however, when I throw a book at you to wake you up, I miss you and hit the student behind you who's awake but not quick enough to get out of the way. It is still a tort — assault and battery — and I am responsible for the injury to the second student. I intended the act — throwing the book — and should have reasonably foreseen the result — possibly hitting someone other than the intended target. I can't raise as a defense to the charge of the intentional tort that I missed the student I was aiming at and hit a different student.

Negligence: When a reasonable person acts unreasonably

Negligence is by far the most common type of tort action. *Negligence* involves the defendant breaching a recognized standard of duty to the plaintiff and the plaintiff suffering an injury as a result.

The most common type of negligence action is seeking monetary compensation after the defendant injures you or your property in some way.

For example, you come across an automobile accident. A car is wrapped around a tree. The driver is unconscious behind the steering wheel. You try to open the car door to get the driver out, but the door won't open. You panic, thinking you have to act immediately because you think you smell gasoline. (In reality, it's your cheap aftershave.) In desperation, you shoot the lock off the car door and remove the driver. Unfortunately, the driver is now deceased, having suffered multiple bullet wounds from your action.

The autopsy reveals that the driver was only momentarily stunned by the accident and, had you done nothing, would have walked away from the crash virtually unscathed.

The driver's family can sue you for negligence because you acted in an unreasonable manner under the facts and circumstances existing at the time. A reasonable response would have been to call 911 and wait for help or perhaps break the window glass to gain access and assist the driver from the car.

Most negligence claims are the result of automobile accidents, a trip and fall on broken sidewalks, ice, or debris on the floor of stores. These are rarely brought in small claims court because they require the skill and expertise of an attorney. Negligence actions usually seek money damages far in excess of the monetary limits of small claims courts. Another difference between negligence and intentional torts is that if the defendant has insurance, it will usually cover a negligence claim but insurance generally won't cover intentional torts.

It's very easy to find a personal injury lawyer, as you know if you watch late-night television. Not having a lawyer makes your case immediately suspect because you normally have to fight off personal injury lawyers, not beg one to take your case. Don't show up in court without a lawyer in a personal injury case.

Strict liability actions: Doing everything right and still paying damages

A third class of tort law is called *strict liability in tort*. The idea in these kinds of cases is that that the defendant engaged in an ultra-hazardous activity and that the plaintiff suffered an injury as a result of it. The defendant can't claim that she did everything correctly and had no intention of causing an injury. The law permits the plaintiff to receive monies because the defendant's activity is inherently dangerous and even if the defendant does everything correctly, an injury may still occur.

Strict liability actions are rarely brought in small claims court because the legal issues are often very complicated and the damages suffered are often extensive, making the potential recovery beyond the monetary limits of the court.

As an example, say you're hired to demolish a building. You follow all the instructions and procedures perfectly. However, because of the concussion of air naturally arising from this activity, the windows on a building a few blocks away are broken. You're strictly liable for the damage suffered. It's not a defense that you did everything properly.

A claim may be brought in small claims court for minor damage to personal or real property. A personal injury or property damage claim would probably be beyond the monetary limits of the small claims court.

Products liability actions

Products liability claims arise when a person is using a manufactured product in the proper manner for which it is designed and for a proper purpose but the person suffers an injury. Products liability combines both contract and tort law theories.

It's very unlikely that this type of litigation would ever be handled in small claims court because of the nature of the injuries received, the complexity of both legal and technical issues, and the fact that the probable defendants may be located in other states or other countries, making them not subject to the jurisdiction of a small claims court. Many of these lawsuits are brought in federal court, because the number of persons injured or who potentially could be injured is beyond that of a single litigant.

Say you buy a new car. The first day you're driving it, the steering wheel comes off in your hands. Under the common law if you sued the car dealer, the dealer would have a defense alleging that it was not negligent because it did not manufacture the car. The dealer would claim it sold you the car so it only had a contractual relationship with you.

If you sued the manufacturer, the manufacturer would defend saying although it made the car, it had no contract relationship with you. It didn't sell you the car. It provided the car to the dealer who sold it to you.

Products liability cases allow the injured party to sue both the manufacturer and the dealer. The manufacturer's liability is based on the idea that it made a product for sale to the general public and put that product into the marketplace knowing someone would buy it. The dealer's liability is based on the idea that it has a duty to inspect or even test the vehicle before selling it.

Determining Who's Really at Fault

The two elements of proof in every court case are liability and damages. In other words, was the defendant to blame, and how much should she pay to make it right? In order to win any case, you must prove both of these things.

It's possible to have a good liability case in which the defendant's fault is undeniable and still have a terrible damages claim because no one was hurt. On the other hand, you can have a terrible liability case, meaning you, the plaintiff, and not the defendant, were really at fault but you suffered serious horrific permanent injuries, therefore making a great damage claim. In both situations, winning your case will be difficult because one of the two key elements of your claim is legally insufficient.

An example of good liability/bad damages is a situation in which the defendant gets drunk and drives up on your lawn. The entire incident is not only viewed by three police officers and every religious leader in your community as they were all engaged in an ecumenical walk, it's recorded on your security camera. Great liability case. However, the only damages are two tire tracks on your grass, which, after your gardener rakes the lawn, disappear. Bad damage claim.

A bad liability/good damages example is when you get drunk, run a red light, lose control of the car and wrap yourself around a telephone pole. You spend six months in a coma and two years in rehab and are left with permanent injuries. Great damages. No liability — you can't sue yourself. This is where you look for a really sharp lawyer to find someone else to blame.

The issue of liability is usually not such a big factor in a contract case, because there will be a written agreement setting out what each party was supposed to do, and figuring out who didn't perform is often not that difficult.

In negligence cases, the issue of liability is a key element of the case. If you don't think you can prove the liability or fault of the defendant, then you probably don't actually have a case. If you can't prove the defendant is at fault, you never get to the issue of damages.

To determine whether you can establish liability, you need to look at the following issues:

- **Contributory and comparative negligence,** which means that you were partly responsible for what happened.

- **Assumption of risk,** which means you knew there was risk involved and did something anyway.

- **Last clear chance,** which means you had one last opportunity to avert disaster and didn't take it.

I discuss these issues in the next sections.

Contributory and comparative negligence

Whether you're partially to blame for an accident matters in negligence cases. Under the common law, the accident would be looked at to see which party was at fault. If it was determined that you as the plaintiff were partially at fault, you would have contributed to the cause of the accident. This is called contributory negligence and would be used to deny any recovery if you suffered an injury.

Contributory negligence means that if you engaged in actions that contributed even one percent to the accident, you're not entitled to any recovery. So even if the defendant was 99 percent responsible and you were the only person injured, you would be denied receiving damages because your actions contributed to the accident.

Take this example: You're leaving work at night during the worst snow storm in a decade. There's a stop sign on the corner, but you know if you make a full stop at it, you'll probably get stuck in the snow. So rather than do a full stop, you slowly inch your car into the intersection. Just then the defendant, driving 100 miles an hour, backwards, on the wrong side of the road, lights off and drunk, comes around the curve and crashes into your car, causing you injury.

Because God protects drunks and children, as the saying goes, the defendant walks away unhurt. The jury finds the defendant 99 percent at fault and you 1 percent at fault, noting that had you made a full stop, the defendant would have gone past the intersection so fast there would have been no accident. Under the common law, you recover nothing because you contributed to the accident. Now that doesn't seem very fair, does it?

Originally most states applied the common law contributory negligence rule. Now most states don't use it, preferring the idea of *comparative negligence,* in which damages are reduced by the percentage of the plaintiff's fault. So if you're ten percent responsible for an accident and the jury awards you $100,000, the award is reduced by — take out your calculator — ten percent or $10,000, making your recovery only $90,000. This sure seems a lot fairer than contributory negligence.

Don't stop reading yet. This is not the end of the story. Not all states follow this rule. Some states are *50 percent* states. In these states, if you're more than 50 percent responsible for the accident, you get nothing. So if a jury finds you 90 percent responsible and the other party only 10 percent at fault, you would be denied recovery. In a non–50 percent state, you still can recover, but only 10 percent of the damage award.

Most states have fortunately abandoned contributory negligence and have adopted comparative negligence as the standard to apply in accident cases.

The standard applies in all negligence actions, not just car accidents. So if you trip and fall because of a hole in your neighbor's sidewalk, the jury could apply the "Why didn't you look where you're going, stupid" standard to you and apportion the fault between you and your neighbor.

Understanding assumption of risk

One defense to any negligence action is called *assumption of risk*. This means that you understood that there was some risk involved in the activity and still engaged in it. If you're injured and sue, the defendant must establish that you were told of the risk and understood what the risk was.

Say you're going ice skating for the first time at the skating rink. You slip and fall on the ice and break your wrist. Most juries would deny you recovery because it is commonly known that ice is slippery and common sense tells you that you can slip and fall on ice even if you do everything properly. A jury would conclude you assumed the risk that you could fall and get hurt when you went on the ice.

I said most juries would do that because there is probably one jury somewhere who could be convinced by a talented lawyer that the rink should have a big sign posted saying "ICE IS SLIPPERY. YOU CAN FALL AND GET HURT." And because there was no sign posted, the rink is liable.

It would probably also help your case if you could convince the jury that you just flew into town having been raised in a tropical jungle by wild animals and the first thing you did when you got off the plane was go to the skating rink, having no idea that this activity could be dangerous.

Remember the point in the exculpatory clause section about going to a baseball game and getting hit by a foul ball? That situation is also one where the law presumes you understand the risk of being hit by a foul ball because you're presumed to know about baseball and therefore assumed the risk of being hit.

Pointing the finger — last clear chance

Because contributory negligence resulted in such harsh judgments, the common law developed theories to lessen its impact and permit you to recover even if you were partially at fault. One of these theories is called last clear chance. The idea of *last clear chance* is that the court doesn't determine who was primarily at fault but looks to see which party had the "last clear chance" to avoid the accident.

Picking a dollar amount in personal injury cases

You may have wondered how the lawyers come up with the astronomical sums they ask for in personal injury cases. If it seems as if they pluck them out of thin air, you're not too far off. An attorney may ask a client claiming to have suffered personal injuries "What is your telephone number?" This is not being asked for informational purposes.

More likely than not, the lawyer wants a seven-digit number to serve as the amount of damages to be initially demanded from the defendant. The lawyer does this because in many states, you can only recover the amount of money you sue for. So even if the jury or judge made an award of damages for more than your lawyer asked in the lawsuit, you'd only get the amount you asked for initially. On the other hand, many states

only require the plaintiff to ask for damages or damages in an amount to be determined at trial. This isn't an issue in small claims court, because in all likelihood you'll ask for the maximum allowed. Remember, small claims courts have monetary limits on the amount you can sue for, which is why personal injury cases rarely are brought there.

Most clients in this situation are not very understanding. They aren't satisfied that they won and got some money; they want all the money the jury awarded. In this situation, the attorney may end up contacting her malpractice insurance carrier to defend a legal malpractice claim for being a better lawyer than she thought she was. The way to avoid this is to ask for a lot of money for damages initially.

For example, you're driving your car and see a person lying in the middle of your driving lane in the middle of the block outside the town's favorite watering hole. You decide to run the inebriated fellow over — after all, you have the right of way and he is sleeping in your lane of traffic.

Under a strict contributory negligence theory, you could do that because the drunken fellow had contributed to the accident by being drunk, crossing in the middle of the block, and passing out in the road. Under last clear chance, however, you would still be responsible because you had the last clear chance to do something to avoid the accident by stopping your car and not running over the poor fellow.

Realizing Why Personal Injury Claims Aren't Brought in Small Claims Court

In personal injury cases, the plaintiffs usually ask for large sums of money, usually amounts far in excess of the monetary jurisdiction of small claims court. If you're bringing a personal injury action in small claims court, there's a good chance the defendant won't treat the case very seriously because no one brings cases involving really extensive injuries in small claims court.

Generally speaking, if the amount demanded in the complaint by the plaintiff is less than seven figures, the automobile accident was probably a fender-bender that the police weren't called to, and both sides just exchanged information and drove away from the scene.

If there is insurance coverage involved, the insurance carrier is generally required to provide a defense to the person you're suing. This means that in all likelihood the defendant will have an attorney. As a plaintiff, you may want to have an attorney as well, especially if proving who caused the accident is an issue.

Acting Fast: Time Is of the Essence

Time is generally not on your side in the legal system, and the sooner you bring your case to court the better. Defendants leave the state, people die, retire, or become too ill or too befuddled to testify, and over time, your case may take on less of a sense of urgency to anyone but you — and sometimes even to you. After you're sure you have a case, you have nothing to gain by holding off filing.

Time's up! Checking out the statutes of limitations

Different classifications of lawsuit have specific time frames in which an injured party — that's you — may bring a cause of action. The legislature of each state sets the state's time periods, which is why you must always check your state's laws. The law that determines time frames in each state is called the *statute of limitations*.

 If you fail to start an action before the statute of limitations has run out, your claim could be dismissed with prejudice. That means the lawsuit will never see the light of day. This is a defense that the defendant has to raise when the defendant answers your complaint. If the defendant fails to bring the issue to the judge's attention when the answer is due, the defense is said to have been waived.

In some states, unless the defendant raises the statute of limitations as a defense, it isn't a valid defense; the court doesn't have to tell a defendant that the statute of limitations has expired — if it even knows. After a case is underway, generally it's too late.

In other states, the statute of limitations may be raised at any time and cannot be waived. This means that a defendant can raise the fact that the statute of limitations has passed even after the trial is over. Whatever the results of the trial are, they're moot because the law in that state would have prevented the case from going forward initially.

States may also have rules which allow the statute of limitations to be *tolled* or *stayed* meaning that the time is not running on the plaintiff to start the lawsuit. If the defendant has moved out of the state, this may be a reason the statute of limitations would be tolled. If the defendant has never left the state, and the plaintiff simply cannot find her, this generally does not toll the statute of limitations.

Advice as to whether or not the statute of limitations has run out is not something that the clerk of the small claims court can give. It's something that you have to research yourself. If you can't find the answer, consult an attorney or some public interest entity for advice about statutes of limitations.

Clerks generally can't give legal advice at all, let alone advice as to what the statute of limitations period is for a particular kind of action and whether or not it has run out. This is legal advice, and most states require that only lawyers give legal advice. There's a good reason for this rule. If you're wrong about the type of case you have and wait too long to file it, your case would be dismissed on the merits. Court employees don't want to open themselves up for a lawsuit if they gave the wrong advice.

Statutes of limitations in different states

There's no standardization in the statutes of limitations between states. You may be able to see an action brought for breach of contract for six years in one state and four years in another. Some lawsuits such as those for intentional torts may have to be brought in as little as one year after the incident. Some contract actions may be governed by a specific statute that applies only to specific breaches of contract, such as the Uniform Commercial Code. For those of you who are somewhat curious, the Uniform Commercial Code is a statute that has been adopted in almost in its entirety in some form in every state. It's an attempt to have certain types of business transactions common in interstate commerce treated the same way in every state.

For example, in New York, a common law contract action has a six-year statute of limitations, although a contract action subject to the Uniform Commercial Code has a four-year statute of limitations period.

Personal injury lawsuits can also be subject to different statutes of limitations in different states. Even if the states are close neighbors connected by large bridges that millions of people travel every day, such as New York and New Jersey, they won't necessarily have the same statute of limitations.

Here's another example: There are four bridges and two tunnels for motor vehicles between New York and New Jersey. How long you have to file suit for damages resulting from an automobile accident on one of those bridges or tunnels is determined by where the accident took place. If the accident was on the New York side of the bridge or tunnel, the statute of limitations is three years. If on the New Jersey side, you have two years. Same cause of the accident. Same injuries received. Different time to sue.

If you think you have a contract action, but what you really have is a negligence claim, you may miss the filing date and have the case dismissed. Knowing how to classify your claim is very important; knowing when to bring it is a key component of any lawsuit. This is not one of those rules that is forgotten about or viewed more liberally just because the case is brought in small claims court or just because you don't have a lawyer. If you blow the statute of limitations, your case is over.

Say you want to sue your lawyer for legal malpractice because she failed to file the case in a timely fashion. You believe that because you have a written retainer with her, you have a breach of contract action against her, and in your state, New York, breach of contract has a six-year statute of limitations. Unfortunately for you, in New York and other states, the mere fact that there is a retainer does not make it a contract case. New York considers it a negligence-malpractice claim and the statute of limitations is only three years.

Classifying your claim and understanding the relevant statute of limitations can get complicated; paying the money to speak to lawyer can make the difference between winning a case and never being able to file it because the statute of limitations has run out.

Laches can lock your case out of court

Sometimes a defendant can have the plaintiff's case dismissed even if the statute of limitations has not run out. If the defendant can establish that the plaintiff waited such a long time to bring the suit that it is unfair to allow it to continue, a court may dismiss the case based on the equitable defense of laches. *Laches* is the idea that too much time has passed, making it impossible for the defendant to properly defend the claim.

For example, the statute of limitations is six years for breach of contract in a particular state. The plaintiff waits 5 years, 11 months, and 29 days to bring the action. Although this lawsuit was timely under the statute of limitations and the defendant could not raise that as a legal defense, the defendant can claim that it's unfair to have to defend this lawsuit because so much time had passed, making it impossible to get witnesses or produce records. The defendant would raise the equitable defense of laches.

The lesson to be learned here is simple: If you're a plaintiff who thinks you have a good case, don't wait to bring your lawsuit. Unlike cheese and fine wine, your case will not get any better with age.

Chapter 5

What's the Damage: Understanding Different Types of Damages

*M*ost people who go to small claims court have one main motive: to get the defendant to pay for something he did to them. There may be other motives, too — to embarrass the defendant, to get even, or to satisfy some other emotional goal. But at the bottom of most small claims cases lies one motivator: money.

Determining how much money to ask for if you're the plaintiff in a small claims case can be easy or difficult, depending on how easy it is to determine the value of what you lost.

Because you need to put a set amount in your complaint at the time you file with the clerk, spend some time going over figures to come up with a plausible number. (I talk more about the clerk's role in your case in Chapter 7.)

In this chapter, I provide insight into the monetary rules of the court to help you come up with a figure that helps you present your case in the best possible light as well as compensate you fairly for your losses.

Classifying Your Damage Claim

Damages in the legal world fall into four general categories. Not all will put money back in your pocket. They are:

- ✔ **Compensatory damages:** An award of money to give you back what you lost.
- ✔ **Consequential damages:** Damages that occur from the defendant's actions and that could have been foreseen.
- ✔ **Nominal damages:** Damages that acknowledge that you're right, but don't award you any money.
- ✔ **Punitive damages:** Judgments aimed at punishing the defendant beyond the compensatory damage he must pay.

Making you whole: Compensatory damages in contract cases

The goal of suing for compensatory damages is to restore you — financially, at least — to the state you would have been in if you hadn't gotten involved with the defendant.

The amount you can collect cannot exceed the amount you lost. In contract cases, the amount you lost is always the same as the amount you spent or would have realized had the defendant kept his end of whatever bargain or understanding you had, as the following cases demonstrate.

Time for an example: You hire the defendant to paint your house before the weekend of your daughter's engagement party. By a written contract, you agree to pay him $5,000 if he completes the job by Thursday, and he agrees to do that.

On Wednesday, the defendant calls and says he never finished the last job he was doing and now he can't get to your house for at least another week. To get the job done, you now have to hire another painter who agrees to do the job on short notice but for $10,000.

How much money can you collect in this scenario?

- ✔ Is it $10,000 — what you had to pay to have the house painted by the second painter?
- ✔ Is it $5,000 — the difference between what you paid the second painter and what you agreed to pay the defendant?
- ✔ Or is it nothing because you really didn't have to have the house painted and you hired the most expensive guy?

The answer is $5,000, the difference between what you paid and what you would have paid had the defendant done what he was contracted to do. You would have paid $5,000 to the first painter if he had done his job, so your damages are the additional costs you incurred because the defendant breached the contract.

Now, take the same scenario, except that the defendant actually paints your house, but uses defective paint. It rains on Wednesday, causing all the paint to wash away. You now hire the second painter for $10,000 on short notice. In this case, you can recover the entire $10,000, because your damages would be what it takes to correct the defendant's worthless work.

You may even be able to collect $15,000 — the $5,000 you wasted on the first painter plus the $10,000 you had to pay the second painter if you can establish that the first painter made the job worse and you didn't have to pay the extra money merely because of the rush nature of the job.

One more example: You order a new couch from your local furniture store and prepay the entire purchase price. The couch is never delivered. You can sue to get your money back. You may prefer to sue to get the couch delivered, but the goal of small claims court is generally to award you money, not goods.

Compensatory damages in negligence cases

In a negligence case in which you suffer either personal injury or property damage because of the defendant's negligence, the money you receive is also designed to make you whole. But you may also be able to recover money for "conscious pain and suffering," in addition to lost wages, medical expenses, and the like.

Personal injury means actual physical or psychological harm you suffered as opposed to something that you took personally or that offended you but that didn't actually cause you any harm.

Suffering personal injury

Establishing pain and suffering is a more difficult undertaking than establishing a cut-and-dried monetary claim. You must produce medical records and medical testimony as well as establish a subjective standard of how much pain you suffered as a result of the defendant's negligence.

Because of the complications involved in proving pain and suffering in personal injury cases, these cases are almost never tried in small claims court. For one thing, the cost of having a doctor testify generally exceeds the monetary limit of small claims court.

In reality, an insurance company won't take a personal injury case brought in small claims court very seriously because these cases are usually brought in the regular civil court where the plaintiff's potential dollar recovery is much greater.

Truthfully, the only personal injury cases in small claims cases are those where the plaintiff doesn't have a lawyer because:

- ✔ The plaintiff is a difficult client — to put it politely.
- ✔ The defendant's liability is difficult to prove.
- ✔ The injuries to the plaintiff are so inconsequential that no lawyer would waste time taking the case.

Pursuing personal injury claims is one of the more profitable areas of the law, so if a plaintiff can't find a lawyer willing to take the case, it creates an impression that the case has little real value and cannot be proven.

Medical expenses, lost wages, and other out-of-pocket costs are easy to prove if you have the proper documentation, but loss of enjoyment of life and other similar damages are harder to evaluate.

Loss of enjoyment of life is a separate complaint than physical or mental pain and suffering. It refers to any damages that result in the plaintiff being unable to partake in activities or participate in pleasures of life as he could previously. For example, a person who was left paralyzed after being hit by a drunk driver can claim loss of enjoyment of life because he can no longer play with his children.

Experts are often needed to prove future lost wages and future medical expenses in personal injury cases. Because no one can predict what future expenses will be with any certainty, experts are required to make educated guesses. Without expert witnesses, such damages are considered speculative and uncertain.

The law prohibits judges and juries from awarding damages that are completely speculative. There must be some factual basis to support an award.

To establish psychological damages, you must prove your response is beyond a normal reaction and resulted in a change in behavior. For instance, if a dog bites you, it's normal to now be afraid of dogs. So bringing that statement into court will only result in a minimal damage award, for instance the medical costs incurred and the monetary value of the scar resulting from the bite or the stitches you received.

But if you testify that you're now afraid to leave the house, require someone to be with you at all times, can't sleep at night, and are scared of the dark and must leave all your lights on, you establish a change in behavior beyond the normal reaction. This may result in a greater damage award.

Scars on women are worth more than scars on men, although this may well be considered sexism. A scar on a guy makes him look tougher and gets him more respect in certain neighborhoods; however, a scar on a woman typically has nothing but negative associations. As you may imagine, facial scars are considered more serious than scars on other body parts.

Show me the money: Getting money after a car accident

Damage to personal property also has its own rules. If your car is damaged in an accident, then the amount of damages is the cost of repairs. You aren't getting a new car from the accident; you're only getting the value of the car on the date of loss.

Several things can happen after a car accident:

- ✔ **You accept the defendant's insurance company's estimate, and take the money it determines it will cost to have the car repaired.** In this case, you do not need to involve the court. This is what insurance is for.

- ✔ **You reject the insurance company's estimate, pay for the repairs out-of-pocket, and take the defendant to small claims court for the difference.** You'll have to establish why the insurance company's offer wasn't enough to repair your car. For example, you may have the mechanic come in and explain why what he had to do cost more than the insurance carrier wanted to pay.

- ✔ **You reject the insurance company's estimate but can't afford to pay for the repairs until you collect from the defendant.** You may have to produce at least two repair estimates. Some courts award you the average of cost estimates from both you and the defendant. Other courts take the lowest estimate, feeling that if the scope of the repairs is the same in all of the estimates, you should go with the lowest one.

- ✔ **The cost of repairs exceeds the value of the vehicle.** You get the book value of the vehicle paid by the defendant's insurance and the car doesn't get repaired.

    To counter this possibility, you may need to have your mechanic come in and establish the mileage and the condition of the car. You can also go to websites or books recognized in the auto industry as accurately evaluating the value of used vehicles. This is a problem with old cars, when the value of the vehicle to the plaintiff exceeds the actual market value of the car.

You must establish both the liability of the defendant and the amount of damages you suffered.

Unfortunately, you may be left without a car because it's *totaled,* meaning it's worth less than the cost to repair it, or is so old that it's *out of book* and not listed in used car evaluation guides any longer. In this case, the payment from the defendant's insurance carrier is too little to buy a new car.

If you do get an offer from the defendant's insurance company, the amount may be reduced by the percentage of fault the defendant attributes to you in causing the accident. It's a common practice for the defendant's carrier to produce an estimate saying, for instance, that the damage to your car was $5,000 but because you were 50 percent at fault, they're offering just half, or $2,500.

You can only get the defendant to pay for the damage you prove he did to your car. If you were using it in demolition derbies and the vehicle had pre-existing damage, the defendant isn't paying to fix it.

You also can't just show the judge a picture of your car and ask the court to put a dollar amount on the cost of the repairs. It's your obligation to prove the repair cost as part of your case.

If you produce a picture of your car or the defendant's car, make sure that the photo includes the license plate or some other distinctive marking on the vehicle. In this day and age when everyone has a cellphone, unless you're injured in the accident, there really is no excuse as to why you wouldn't have a photo taken at the scene.

It can also be important to be able to establish when the pictures were taken, either with a date and time stamp on the photo itself or digital information in the photo file.

Getting personal: Claiming personal property damage

When other types of personal property are involved, such as if your basement floods or the cleaner ruins your clothes, the amount you can recover as damages is the value of the property on the date of loss.

This means if your ten-year-old couch is ruined by a sewer backup, you get the value of a ten-year-old couch. The court won't award you what you paid for the couch ten years ago or the cost of going out to the furniture store and buying a new couch.

Trying to prove the value of old items of personal property is difficult. What you paid for it is not the measure of damages, nor is what it costs today to replace it. If you have a great deal of personal property damaged, it pays to hire an insurance adjuster to prepare a statement as to the value of the property on the date of loss, called the *actual cash value.*

Using your insurance as intended

It never ceases to amaze me when people with property damage claims to the contents of their homes decide, for some reason, not to notify their homeowners' insurance companies and seek coverage. After all, isn't that why you buy insurance?

If you have insurance that covers something that got damaged, you call your agent, and the carrier sends out an adjuster to appraise the loss and determine the value of your property. If the loss exceeds your coverage, you can use your insurance company's estimate as part of a case against the defendant for the difference between what you received and your actual loss. The adjuster from your carrier may also be able to testify on your behalf at the trial. But go to your insurance company first!

But you can't recover twice. If you collect from your carrier, you can't then collect the entire amount from the defendant. You can only collect what you actually lost.

Your insurance carrier may also bring its own lawsuit against the defendant to recover the amount they paid on your claim, which was caused by the negligence of the defendant. In that situation, you may have to go and testify on behalf of the insurance company. This may be an inconvenience, but look on the bright side — you've been paid and the carrier is underwriting all of the litigation costs. And, the terms of your insurance policy may require you to cooperate with all collection efforts, which would include participating in the trial.

Some courts use tables established by the Internal Revenue Service or accepted by the accounting profession as a standard to calculate the depreciated value of the property on the date of loss. If you're planning to use some outside source, choose one recognized as reliable in the industry.

Some merchants, such as cleaning establishments, have dollar limits on the amount you can collect if they damage something. If this information is prominently posted, and you know about it before you bring your clothing in, most courts enforce such limits. So if the posted limit is "not responsible for damage to property in excess of $75," that's all you can recover for your $300 suit. The idea is that if you don't like the limitation, go locate a cleaner without one.

Knowing the consequences: Collecting on consequential damages

Consequential damages are damages that don't directly arise from the defendant's actions but that could have reasonably been foreseen to have resulted from them. That's a mouthful, but the following case help make it clear:

You hire a messenger service to pay your credit card bill at the bank on or before May 1. You tell them that it is a credit card bill and if it's not paid on time, you'll have to pay additional charges and interest. The messenger agrees to make the payment, understanding the importance of the timely payment. But the messenger forgets and pays the bill late.

Obviously, you could have the fee you paid to the messenger refunded because he did not perform as agreed. However, you also want to recover consequential damages to compensate you for the money you had to pay to the credit card company for late charges and penalties, as these were reasonably foreseeable as arising from the failure to make the delivery.

Another for-instance is the case of your car suffering damage as a result of the defendant's negligence. The defendant is 100 percent responsible and the defendant's insurance company is going to pay for all of the repairs without question. Your car will be in the repair shop for three weeks. Your compensatory damages are the cost of the repairs. Your consequential damage is the money you have to lay out for car rental expenses or for taxi services while your car is being repaired.

Under the common law, lost profits were not considered consequential damages because a business could not prove that it would have any profits. Profits are considered speculative.

Modern case law permits the recovery of lost profits when you can establish an ongoing business, as well as past dealings with the defendant or industry standards applicable to such a transaction.

Imagine you own a truck and have a contract to deliver lumber to a construction site next Monday. You take the truck to the mechanic to service and tell him that you need the truck by Saturday so that you can deliver the lumber on Monday.

The mechanic, now aware of why you need the truck, says, "No problem, you'll have it by Saturday," but doesn't deliver the truck on time because he forgets to work on it. You would have a viable claim for the profits you lost by not showing up to haul the lumber.

When you'd rather be right than rich — nominal damages

Nominal damages are really not very satisfying. Sort of like when your spouse says you're having burgers for dinner and you expect a thick, juicy all-American pile of beef, but when you get home, the burger is a slab of tofu on a bed of lettuce.

When football leagues collide

The United States Football League (USFL) sued the National Football League (NFL) alleging the NFL was a monopoly, and because it was a monopoly the USFL was out of business. The case resulted in a finding that the USFL was legally correct, that the NFL was a monopoly; however, there were other reasons why the USFL failed irrespective of the NFL monopoly. The USFL received nominal damages of one dollar.

In addition, because it was a case where a monopoly was established, treble damages were awarded so the USFL received another three dollars. Fear not, however: Because they proved the NFL was a monopoly, the USFL lawyers as the prevailing party were paid by the NFL. It's stories like this that warm the cockles of a lawyer's heart.

Nominal damages are awarded when you prove the allegations of your complaint that the defendant has legal liability, but in reality you have not suffered any real damages. In other words, you proved your point but haven't suffered any economic loss.

For example: You proved that the defendant entered your property without permission to trim some dead branches from a tree on your property that hangs over his property. The defendant testifies that the tree had to be trimmed before the branches fell and hurt someone.

You can establish that the defendant committed the tort of trespass to real property, yet what damages did you actually suffer? Some bent blades of grass? There isn't enough damage to qualify as compensatory damages. In a situation like this, the court may award you a minimal amount, such as one dollar as nominal damages. In other words: You won, so what?

If, on the other hand, the defendant came on the property without permission to trim the tree and the branch he cut fell and damaged your fence, compensatory or actual damages would be awarded upon your proving the facts.

Behaving badly can be costly — punitive damages

Punitive damages are damages designed to punish the defendant for outrageous behavior — punish him above and beyond the actual monetary loss to discourage him and everyone else from doing such a thing again.

Punitive damages are awarded frequently in intentional tort cases, such as defamation. They're also sometimes awarded in business situations such as when a bill collector's actions threaten or harass a debtor.

Say you've been out of work for two years and you finally get a new job. Bill collectors have been calling you at all hours of the day and night on a regular basis threatening you with all kinds of dire consequences, including calling your new boss and telling him what a deadbeat you are. (You could point out that this would probably get you fired, ending any possibility that they'd ever get paid, but collection agencies often don't understand these fine points.)

Most states now prohibit such activities and allow you to maintain an action for harassment and collect actual and punitive damages from the harasser.

A common source of punitive damages is when the legislature creates a right to sue in a certain situation and, as part of the law, gives an injured party an additional right to seek damages beyond those actually suffered. So punitive damages are awarded if a business or an individual violates a statute that the legislature passed to restrict those certain behaviors and activities.

In some cases, the court can make the defendant pay treble damages, so you can collect three times the actual damages you suffered because of the defendant's actions.

Punitive damages aren't generally awarded in small clams cases because small claims cases don't usually fit the profile of punitive damage cases. One exception is if the defendant's actions constituted a deceptive or unfair business practice under the law or if an employer failed to pay wages to an employee.

Typical *deceptive practices* include the following:

✔ Putting the name of a phony corporation on the company's billhead (paper used for billing, on which corporation name and address is printed).

✔ Indicating that the business is properly licensed when it's not.

✔ Engaging in any practice deliberately designed to trick a consumer.

A quick computer search or a call to the agency that licenses the type of business the defendant runs can help you determine whether you can sue for punitive damages.

Liquid Gold: Dealing with Liquidated Damages

Liquidated in this case doesn't mean things being soled for bargain-basement prices, like it does on the late-night infomercials. Liquidated — and unliquidated — damages are specific types of damages that can affect whether or not you can sue and how much you can collect.

Agreeing ahead of time on liquidated damages

Liquidated damage clauses often show up in contracts. In these clauses, the parties agree in advance that they won't sue each other if there's a breach of the contract. They pick an amount of money both agree is a fair estimate of the damage each side suffers if the other side breaches the contract.

These cases sound like they would never end up in court because the settlement details are worked out ahead of time, but that's not necessarily the case. First, both parties must agree which side caused the breach. If they do, there's no need to go to court.

If they don't, however, the party suing must prove the other party broke the contract. Even if the case is won, damages may be limited to the amount of the liquidated damage clause, even if the actual damages are more.

 You can't set the liquidated damage clause at such a high amount that the court may think it's a penalty. The amount of the clause must be reasonable related to the damages suffered. If a court deems that the amount selected is a penalty, the court won't enforce a liquidated damage clause. What this means is that if you and the defendant can't resolve the dispute without going to court, you'll still have to prove your actual damages and hope they're pretty close to the amount in the liquidated damage clause.

Suppose you're interested in buying a piece of vacant land from the defendant for $100,000 but aren't sure whether the town will permit you to build what you want on the property. You enter into a contract with the defendant that says that if you don't close title in 60 days the parties agree that there will be liquidated damages of $5,000.

If you decide not to buy the property, and the seller sues you for breach, the court may honor the liquidated damage clause because $5,000 was about the amount of money he had to expend for the two months for real estate taxes and insurance.

If the seller breaches the contract and decides not to sell and you sue him for damages, the court may honor the $5,000 clause because it was pretty close to your actual expenses for an engineer or architect and other planning expenses.

In each case, so long as the actual damages were reasonable and related to the party's actual loss, the court will honor the clause.

If the liquidated damage clause for the same piece of property is $50,0000, this amount would likely be considered a penalty because absent some really extraordinary circumstance, there's no way the clause was reasonably related to either party's actual damages.

Differentiating between liquidated and unliquidated debts

Everyone is aware of the concept of debt — the idea that you owe someone money. But under the law, debt has two different classifications — liquidated and unliquidated. Liquidated debt may sound like something you'd run up at the local watering hole, but that isn't correct. For clarification, read on:

✔ **A liquidated debt** is an undisputed amount owed. It is a *sum certain*, which is a set amount owed.

  For example, you borrowed $1,000 at five percent interest. You didn't pay anything. The plaintiff sues you and produces the note and the business record showing no payments. None of the facts is in dispute. You owe the money.

✔ **An unliquidated debt** is an amount owed but the exact amount is in dispute; you need to prove the amount.

  In this example, you're in a car accident and want to sue the defendant for the damage to your car. His insurance company says you're to blame for the accident. You deny it. You have two estimates for the repair of your car, one for $1,500 the other for $1,600. The insurance company says the damages are only $1,200. This case has to be tried because the amount of damages you suffered is in dispute.

One way the two types of debt differ has to do with payment of the debt:

✔ If the defendant sends you a check for less than the total amount due marked "payment in full" of a liquidated debt and you accept it, it generally doesn't cancel the entire obligation, because you're owed a set amount and got something less than that. Unless you previously agreed in writing to such a settlement, you can still sue for the entire amount.

Example time: You owe your credit card issuer $1,000. You send them a check for $10 marked "payment in full." Do you really think this will effectively discharge your debt? Such a possibility would destroy commercial and credit transactions.

At one time, the creditor had to reject the payment because it was marked payment in full. That's no longer the law unless the creditor issues a written release acknowledging that he accepts that amount as payment in full. Now the law is that the creditor can accept and cash the check and you only owe $990.

✔ If you accept a check in full payment of an unliquidated debt, the debt is discharged because the amount owed is in dispute.

Say that after a fender-bender, you get out of your car and it looks like just your bumper is bent. The defendant says, "You don't really want to put this through insurance do you? It'll take time and jack our rates. I'll give you $500 in full payment for damages." You agree and take the check marked "payment in full for property damage car accident January 1."

You then take the car to the body shop where to your chagrin, you learn that the frame of the car is bent and it will take $5,000 to repair the car. Because this was an unliquidated debt, you're out of luck. After you accept the check, the defendant is released from liability.

Getting What's Coming to You — And Then Some

After you win your case, you may become a little greedy and start wondering what else you can get out of the defendant.

The good news is that you can receive interest or collect some of the money you spent on getting justice. The bad news is that you can't collect every penny you spent.

Collecting interest and other additional monies

In addition to receiving money as damages, you may also be awarded costs, disbursements, and interest.

The court may award you the *statutory costs* incurred including the filing fees, and if the court does the mailing of the summons and complaint, the mailing costs.

You may spend additional monies on your case, on such things as paying expert witnesses, copying records, paying a private process server, and the like. In general, you either won't be compensated for these expenses and disbursements at all, or if a statute or court rule sets out a right to some reimbursement for them, the amount is probably less than the actual expense.

For instance, the process server may have charged you $100 to serve the defendant, but the statute only allows $20 for such an expense. The court can award one of two types of interest:

- ✔ Any interest that was supposed to be charged as part of the agreement.

- ✔ Statutory interest, interest the court awards to you as the winner, is the more common of the two.

    In a contract action, statutory interest may be calculated from the date of the breach of the contract, because that's how long you've been denied the use of your money or the product value.

    The statutory interest rate may be far in excess of any bank rate. For example, in New York, it's nine percent.

And yes, it's time for another example: You loaned money to your deadbeat brother-in-law — $1,000 for one year at five percent interest. He doesn't pay you a dime. You can sue initially for the $1,050 which you're owed at the end of the year or sue for the $1,000 and ask the court to calculate the interest from the date of the breach until the date of the court judgment.

In some states, if the interest puts your damages over the monetary limit of the small claims court, you'll only get up to the court limit. In other states, they may allow the additional money even if it exceeds the limit. Most states say that the damage award is exclusive of interest and costs, so these figures get added to the judgment but don't count in the monetary limit.

In some cases, the interest is calculated from the *date of judgment,* which is the date the small claims court case is decided. This is more common in negligence cases, because in these lawsuits the defendant's fault isn't established until the trial. So the interest can't be assessed until the court determines who is liable.

Expenses that aren't really damages

Invariably every litigant in small claims court — whether it's the plaintiff or the defendant or the witnesses — wants to be compensated for the time they have to expend in bringing the case or defending the case.

I hate to be the bearer of bad news (or, if this is the naked truth, the barer of bad news), but in American jurisprudence, that is, the American court system, each side incurs the expenses of litigating the case. Or, as they say in Brooklyn, "Fuhgedabouddit."

No one can recover for his time or inconvenience in bringing or defending a small claims suit. This extends to claims for legal fees and other expenses incurred to bring or defend the lawsuit.

The only exceptions are if

- ✔ There's a written contract between the parties which specifically allows the recovery of all such costs and expenses by the prevailing party in litigation.
- ✔ There's a statute which permits such recovery.

A common clause in contracts is one that permits the non-breaching party to recover "reasonable" attorney's fees as well as the costs, disbursements, and expenses incurred in bringing any lawsuit to enforce the terms of the contract. But even in these situations, you most likely would be prohibited from collecting any damages for your lost time.

Some cases and statutes say that only the winner, or *prevailing party,* can collect legal fees and costs. The prevailing party may not be the one who brings the case to court. This applies even to contracts which, by their terms, give the right only to one side in the agreement.

Residential leases often include a clause that says that if the landlord has to bring a lawsuit to enforce the terms of the lease, the landlord can recover legal fees and expenses. The lease is silent as to what happens if the tenant wins the suit or brings his own suit against the landlord for breach. In many states, by court decision or statute, this clause applies to both the landlord and the tenant. It becomes a mutual right.

Outside of those situations, don't count on getting compensated for your lost time.

Mitigation of damages: Reducing what the defendant owes you

As unfair as it may seem, in some cases you, the plaintiff, must take steps to reduce the damages the defendant may be responsible for. This is called *mitigation of damages* and occurs primarily in contract situations. The following example helps make this clear:

The defendant signs a two-year lease agreeing to rent an apartment for $1,000 a month. The defendant moves after one year. In theory, you, the plaintiff-landlord, can sit and wait another entire year and then sue the defendant-tenant for breaching the lease. You would sue for the balance of $12,000 due on the lease.

Under the idea of mitigation of damages, the law says that you must take steps to try to re-rent the premises to a new tenant before that year is up and reduce the damages you suffered because of the defendant's breach.

So if you re-rented the premises for $500 a month, then the defendant would only be responsible for $6,000 — the amount left after the defendant gets credit for the $500 a month paid by the new tenant.

If you re-rented the premises for $1,000 a month or more, the defendant would not have any liability because the plaintiff would have no damages.

If you can't re-rent the premises, you can sue the defendant for the $12,000 lost rent when the year is up. But you would have to show what steps you took to re-rent the apartment, such as listing it with real estate brokers, advertising in newspapers or online, and so on.

Also you couldn't advertise the apartment for a monthly rental rate, such as $5,000, that makes it impossible to find a tenant. The law would only award you the fair market value in that situation.

Likewise, if the tenant says he's breaking the lease and leaving early but gives you 30 days or some other notice and you re-rent the place the next day without any break in receiving rent, you have no damages.

Of course, any expenses you incur in re-renting the premises, such as advertising, are recoverable as damages.

Part II
Getting Ready to Go to Court

Five tips before you head to court

- ✔ **Think twice.** You may think court is your only option, but one final time, consider the alternative, including mediation or conciliation.

- ✔ **Get your names straight.** Sounds obvious, maybe, but make sure you're suing the right person, with the right spelling, at the right address.

- ✔ **Don't be a jerk to your clerk.** Be cordial with your clerk when filing your papers.

- ✔ **Brevity is the soul of small claims success.** Tell your story clearly in one or two lines on the complaint form.

- ✔ **A good defense stops a good offense.** Don't expect the defendant not to fight. Anticipate the other side's response.

web extras

Find out where you can get free or nearly-free legal information at www.dummies.com/extras/filingandwinningsmallclaims.

In this part . . .

✔ Before you can go to court, you have to know exactly whom is responsible for the damages you've suffered (a company? an individual?) and what exactly the defendant's address is.

✔ Understand that the court clerk can make your life exponentially easier when it comes to preparing and filing your case, and the reasons you should always respect the clerk and his knowledge.

✔ Prepare to serve your defendant or know what to expect if you are the person served; understand the various methods of informing a defendant that she is being sued and which is the best for your particular situation.

✔ Brush up on alternatives to settling disputes in court, such as using a mediator or going through arbitration. Court is costly, time-consuming, and stressful — make sure it's your best option.

✔ Check out www.dummies.com/extras/filingand winningsmallclaims online for information on things to consider before going to court.

Chapter 6

Just the Facts, Jack: Gathering Your Information

In This Chapter

▶ Identifying and finding the defendant

▶ Filing in the right place

▶ Assembling all the pertinent information

*E*ven if you know your case backwards and forwards, you won't get far if you don't know whom your opponent really is and how to find her. And if you don't know your case backwards and forwards before you ever walk in the doors of the courtroom, you may as well stay home for all the hopes you have of winning.

In this chapter, I lay out the basics of reviewing your case, as well as discuss how to identify your defendant and how to find an elusive defendant — which sometimes isn't so easy.

Determining Who Your Defendant 1s

This may seem like a no-brainer — shouldn't you know, without thinking about it, who you're suing? But things aren't always so clear in the legal world, especially if you're dealing with someone hiding her identity behind storefronts or corporations.

Properly identifying the name of the defendant, whether you're dealing with an individual or a business, is a key element of your case. If you don't have the correct name, you may not get *personal jurisdiction over the defendant,* which means that even though the summons and complaint (legal documents I discuss in Chapter 8) were served on the defendant, she doesn't have to respond to them if she's not properly identified or if she's misidentified. Even if the defendant does respond, your case may be dismissed because you sued the wrong — or a nonexistent — party.

If you do obtain a judgment against the defendant and it turns out her legal name is different from her actual name, the sheriff or marshal you contacted to enforce the judgment may not do so because the name is incorrect. The name of the judgment debtor — the person that you beat in court and from whom you want to get the money — must match the name of the person who owns the asset the sheriff or marshal is seeking to enforce the judgment against. Otherwise, the sheriff or marshal will not take money or property from the judgment debtor that the law permits to be taken.

It's good practice for a judge or whoever is hearing the case to ask both parties to verify their names, but if that doesn't happen, ask the judge to confirm the proper identity of your opponent.

As a plaintiff you want the defendant's real information so that you can collect on a judgment. If you're a defendant being sued by a business (in a situation in which a business can use small claims court), you want to confirm the plaintiff's name because if the business is a corporation that isn't properly registered or filed, it may be prohibited from using the court system. For example, a person or company is conducting its activities under an assumed name. These persons or corporations are known as a d/b/a (short for *doing business as*). A business operating under an assumed name must be properly filed as a d/b/a to use the court system.

For instance, it's unlikely that Mister Mxyzptlk would operate a kryptonite store under Mxyzptlk Emporium. It's more likely that he had registered as Mister Mxyzptlk d/b/a Kryptonite R Us, with the awning reading just Kryptonite R Us. So if the supply of kryptonite he purchased from you failed to stop Superman, he would have to sue using the full d/b/a name and not just the name that was on the awning.

Providing the defendant's address

When you first visit the court clerk (see Chapter 7 for more on how to prepare for this), you need the defendant's address. You'll get nowhere without this, because

- That's where the summons and complaint is served. If you don't know the defendant's address, how can you give her notice that you're suing her? If the defendant doesn't get notice, you can't have a trial.

- The clerk needs to check if the defendant is *present* in the jurisdiction of the court. *Present* in this context means that the defendant has done something locally so that it's fair to serve her under the rules of the court. Jurisdiction here is used to determine if your county or area is the correct court to hear the case. If the defendant doesn't live in the county or work or conduct business in the county, the clerk may not accept your papers for filing.

When the clerk tells you that the rules don't allow you to sue the defendant locally, don't throw a hissy fit. You don't want the clerk to take your money for the filing fee, let you take time off from work for the trial, and pay a witness only to find out from the judge that your case is being tossed and the clerk should never have accepted the filing. You won't get your money back in this case so listen to the clerk and find the right county to file.

For example, you hire a company from the next county to fix your roof. The company doesn't do the job properly and you want to sue the owner. Because she's from another county or in some cases, even from another state, she may not be subject to the jurisdiction of the small claims court in your county. She doesn't live here; she isn't employed here, nor is her place of business here. If she's not subject to your local court's jurisdiction, you have to discover where she's located and file there. Another option is to use the regular civil court, which probably doesn't have such a restriction on who can be sued there.

If you don't have the address of the defendant, you have a problem.

Identifying the defendant

You have the burden to properly identify the defendant. If the person is your next-door neighbor, this isn't terribly difficult. But if you're suing a guy who knocked on your door and offered to pave your driveway, you may have more difficulty.

You need to determine what category the defendant is: an individual or a business. If an individual, make sure the name is complete and properly spelled. If a business, you need to find out if the business is a sole proprietorship, meaning it's owned by one person, or a partnership or some other unincorporated entity.

The defendant may also be a corporation or some other entity that is required to register with some state agency in order to be created or carry on business in your state. If a corporation, is it a nonprofit corporation?

In most instances, it won't matter which category of corporation you're suing. However, if it's a nonprofit corporation you may find yourself limited in what you can recover from it by the doctrine of charitable immunity. Hop over to Chapter 2 for more on that.

If you're suing a business, you need to discover whether the name of the business is its legal name or whether the legal owner is a person or entity doing business under that name, commonly called a d/b/a.

To show the importance of the right name, say you sue "Joe the Cleaner" because that's the name of the business that damaged your clothes and refused to make good. In fact, the person answering to the name Joe is really Nunzio Bacciagalupe, who decided to call himself Joe because no one could pronounce his name.

If you list Joe as the defendant, you're not going to get very far. The correct defendant may be Nunzio Bacciagalupe doing business as Joe the Cleaner or the 13 Main Street Corporation doing business as Joe the Cleaner. Or, it may not be a corporation at all, but an individual such as Soapy Sudds doing business as "Take Me To The Cleaners." In this situation, an individual is doing business under an assumed name. Suing "Take Me To The Cleaners" may not get you the relief you want because in reality there is no legal entity with that name to bring to court.

You may think, "Hey, what's the big deal? I've got the basic info." Well, the big deal is that if you get a judgment against the defendant and you don't have the correct name, you may not be able to collect any money.

A common error people make in property damage cases, such as car accidents, is failing to bring the claim in the name of the owner of the property. Often, the person in possession of the property is not the person who owns the property. In a car accident, the owner of one car should sue the owner and the driver of the other car. If your kid is driving your car and is involved in an accident that's not her fault, she's not the plaintiff — you are, even though she was driving. She may be a witness, but should not be bringing the lawsuit.

Looking for the right business

If you know you're looking for a corporation or other business that might have several names, you need to dig in the right areas to find the proper entity to sue. It should be obvious that not naming the proper entity can waste your time and your money, and if you took your time in bringing the suit, it can also result in having the statute of limitations expire on your claim, permanently barring any potential relief for you.

Starting with the secretary of state

Because a corporation has to be formed in accordance with a state statute, all corporations are registered with a state agency. Generally, the secretary of state registers all businesses in a state. Don't confuse this state office with the Secretary of State of the United States, who could not care less about the names of local corporations.

The following types of businesses are registered with the secretary of state:

✔ **For-profit corporation:** The most common business entity.

A corporation generally has one of these words in its name: corporation (Corp.), incorporated (Inc.), limited (Ltd.), or company (Co.). So identifying a corporation is easy, right? Not necessarily. For instance, in New York the word "company" indicates a partnership and not a corporation.

✔ **Not-for-profit** or **nonprofit corporation:** The purpose of a nonprofit is to use any money it makes to continue to work to achieve the organization's goals, which are charitable in nature. However, just because a business is a not-for-profit corporation doesn't mean that it doesn't have any assets or that it can't make money. You generally can sue nonprofit organizations although some states do restrict this right.

✔ **Other corporations:** Professional corporations (PC), limited liability partnerships (LLP), limited liability companies (LLC), professional limited liability companies (PLLC), and all relatively newly recognized legal entities designed to limit the liability of their members, but having nothing to do with your right to sue them.

Many states allow you online access to business filings with the secretary of state. This information is generally available either for free or for a small fee. This makes it easy for you to verify the correct name of the business. If the information is not available online, you may have to hire someone to conduct a name search for you so you have the correct party to sue. You can find companies who do this work online or speak to a lawyer who handles corporate work.

Checking with the county clerk

In order to research the status of a "doing business as" entity, you generally have to check with the county clerk or at the county seat. Some states may have a central registration for businesses operating under a so-called "assumed" name (d/b/a), but mostly this registration is considered a local activity.

If a business is required to be registered and is not, it may be prohibited from bringing any litigation in any court. This can be an important defense a defendant can raise against a plaintiff who didn't properly register her business.

Tracking an elusive defendant

You may be able to figure out the defendant's legal name or designation, but if your defendant is elusive, try the following ways of tracking her down:

✔ If you're suing a store, look to see if there are any licenses posted somewhere within the store. If you're in a place like New York City, just about every business must have some sort of license, and they're required to be posted.

- ✔ If you have a contract, bill of sale, or invoice from the defendant, it should include the legal name of the entity. In some places, if the business is licensed, the license number should be on the document. You can then contact the licensing agency, give them the number and get the correct name of the defendant.

- ✔ If you paid by check, look at the back of the check to see how it was endorsed and the name of the account the money went into.

- ✔ If you paid by credit or debit card, check your monthly statement for the correct name or contact your card issuer to verify to whom the payment was made.

- ✔ If you know the address of the property where the business is located, check the county clerk records and see who owns the property. If there's a mortgage on it, find out whose name is on it as the borrower. If your lawsuit arises out of an incident concerning the condition of the property, this is a good way to get the name of the owner to name as the defendant in the lawsuit. But be warned: If you're merely looking for the correct name of the business operating at that address, the business may not be the owner — it may be the tenant, so the name of the owner won't help. However, in some states, leases are recorded as well and the name of the tenant which could be the business you're after may be named in the recorded lease.

Knowing your role: Recognizing who you are in court

After you file your case with the court, you get a new name. Most courts refer to the person bringing a lawsuit as the *plaintiff* — although you may be referred to as the *claimant* or *petitioner* in some states. The person being sued also gets a title: *defendant*. The term *respondent* may be used in states that call the person bringing the suit the *petitioner*.

The *court* — meaning the judge — won't refer to you by your given name; for the court's purpose, your name is either *plaintiff* or *defendant*.

It's important to keep this in mind because sometimes the clerk or the judge calling the case says, "When I call your case, please answer plaintiff or defendant." If you don't answer, you will be marked down as not appearing for trial and, if you're the plaintiff, your case will be dismissed. If you're the defendant, a default will be entered against you.

You really don't want to be looking for the clerk after the calendar call trying to explain why you didn't know which party you were so you didn't answer.

Making a minor point: Cases involving minors

Cases involving people under age 18 or those with developmental or some other disability fall into special categories and can require a change in plaintiff or defendant. If you're under the age of 18 and unemancipated, which means still dependent on your parents for support, your parent or guardian has to bring a suit on your behalf.

Likewise, if the person you are suing, the defendant, is under the age of 18, you may have to name the minor's parent because the minor doesn't have the legal capacity to be sued.

Say your daughter and another seventeen-year-old are involved in an automobile accident. Both of the persons involved in the accident are minors and lack the legal capacity to sue in their own names. If you're bringing a personal injury action as the "parent and natural guardian," you would sue the "parent and natural guardian" of the defendant minor. However, if you're bringing a property damage claim, then the fact that your kids are involved won't be important as the owner of each car is the proper plaintiff and defendant.

Persons with developmental disabilities or suffering from a medical condition which prevents them from participating fully in the litigation may need to have a guardian appointed by the court in your state that handles those issues because they may lack the legal capacity to either bring or defend a lawsuit.

If you're the parent of a developmentally disabled child, don't assume that you're always going to be the person making decisions for your child. A person who reaches the age of 18 is legally considered an adult with all the rights and obligations of an adult, developmental disabilities notwithstanding. If your child is unable to take of herself, as the parent you must take steps to have yourself named legal guardian; otherwise, the law presumes that she can act on her own behalf.

As the parent of a developmentally disabled child, I can tell you from personal experience that you must act to have you or your spouse or some other adult appointed as guardian of your child when she reaches legal age. You don't want to find yourself in the hospital emergency room arguing about who is legally able to make decisions in regard to treatment.

Bringing a Case to the Right Location

Venue is the legal term for the physical location of the court. Basically, the question of venue determines which county is the proper place to bring the lawsuit. The three potential places for any lawsuit to be started are:

- ✔ **Where the defendant lives, works, or has a place of business.**
- ✔ **Where the action that caused the lawsuit happened.** This may be where the accident took place, where the contract was made, or where the contract was to be performed. If the dispute involves real property, the lawsuit almost always may be brought where the real property is located.
- ✔ **Where the plaintiff lives, works, or has a place of business.**

Choosing to bring a case where the plaintiff lives is frowned upon because it doesn't appear to be fair to the defendant. On the other hand, bringing the case where the defendant resides is always considered to be fair because the defendant can't claim prejudice or bias or that the plaintiff has a home field advantage.

If you file your papers in the wrong county, in most situations the case will not be dismissed and will proceed in the wrong court. Notice I said in the wrong county, not the wrong court. If you're in the wrong level court, you have a subject matter jurisdiction problem, not a venue problem. (See Chapter 2 for more on this issue.) Where the venue is improper, the case may be transferred

- ✔ **By the court on its own without anyone asking it to do so.** The court may change venue on its own in an instance in which an employee of the court system is a litigant or if one of the parties knows the judge, who's the only small claims judge in the county. The judge would transfer the case to ensure fairness.
- ✔ **By the defendant requesting that the court moves it to the right county.**

Notice I didn't list the plaintiff asking to have the venue changed. As the plaintiff you picked the court, so why would you want to change the location?

The court may actually hear the case even if it's not in the correct county if neither party objects; Venue is presumed to be correct unless someone objects. Also some states have a rule that to change the venue, you have to make an application in the county you think is the correct one. This can be complicated for unrepresented litigants.

You may not have any choice as to where the case is brought if you agreed upon a location in advance or if a statute or administrative rule says the case has to be brought in a particular county.

For example: You enter into a written contract — you can do it by mail, on the Internet, or any other way you can think of to enter into a written contract. Like everyone else in the world, other than looking at the price and the delivery date you don't read any of the small print on the contract. A dispute arises and you sue in your local small claims court.

The next thing you know, your case is being transferred to some county in the middle of nowhere because that's where you agreed to have all lawsuits brought in the small print on the contract. So if you ordered a computer from the Knotwerk Computer Company, from Knotwerk City in Knotwerk County, all named after the founder of the town, Y. Knotwerk, guess where your trial is likely to be. The fact that it is inconvenient to you won't help; you agreed to the terms by signing the contract.

In a similar instance, if you want to sue a government agency, a statute may say that the venue where you have to bring the lawsuit is the county seat or the state capital. So be prepared to pack your bags and put on your travelin' clothes.

If you're suing a business, make sure that the business is present in the county where you want to bring the lawsuit. A business is *present* if it transacts business at a particular location. This usually means something more than one commercial transaction in a state. The mere fact that the business delivered something to you does not necessarily mean you can sue them where you are.

Gathering Your Facts

By putting in a little time before you bring your case, you may save yourself a considerable amount of grief in filing your claim, prepping for trial, and trying your case. Courts aren't a place where you find the social theory of equality of results being applied. In other words, in litigation, there's a winner and a loser, and unlike your kid's after-school sports program, everyone doesn't get a certificate for participating.

Making a list and checking it twice

Gathering your facts in an organized manner before you file your case also helps you get organized to present your case.

At the very minimum, have these facts down cold:

- ✔ Where the event took place, including the exact address
- ✔ When the event took place — the exact date (and time, if relevant)
- ✔ Who was present, with the exact name of the defendant
- ✔ What exactly happened
- ✔ How the defendant could have prevented the event or result
- ✔ Why you feel the defendant owes you

Writing it down for the clerk

If you've carefully prepared your case, you know what kind of case you have and how much money you're suing for. So you'll be prepared when the clerk hands you a piece of paper with space to record your sad tale, also known as the complaint form. The *complaint form* is a brief description of why you're suing the defendant. It should be a short, concise statement advising the defendant of the nature of your claim.

This statement should not include so much detail that it makes Tolstoy's *War and Peace* look like a short story, but it shouldn't be so devoid of information that when the defendant gets to court she says to the judge, "Your honor, I have no idea who this person is and why I'm being sued." A complaint saying, "damage from a car accident," is too sketchy to inform the defendant why she is being sued. This is especially true if the defendant has several car accident claims pending. A better pleading is "Car accident on January 1, 2012, at Main Street and First Avenue." Likewise, a claim listing "rent" as the cause of the suit isn't sufficient. The defendant needs to know what period you're claiming the rent was due. A more acceptable statement would be "Rent due for January 2012 for 123 Main St."

If the rent is $1,000 a month and you're only suing for one month's rent, don't sue for $5,000. You'll look disingenuous before the judge.

If you're suing for damage to your property and the amount due is in dispute or who was at fault is an issue, you can sue for the small claims court's maximum amount. The judge will award the amount you can prove you merit or that the judge feels is reasonable under the circumstances.

Chapter 7

Dealing with the Clerk

*I*f you haven't spent much time in court, you probably have no idea that one person can affect your case more than almost any other — and it's not the judge. Meet the clerk, the person who can make life easy or difficult for you in the court world.

In this chapter, I introduce you to the clerk and fill you in on how to get the most out of your working relationship. After you decide to file in small claims court, every case begins at the clerk's desk. Giving him the information he needs, making a positive impression and, most of all, respecting the power he holds in your court case will simplify your life as you prepare and file your small claims suit.

Understanding How and Why Clerks Rule the Legal World

Judges and lawyers just think they control the courtroom, but not so: Clerks do. Newcomers to court often don't grasp this, and it often causes great sorrow down their path to justice. Before you set foot in the courthouse, keep in mind the following rules:

> ✔ **Rule #1:** The clerk is the most important person in the room. He also has the most relevant knowledge to help you.

> ✔ **Rule #2:** Even if you have a law degree from Yale, a medical degree from Harvard, and a PhD from Oxford, Rule #1 still applies.

Respecting the clerk's knowledge

Why is the clerk the most important person in the room when you file a small claims suit? Because if you're rude or disrespectful to the court clerk, you may not get the help you need. You will probably get what the letter of the law requires him to give, but not one thing more.

But more than that, the clerk knows his stuff. He deals with people filing cases every day and is far more familiar with the paperwork and the problems inexperienced litigants encounter than you are. In addition to knowing where the bodies are buried, the clerk also knows the right way to get things done in the courthouse. The clerk can tell you about errors in your paperwork before you start the process, and thus prevent you from making a mistake that would get your case dismissed, sometimes without even getting to a hearing on the merits.

If you have an attitude with the clerk, don't be surprised if your incorrect papers get filed and your case winds up getting dismissed by the judge because of those errors. A wrong filing means you have to start over again. Or, in the worst case, it means having your case dismissed by the court with prejudice, which means you can't restart it.

Getting off on the right foot with the clerk

Sometimes it may seem that the clerk is being uncooperative, but this is the exception and not the rule. In urban courts, clerks deal with hundreds of people filing papers every day, and almost all of these litigants file papers on their own, without using a lawyer. Whereas lawyers generally know what they're doing in court, the average person does not, unless he reads a book like this one. You can imagine that dealing with a constant barrage of inexperienced litigants is sometimes frustrating for the clerk.

Clerks deal with people who are angry about being sued, with people who may not be able to understand instructions either because of language problems or some learning disability, and with people who think they are smarter than the clerk and feel that they really should not have to be wasting their valuable time responding to a baseless lawsuit.

You can start off on the wrong foot just by showing how annoyed you are at having to stand in line. Try to chill on the outside, even if you're seething on the inside. It's not the clerk's fault that ten people got in the line before you did. Besides, you probably spend as much time at your local drive-through fast-food joint.

Never say, "The clerk made me do it"

As a judge, one thing I hate to hear from a plaintiff is, "The clerk told me to do it this way." This is no way to win the judge over, for a couple of reasons: First, the clerk isn't supposed to give you legal advice; and second, a plaintiff who uses this excuse is usually doing things so far removed from the proper way to handle a case that I find it hard to believe that anyone would have told the plaintiff to do it that way, let alone a clerk.

A good way to make a bad situation worse is to insist that the clerk's advice is correct and ignore the advice the judge gives you. This type of exchange usually ends with a judicial response like "When the clerk goes to law school and starts wearing robes, you can follow the clerk's advice." Don't start off on the wrong foot by undermining the judge!

 It's always better to approach the clerk with the attitude that you don't know what you're doing and would appreciate any advice he can offer. This probably isn't far from the truth, anyway. Although you don't want to come across as a bumbling idiot who will need excessive hand-holding during the entire procedure, acting as if you could use a friendly face and a guiding hand will get you more genuine help than a know-it-all attitude. Remember, however, that clerks are not authorized to give legal advice.

Being prepared for meeting the clerk

Being prepared isn't only a good philosophy for Boy Scouts. You win Brownie points with the clerk by having your paperwork ready to file. You are responsible for having all of your information in order when you show up at the clerk's office to file your papers.

Many small claims courts have books or pamphlets available either at the clerk's office, by mail, or online. Read the book or review this information before you pay your first visit to the courthouse. If you didn't go over the rules for your small claims court before you filed your case, it's imperative that you do so before you appear for your trial. Many courts also have help centers staffed by lawyers or other volunteers to assist you with understanding the process. Generally they can't give legal advice but can explain the forms being used, and answer your questions about the small claims court procedure.

Just because you don't have an attorney doesn't mean that you won't be expected to know the rules and what is expected of you, whether you're the plaintiff or the defendant.

Many courts now permit small claims cases to be filed online. You still have to provide the same information as with a paper filing, but you don't have to show up at court to do it. Although this saves you the hassle of standing in line, it also distances you from the clerk. If you think you may need some help with filing correctly, see the clerk in person. Also some courts charge extra if you file on line because you'll be paying by credit card.

Information Every Clerk Needs

Your paperwork will proceed more smoothly if the clerk has all the information he needs. Some information comes from the form you fill out to get your case started. You may need to volunteer other information yourself to help the clerk help you, which is another reason to be prepared before you show up in the clerk's office.

Determining whether you want a jury trial

One of the questions the clerk may ask you or that you must answer on your claim form is, "Do you want a jury trial?" The proper answer is "no." If you answer "yes," you'll not only have to pay a larger filing fee, you'll also be subjected to the humiliation of the clerk and everyone else in their cubicles laughing at you.

Cop and lawyer shows on television certainly make it look easy to try a case in front of a jury, but looks can be deceiving. If you're filing in small claims court, you don't want a jury trial for a number of reasons including the following:

✔ Most states prohibit jury trials in small claims actions. If you think you want a jury trial, check with the clerk to see if you can even do it.

✔ Additional costs may be imposed by the court system in a jury trial.

✔ Opting for a jury trial may delay your case because it puts an additional strain on the court facilities and causes scheduling problems with the regular civil calendar.

✔ Picking a jury is complicated and, unless you're a lawyer, probably way beyond your skill level. Even many lawyers don't know how to pick a jury well, and cases are won and lost in the jury selection process. In fact, an entire industry has grown up around the jury selection process, with experts brought in to instruct attorneys on how to pick a favorable jury and how to understand the demographics of a jury pool. Obviously this doesn't happen in small claims courts.

✔ The judge isn't going to be thrilled about having a novice non-attorney conduct a jury trial. A case with a novice attorney means extra work for the judge because he has to make sure that the lawyer's inexperience doesn't result in an unjust outcome; when a non-lawyer tries a case before a jury, the role of the judge gets even more difficult.

✔ If you decide on a jury trial without using counsel and the defendant gets an attorney, the case can turn against you in an instant. Think the battlefield is going to be level if you're up against an attorney in front of the jury? No amount of television watching can prepare you for the real thing.

✔ Although the aim of a small claims court proceeding is an outcome based on *substantial justice,* a judge hearing a jury trial may be less likely to cut you slack when you make mistakes, less likely to ask questions to witnesses when you get tongue-tied, and less likely to relax evidence rules.

If you have a lawyer representing you, discuss having a jury trial with him. Yours may be the type of case where a jury of your peers will be more sympathetic to you than a judge may be.

Say what? Arranging for an interpreter

If you don't speak English, you're entitled to have someone who speaks your native language assist you. Either the plaintiff or the defendant can request an interpreter.

If you're the plaintiff, tell the clerk you need an interpreter when you file your complaint. If you're the defendant:

✔ If no written answer is required, notify the clerk before the scheduled trial date of the trial.

✔ If you need to file a written answer include your request for an interpreter when you file your answer or on the first date scheduled by the court for the parties to appear on the case.

If you have a witness who needs an interpreter, you must also notify the clerk of this. Failure to have an interpreter present can result in the case being adjourned until you get one. In fact, if you know the defendant will need an interpreter because the two of you conversed in your native language when you entered into your contract, you should let the clerk know that when you file your papers.

In some courts, such as New York City, the interpreters are all either court employees or private individuals who have been certified by the court as interpreters of a particular language and are compensated by the court system.

In some states, the rules permit a family friend or relative to serve as an interpreter. The problem with this situation is that no one knows if the person is translating accurately, which can be a problem if the case involves legal or technical terms. There may not be an accurately descriptive word in that person's native language and the untrained interpreter may not translate correctly.

Be absolutely sure your interpreter knows his stuff. In a case I tried, one party had an interpreter. At a break in the trial, a juror sent me a note saying that she was fluent in that language and that the interpreter, who had been court approved, was not accurately translating what was being said. We were able to resolve the problem by having a new interpreter assigned to the case and avoided a mistrial — and having to try the case over.

If it becomes obvious that your opponent needs an interpreter, don't oppose an adjournment so that one can be found. One of the easiest ways to trigger a retrial is for your opponent to say, "I don't understand English" when filing his appeal.

Judges don't particularly like having to try cases over again, especially for something that could have been dealt with before the trial started if someone had said something.

Let me share something that always amazes me: The number of defendants who, after having negotiated a contract with the plaintiff and having it reduced to a writing signed by the parties, get to court and suddenly can no longer understand English. In a situation like this, instead of standing there insisting that the defendant speaks better English than Samuel Johnson, agree to have an interpreter present and adjourn the case. Even if the judge believes you, if the defendant loses and convinces an appeals court his rights were ignored, you will be trying the case over.

Proclaiming yourself a senior citizen

Some small claims courts have special rules for senior citizens. In places where small claims court is in session primarily at night, seniors may be permitted to bring their cases in the day. Courts recognize that seniors may have trouble traveling at night so sometimes accommodations are made. If you're a senior, check with the clerk of your local small claims court for any special rules that apply to you.

Making the clerk aware if you have a disability

If you have a disability that affects your ability to file or present your case at trial, the court system must take steps to accommodate you. If you have trouble walking and need a wheelchair-accessible courtroom, if you're hearing impaired and need amplification or a sign-language translator, or if you're visually impaired and need a visual interpreter, let the court know in advance so that an accommodation can be made. If you wait until the date of trial, it may result in the case being adjourned.

It's imperative that you let the clerk of the court know of your needs as soon as possible — when you file the case if you're the plaintiff or when you receive the summons and complaint if you're the defendant. Any witness who needs assistance must also be accommodated. If no one tells the court personnel in advance, and you wait until the time of trial to raise the issue, you only delay the case and make an adjournment necessary.

If you're illiterate, let the clerk know this also. But in all my years on the bench, I have never had an adult admit they're illiterate and could not read the contract that the suit is about or that they can't read the settlement agreement they're signing in court.

Pay Up: The Filing Fee

Each state charges a minimum fee to file your small claims suit. Some states have a sliding scale for the fees, which means that the greater the amount you're suing for, the higher the fee you pay. Generally, the filing fees are less than $100. However, check with the court clerk; with the budgetary crises facing many states, the legislature may have raised the filing fees to generate revenue.

In most states, the filing fee in small claims court is generally less than the fees charged in regular civil courts. If you can file online, you may pay an additional fee for the convenience.

If you can't afford the filing fees, you may be entitled to have the fee waived. You have to file an affidavit explaining why you need the fee waived and may have to provide proof of income or lack thereof. Even though you make an application for the waiver of fees, your request may not be granted. It's up to the judge or other official who makes the determination.

As the plaintiff, you're bringing the suit and are required to pay the fee to start your case. If you win, most states permit you to recover the filing fee as part of your judgment. If you lose, you won't get the fee back.

Paying the filing fee

States have different rules about paying filing fees. Some courts only take cash or a certified check. If cash is required, you may have to bring the exact amount, as the clerk will not make change. The clerk may be prohibited from keeping an overpayment even if you consent to it. So if the charge to file is $15.96, that amount and not one penny more or less is what you have to give the clerk.

Most courts won't take a personal check for the payment of the filing fee. It may not clear on time, especially if your small claims case is placed on the court calendar quickly. Also, bouncing a check is a crime in most states. And although in places like New York, it's unlikely that anyone would have you arrested for passing a bad check, in small towns, officers of the law may not be so tolerant. You really wouldn't want to go directly to jail after your small claims appearance, would you? Many courts now take credit cards or debit cards for the payment of the filing fees. However, this is not a universally accepted payment method and there may be an additional charge involved.

Filing more than one case at a time

Perhaps you have several cases you want to bring in small claims court against different defendants and wonder if you can bring them all at the same time. The answer is, it depends on the rule in the state where you live. Your state may

- Place no limit to how many cases you can file at one time.

- Restrict the number of cases that can be filed in a particular time period, such as a month or a year.

- Charge higher filing fees after you reach a certain number of cases. This is one time when you don't get a cut rate for buying in bulk.

The rules are primarily designed to prevent commercial plaintiffs from dominating the court with their litigation and preventing other members of the general public from bringing cases. Assume, for example, that your state permits condominium associations to sue in small claims court for unpaid common charges assessed against each unit owner. If there's no limit on the number of cases that can be filed, the condominium could sue all 100 homeowners at the same time and dominate the entire calendar, effectively shutting out all other plaintiffs for that day or night.

Chapter 8

Informing the Defendant About the Case

In This Chapter

▶ Understanding the options for serving papers

▶ Preparing for the defendant's reaction

▶ Responding to counterclaims

▶ Looking at cross-claims

*Y*ou've done your research. You know what kind of case you have, how much money you want, the real name of the defendant, and where she's located (if you don't, hop over to Chapter 6, then meet me back here). You went to the clerk's office and filed your papers.

There's one slight problem: The defendant doesn't have the slightest idea that she's about to be sued. And you won't get far in court unless you let her in on what's going on.

We've all seen "you've been served" scenes on television legal dramas, and that's what I fill you in on now: serving papers.

In this chapter, I review the procedure for serving your opponent with papers that let her know she's being sued, including the different ways papers can be served, and then I prepare you for the types of defendant responses you should be prepared to handle — such as what to do if the object of your disaffection turns around and sues you back.

Serving Papers: The Service of Process

If the defendant is your neighbor or a local merchant, she may know you're dissatisfied with something she did. You may have said something to her directly or resorted to the less diplomatic method of bad-mouthing her every chance you get to everyone you meet.

That's one way to get your point across, but it won't get you any cash reward. Unless she receives your equivalent of a lawyer's letter threatening to bring suit unless the dispute is resolved, it's unlikely that she knows she'll soon be adding the title of "defendant" to her name.

You may want to run right over to her house and hand the scoundrel a copy of your complaint or nail it to her door, like Martin Luther did some time ago with the 95 theses. You may want to do this — but you shouldn't, and as a matter of fact in most states, you legally can't.

The specific procedure in the court system for giving notice to the defendant is called *service of process*. If you don't do this correctly, you can mess up your entire case and lose any chance you had at receiving any reward.

Before you can drag someone into court, you need to get what is called personal jurisdiction over that person. *Personal jurisdiction* refers to the power or authority of the court to bring the defendant before it to have the defendant defend the case. It must be done in a manner to insure fairness. To establish personal jurisdiction, the defendant must be given notice of the lawsuit by a procedure established by court rules.

After all, how fair would it be to have a trial without giving the defendant a chance to present her side? Part of the concept of fairness is that even if you're in the proper court for jurisdictional issues, the defendant has the right to hear what you say and have the right to defend herself.

The following sections review the different methods you can use to legally serve pleadings, which consist of the summons and complaint. These include mail delivery or handing directly to the defendant or other person.

There are several different methods of obtaining *personal service of process* on a defendant, which is simply legalese for serving legal papers. Personal service of process refers to the various means of giving a defendant notice that you've started a lawsuit against her.

CHECKOUT SLIP
DELPHOS PUBLIC LIBRARY
309 W SECOND ST
DELPHOS OH 45833
419-695-4015

Date charged: 7/20/2016,15:47
Title: Filing & winning small claims for d
ummies
Item ID: 33064009403319
Date due: 8/19/2016,23:59

.
.
.

- ✔ **Mail service:** Sending it through the U.S. Postal Service to the defendant at her last known resident or business address.

- ✔ **Personal delivery:** Having someone — not you — hand-deliver it to the named defendant.

- ✔ **Substituted service:** Handing it to someone, such as a family member, who will give it to the defendant.

- ✔ **Conspicuous service:** Taping the summons and complaint or otherwise attaching — the law uses the term "affixing" — it to the defendant's door.

You've got mail: Delivering through the post

Because small claims court is designed to keep litigation costs down, the most common method of giving notice to the defendant in small claims court is by mail. Mail is the cheapest method.

Interestingly, snail mail is the least-preferred method in almost all other courts because it lacks the certainty of all the other delivery methods. If mail service is not successful, the rules of small claims court authorize another method of personal service to be used.

In most small claims courts, the clerk does the mailing. The mailing is made by regular first class mail, certified mail return receipt requested, registered mail, priority mail, overnight mail, or by a combination. The rules or the clerk of your small claims court will tell you which method is used.

The mail service method authorized usually provides some mechanism so that the sender gets proof that the defendant actually received the papers. If the clerk does the mailing, you pay an additional fee to the court for the cost of the mailing. This fee is collected when you file your complaint and is usually included in the filing fee.

In all likelihood, the clerk will mail two notices to the defendant: one by regular mail and one by certified mail return receipt requested. If both notices are returned as undeliverable, you will have to look to getting a better address for mail service or try one of the other notification methods listed in the following sections.

There's one recurring problem with the commonly used service by certified mail return receipt: Often, if the letter is unclaimed or undelivered, the court doesn't receive notice of the failure until after the scheduled trial date.

As the plaintiff, you may obtain a default judgment because the defendant never appeared. But, at some point, the defendant will find out about the judgment and try to get the case restored to the calendar for a hearing on the merits. Remember small claims court tries to give everyone their day in court so if the defendant can establish that she never got the mail notice, it's likely the case will be restored for a trial.

If the court record shows that the mail was *unclaimed,* meaning the address was accurate and the defendant ignored the notice, rather than *undeliverable,* meaning the address was incorrect or the person you're suing doesn't live there, the court may allow you to go forward, feeling the defendant is trying to ignore the service of process.

If the court record shows that the address is accurate but the mailing was returned *unclaimed,* it usually means that the notice was received but ignored, and the court may decline the defendant's request to schedule a new trial. Courts generally are not that sympathetic to litigants who are too busy to pick up or accept certified mail.

But in many small claims courts, no matter how long after you got the judgment, and no matter that the defendant chose not to respond to the service of process, the court may decide to put the case back on the court calendar for a trial on the merits, as it is the policy of most small claims courts to give all litigants their day in court.

If the mailing is returned as "moved, left no forwarding address," then it's obvious you won't have a valid judgment because the defendant didn't get notice. In this case, you can ask for a new court date or withdraw the case without prejudice and bring the case back when you locate a new address where you can serve the defendant.

If given the choice, go ahead and get the judgment. For one thing, maybe the defendant will just pay it when she receives notice of the judgment. Or the court may deny her application to restore the case, which means your judgment is valid. If the defendant tries to get a new trial date, you have current contact info, because she's shown up in court to make the application, and maybe you can settle the case.

Worst-case scenario is you have to try the case again. But now that you have had the experience of trying a case, you're familiar with court process and know what evidence the judge felt was important in awarding you the judgment, all of which gives you an advantage in court for the second go-around.

If you get a notice from the court that the defendant has filed an application to have the case restored to the calendar, don't you ignore it. Show up on the court date of that application and be prepared and ready to go.

Often plaintiffs get a copy of the notice to restore the case and don't appear on the return date because they are consenting to the restoration of the case for trial. Unfortunately in some courts, the judge will grant the defendant's application to restore the case for that date and if you're not there your case will be dismissed. The better practice is to show up and, if you're not ready, consent to the case being restored and ask the court for a new trial date.

There's also the possible advantage that if you show up on the return date of the defendant's application and you're prepared but the defendant isn't, the judge may deny the application and let the judgment stand.

Making it personal: Handing it over via personal delivery

Personal delivery, having the pleadings actually handed to the named defendant, is the best way to give the defendant notice.

Obviously, personal delivery is the most efficient way to tell someone that she's being sued. It is hard for a defendant to claim she didn't know about the case if the summons and complaint were served by personal delivery.

However, personal delivery is also one of the most expensive and time-consuming service of process methods because the papers must actually be given to the named defendant. You have to pay either a licensed process server or a public official such as the constable, sheriff, or marshal to serve the pleadings.

Because of the expense involved in personal delivery service, most small claims courts do not require this type of delivery initially. However, if the court's preferred method of service, usually mail, fails and the defendant doesn't respond to the initial summons, the court may require personal delivery.

The added cost of personal delivery may be recoverable if you win your case depending on the rules in your state.

Personal delivery is the most difficult method of service to complete, because the papers must be handed to the named defendant. Processes servers often have to be fleet of foot because, hard as it is to believe, people actually don't like to be sued. Sometimes defendants get downright annoyed and chase the process server.

One good reason that you're not allowed to serve the summons yourself is to prevent your civil suit from becoming a criminal matter if you and the defendant take your argument to the next level and someone starts swinging.

It is also not a good idea to go with the process server to watch the fun and then stand there yelling remarks the court would consider baiting, such as any version of "see ya in court." It's an equally bad idea to record the serving of the summons to post on your Facebook profile.

If you think the defendant is going to avoid service of process or deny her identity, give the process server a photograph to help identify the defendant. If you have to go with the process server to ensure delivery to the proper person, stay in the background and don't participate or act out. If you can't behave, have someone else who knows the defendant help pick her out.

If the defendant refuses to open the door and accept service, a process server will know how to properly handle that situation and file an appropriate affidavit of service. You or the friend you convinced to serve process won't — another compelling reason to hire a professional to deliver your summons for you.

Also, even if the defendant decides to turn and sprint away from you yelling some version of "Can't catch me, I'm the gingerbread man," a professional can still find a way to serve the papers.

Back around the time Abe Lincoln was serving process, the law stated that the process server had to physically touch the defendant with the notice — this is no longer the case. Fun fact: Lincoln didn't go to law school — he studied with a lawyer. States that still permit becoming a lawyer without attending law school label such attorneys *Lincoln lawyers*.

Substituted service: Giving it to someone else

Substituted service is when the pleadings cannot be hand-delivered to the named defendant but are delivered to a *person of suitable age and discretion* — generally held to be an individual over the age of 14. This age requirement is only a presumption, which means that the defendant can later establish that the person really wasn't a person of suitable age and discretion. Even though delivery is to someone other than the named defendant it's still a form of personal service.

Someone over the age of 14 who doesn't understand that the papers she's receiving have legal implications will probably not be deemed a person of suitable age and discretion. Delivery to such a person is not valid service meaning you can't get an enforceable judgment against the defendant because the notice requirements of the law haven't been complied with. Additionally, after leaving a copy with the adult, another copy of the summons and complaint has to be mailed to the defendant because actual personal delivery hasn't been made to the named defendant.

The recipient can be a family member, a business associate, or any other person who would presumably deliver the document to the defendant. It can't be a stranger or laborer temporarily at the site.

If the defendant lives in an apartment house with a doorperson and the doorperson refuses you entry to the building, service generally can be made on the doorperson. A similar rule applies at a business where a receptionist or security guard prohibits entry. If the rules of an apartment or office building prevent direct delivery of a pleading, the person preventing the delivery can be an acceptable substitute.

A few examples of valid and invalid substitution service:

- You ask your friend to serve the complaint on your neighbor. Your friend, being a bit of a coward, sees the neighborhood kid delivering the free weekly coupon guide going to the defendant's house and hands her the papers.

  That's probably not going to be good service. There was no obligation for the coupon guide delivery girl to accept the papers initially on behalf of the defendant, nor was there any expectation she would re-deliver them to the defendant. After all, the casually tossed weekly coupon guide is more likely to land in a tree or soak in the porch gutter than to make it in the front of the door, so why would the summons and complaint get any better treatment?

- A process server sees my 30-year-old, developmentally disabled son sitting on the porch and hands him the complaint. My son is non-verbal and can't read or write. That service is not good. Although a person of suitable age, he lacks any discretion. But, as the defendant, I would have to prove this fact to the court.

- The process server sees my ten-year-old daughter, who is a member of the genius group Mensa, on the porch and hands her the complaint. She looks at it and says, "Oh yes, I know what this is. It's an important legal paper. I know because I've seen them in my mom's law office. I'll give it to my dad." This is probably good service because the ten-year-old understands the legal implications of the document and knows to deliver it to the defendant parent.

Conspicuous service: Going to the tape

Conspicuous service, otherwise known as *affix and mail* or *nail and mail service,* occurs when the process server cannot find the defendant at the defendant's home after making several attempts to deliver the pleadings.

These attempts generally have to be made at various hours of the day and night. After making several attempts — most states require three or more — the process server can then affix a copy of the pleadings to the door and mail an additional copy to the defendant. The additional copy is mailed because there wasn't personal delivery to the named defendant.

Affixing means with tape. You can't take out a nail and hammer and attach the complaint to the door, the doorframe, or the like. Using a nail isn't a good idea — especially if it's a glass door. Putting the pleadings in the mailbox is also a no-no.

If a doorperson at an apartment house won't let the process server even come inside the building, in most states, the process server can tape the summons and complaint to the front door of the building.

Although this is not as an effective method of giving notice as personal delivery or substituted service — after all, a tornado can come and remove the papers or perhaps a young person conducting a paper drive may take it — it does give you the psychic lift of knowing that all of the defendant's neighbors now know she's being sued.

Self-service: Serving the defendant yourself

Serving the defendant yourself is a bad idea on several levels, including the fact that it usually isn't permitted. This is because you have a vested interest in saying the defendant was served. If the defendant is served and does not show up to court, you, the plaintiff, can get a default judgment by swearing you complied with all of the rules for service.

You are not reliable in this case, from the court's point of view. It would be very tempting for you to say you served the defendant even if you did not in order to obtain a judgment. That's why it's better to get a disinterested person to serve the process — a licensed process server or a public official such as the sheriff or the marshal.

You can ask a friend to serve the process, but the danger of this is that your friend won't follow the rules for proper service. If the complaint isn't served properly, you don't have personal jurisdiction over the defendant and you can't get a valid enforceable judgment.

Or, your friend may serve the process properly but then forget to fill out the affidavit of service, which has to be filed with the court to prove the complaint was delivered. This may require a special separate hearing called a *traverse hearing* if the defendant claims no service was made.

In a traverse hearing, the defendant appears in court and claims that she was never served at all or wasn't served in the manner set out in the statute for service of process.

The burden then shifts to you to prove your process server complied with the law. The process server must appear and testify as to how she accomplished service.

A traverse hearing can be held before your trial or after your trial if the defendant learns of the lawsuit when you go to enforce your default judgment.

In many courts, the clerk will reject the affidavit outright if it isn't completed properly. If this happens, you usually can correct the defects before the case is on the court calendar.

If the defect is found after the fact, in the best-case scenario, you'll have to have a traverse hearing and establish that the documents were properly delivered. At which point the fact that the person serving the papers filed a false affidavit, even unwittingly, can be used to attack her credibility.

In the worst case scenario, your case will be dismissed for lack of proper service, meaning you have to start over again, and if you waited a long time to bring the case initially, you may have statute of limitations problems.

So if you have to do something other than mail service, hire a professional process server, or better still use the marshal or sheriff if that is the procedure in your state.

What to do if none of the other methods works

Obviously, you can't present your case to the court unless reasonable efforts are made to notify the defendant. The law states that the defendant doesn't actually have to have received the pleading, only that a method "reasonably calculated" to give notice of your claim was used.

So if the defendant claims that gremlins removed something which she saw taped to her door or that a yeti has been stealing her mail on a regular basis, the court may still say that service was good because the method used was designed to give notice.

If for some reason none of the regular methods of service have been successful, you can ask the court to create a reasonable method of service. One common one is to have the summons and complaint published in a local newspaper for one or more days. Faxing a notice to the defendant may also work if you have her fax number.

Fortunately, in small claims court, you generally aren't going to have such problems, because you know where the defendant is and you haven't waited so long to sue that the defendant may have moved. Right? Good.

Preparing for Battle: What to Expect from the Defendant

After the defendant is served, she should follow the directions on the summons and complaint, and either go to small claims court and file a written answer if that is the practice or appear in court on the return date in the summons and file an oral answer — her response to your complaint. Because you filed the complaint, you should know which procedure your small claims court uses.

In the next sections, I deal with what you as the plaintiff may expect in the defendant's answer. Some answers by the defendant may require you to respond in some manner. The defendant's answer may also contain denials, often referred to as the Sergeant Schultz defense:" I know nothing." This means that you have to prove the allegations in your complaint to the court, because the defendant has challenged your assertions by denying the complaint.

A defendant can also come back with what is called an *affirmative defense,* which is a legal response to your claim that the defendant says relieves her of liability. The defendant has the burden of proving her affirmative defenses. (In Chapter 10, I deal with the answer from the defendant's perspective.)

In the following sections, I discuss two potential responses from a defendant that require you to respond in some formal manner: *counterclaims,* in which the defendant turns around and sues you; and *cross-claims,* in which you sue more than one person.

Counterclaims: When the person you're suing sues you

You may be asking yourself, "I started the lawsuit first, but can the defendant also sue me?" The answer is "yes." The defendant can file what's called a *counterclaim* against you. In doing this, the defendant is essentially saying, "What! You're suing me? I should be suing you!"

Counterclaims can arise from the same incident or transaction or from another incident or transaction between you and the defendant.

If the defendant files a counterclaim, your name and the defendant's are reversed on the court documents. The defendant is called the plaintiff on the counterclaim and you're the defendant on the counterclaim. (Think about how many trees could be saved if judges didn't have to keep using all of those descriptive words when writing a decision with counterclaims.)

So, for example, if you're the plaintiff, your opponent is the defendant. However, if there is a counterclaim, the defendant will then be referred to as the plaintiff on the counterclaim and you'll be the defendant on the counterclaim.

In some situations, you have to file a response to the counterclaim. Your answer is the equivalent of the defendant's answer, but it's called a *reply*. In your reply you may issue denials or affirmative defenses like the defendant did to your complaint.

Generally, in small claims court, you don't need to file a reply, especially if the claim and counterclaim arise from the same event. But the safest thing to do is to check with the court clerk to see what the rules are.

Situations that often give rise to counterclaims include

- ✔ **Minor car accident:** You're involved in a fender-bender. You start your action first and claim the defendant was at fault — *negligent,* in legal terms — and that the defendant's negligence caused property damage to your car. The defendant can file a counterclaim against you, alleging you were the person at fault and you caused damage to her car.

- ✔ **A contract lawsuit:** The tenant who moved out of an apartment sues the landlord to get her security deposit back. The landlord may file a counterclaim alleging that the tenant still owes a month's rent, or damaged the apartment in moving, or left the apartment so dirty that she had to hire people to clean and repaint and dispose of abandoned property.

Suppose, however, that when the tenant sues the landlord for the return of the security deposit, the landlord doesn't assert a claim arising from the tenancy, but instead says that a month before she loaned the tenant her car and the tenant damaged it.

This, too, is a valid counterclaim because, although it addresses two different events, it involves the same parties. In this situation, the tenant would want to file a reply to the counterclaim, because the underlying issue is negligence arising from a different event and not the landlord-tenant relationship.

Sometimes, instead of a counterclaim, the defendant starts her own lawsuit against the plaintiff. This can happen when both people go to the courthouse to file shortly after the incident, and service of process hasn't been made in the first filed suit. Just remember, in the defendant's action the defendant is actually the plaintiff and you're the named defendant. So you'll have to respond by answering the complaint in the second action.

If this occurs, either person or both should notify the court and make sure the cases are scheduled at the same time for what's called a *joint trial*. If you don't tell the court and the cases get decided before two different judges, you can end up with two different, inconsistent decisions.

Counterclaims that exceed the court limits

The defendant can file a counterclaim for whatever amount she feels she is owed from the plaintiff. If the counterclaim is less than the monetary jurisdictional limits of the court, this is not a problem. The problem is if it is more than the jurisdictional limit of the court.

Let's say a tenant sues to get back a security deposit of $3,000. The landlord files a counterclaim, asserting that she had to repaint the apartment, redo the floors, and buy new appliances. The bills total $6,000 and the jurisdiction of the small claims court in that state is only $5,000.

Can the defendant counter sue in small claims court? The not-so-straightforward answer is, "It depends." It depends on the law in that particular state:

- ✔ In some states, so long as the counterclaim arises from the same event or transaction, it may remain in the small claims court even though the amount is in excess of the jurisdictional amount.

- ✔ In other states, the entire case would be transferred to the regular civil calendar and tried under the regular civil rules of procedure and not the more liberal small claims rules.

✔ In still other states, the defendant would be given the option of reducing the claim to the jurisdictional amount or having the claim *severed,* essentially separating the two claims. If the claim is severed, your small claims action remains in small claims but the defendant's counterclaim is moved to the regular civil court where the defendant would now be the plaintiff and you would be the defendant on the counterclaim. You may need to file a written answer or reply to the counterclaim in this situation.

From the point of view of judicial economy, severing a claim is the least favored option because it means two trials between the same parties over the same issue in two different courts.

When the person you're suing blames someone else: Third-party actions

You bring your claim against the defendant, but the defendant alleges that she is not responsible for the event but that some other person actually caused the problem. The defendant would file a *third-party complaint* against that person.

In some states, the defendant can do this when she files her written answer. In other states, you need permission from the judge to file a third-party action, because it will delay the current action by the plaintiff. Even though the defendant thinks she has a third-party claim against someone, in reality it's not related to the plaintiff's complaint and shouldn't be tried with the plaintiff's action. In this situation, the court would deny the third party action but allow the defendant to pursue it in a separate lawsuit.

The person the defendant is seeking to bring into the action must have somehow participated in the event. The defendant can't bring in someone who owes her money from a totally separate occurrence.

The defendant can also bring a separate action against the third party claiming the third party is responsible. You may not be part of that suit. The defendant in that case would be called the plaintiff and the third party a separate defendant.

Courts generally don't like these situations because two or more cases can be pending involving the same incident. Courts like everything tried together so as not to waste resources and to prevent inconsistent verdicts.

The following are examples of third party actions:

- ✔ You're stopped at a traffic light when your car is rear-ended. You sue the owner and driver of the car that hit you, making that person the defendant in your lawsuit. The defendant asserts that she was also stopped at the light and the operator of car #3 hit her car and pushed it into yours. The defendant's claim against car #3 is a third party claim if brought in your case.

    As you can see, in a multivehicle car accident, one event can lead to many lawsuits or one lawsuit with a lot of third party actions tagged on.

- ✔ Your local hospital sues you for the medical bills your kid incurred after she tried to copy some stunt she saw on some television show. When you get to court, you tell the judge you have insurance and you have no idea why the claim wasn't paid. The judge may tell you to file a third party action against the insurance company and get them into the case to explain why there was no coverage.

    This isn't a cross-claim situation because the insurance company is not named as a defendant by the plaintiff hospital. In fact, they probably can't sue your insurance company because they have no contractual relationship with your carrier. (The next section explains cross-claims.)

Cross-claims: When defendants point fingers at each other

A *cross-claim* occurs when you sue two different people and each defendant claims the other person is responsible.

The following examples should help you make more sense of this practice:

- ✔ You're a passenger in a car involved in an accident and are injured as a result. It's not clear which driver caused the accident. Your legal position is "Hey, I'm just a passenger sitting here minding my own business, and the next thing I know because of the actions of one or both of you clowns, I'm in the hospital."

    Your position is "Let the courts sort out who's at fault." You sue both drivers as defendants in your case. Each driver would file a cross-claim against the other driver, saying that if she has to compensate you for your injuries, the other driver should have to pay as well or reimburse her for any payments to you.

- ✔ Your neighbor decides to trim the dead branches off the tree that straddles your property line. She hires the A Tree No Longer Grows In

Brooklyn 'Cause I Cut 'em All Down Tree Service to do the work. While trimming the tree, a branch or two fall onto your vegetable garden, turning your entire tomato crop into tomato paste.

You sue both your neighbor for hiring an incompetent company and the tree trimming service for failing to perform the work properly. Your neighbor can file a cross-claim against the tree trimmer asserting that she didn't do anything wrong and if she has to pay you, the tree trimming service should have to reimburse — or *indemnify* — her.

As a plaintiff, cross-claims don't affect what you have to do on your case. You sued both parties, and it's up to you to prove they're both responsible for your injuries and should pay your damages.

The defendants have to be concerned with convincing the court the other guy is wholly at fault. If you prove your case, you'll recover from both defendants if you established each was at fault. If you only prove one of them was responsible, that's the one you'll recover from and the other one is off the hook.

Chapter 9

Looking at Your Options: Considering Alternatives to Trial

*U*nless you're a wannabe lawyer or an ardent fan of television courtroom shows, the thought of going to court can be intimidating and upsetting. Although you want the money you feel you're owed, the thought of appearing in court gives you nightmares. Settling your case outside of court through mediation or arbitration may sound like the answer to your prayers, and it may well be.

In this chapter, I walk you through the different ways to settle your case outside of court, including cases where you must go to arbitration because the contract you signed said you would.

Understanding Alternate Dispute Resolution (ADR)

Most court systems have systems in place to help parties in civil disputes try to resolve their problems without having to go through the time and expense of a trial. Classified under the general heading of *alternate dispute resolution,* these methods include:

✔ **Mediation:** Trying to work out a settlement between the two parties with the aid of a disinterested third party.

✔ **Arbitration:** Submitting the dispute to a disinterested third party who makes a decision favoring one party or the other, but without being subject to the formal court procedures. Some private arbitration proceedings are even conducted just on documents and affidavits submitted by the parties without the need of the parties ever appearing together.

✔ **Pretrial conference:** Court personnel attempts to resolve the dispute and either eliminate unnecessary issues before trial or reach a settlement. The next sections look at the different types of medication and arbitration available; not all are available in all types of cases.

Meeting in the middle through mediation

Mediation is the term used when a neutral third party meets with you and the person you want to sue and tries to get the two of you to reach a mutually agreeable settlement. The idea is that you work out the dispute between yourselves and reach an agreement you both can live with.

Mediation is often successful in disputes between neighbors or relatives, where the issue is more often a feeling that one side is not listening to the other side and not the need to settle a thorny legal problem.

Using mediation is voluntary in most courts. In some courts, mediation is mandatory, meaning you have to go through the process and see if you can either settle the case entirely or at least narrow the issues you want to bring before the judge.

Depending on where you live, the mediators may be court personnel or they may work with private companies that have contracts with the court system to provide the service. Some courts have the mediators available whenever the court is in session, although in other courts you have to request the mediator in advance.

In my court, the outside mediation service provider sifts through the small claims filings when they are first brought and contacts the parties offering them mediation. An advantage of this is that you and the defendant can schedule to meet with the mediator at a mutually convenient time rather than have to appear in the courthouse and wait your turn.

If you think you want mediation, check with the clerk of the court when you first file your complaint as to its availability.

If you chose mediation to settle your case, generally a judge does not participate in the settlement discussions. The mediator brings the parties together, lets them talk about the dispute and helps them prepare a settlement agreement.

If the mediator is successful, the best way to handle the settlement is to have both sides go before the judge with the written agreement prepared by the mediator and have the judge *allocute* both of you on the record. In other words, the judge swears you in, asks you some questions, reviews the terms of the agreement, and asks if you agree to it. Your case then is marked "settled by mediation."

Although you need to prepare for a trial in case mediation fails, if the mediation is successful, there won't be a trial.

The upcoming section "Settling Rather Than Going to Trial" makes some points to consider when you plan to resolve a case by negotiated settlement rather than by trial.

Going through arbitration

Arbitration means submitting the dispute to a disinterested third party who conducts a hearing and renders a decision that may or not be binding. The two types of arbitration are

- Arbitration that's offered by the court system instead of by a judge.
- Arbitration required by the law or by wording in a contract to resolve a dispute.

Arbitration is often used in small claims court to try to settle a case before it goes to court. Generally both sides have to agree to arbitration if it's offered as an alternative to a trial.

Some contracts contain an arbitration clause, so you may have agreed to use arbitration by a recognized arbitration service when you signed a contact with the defendant. This type of arbitration is often more expensive than the small claims process.

If you agreed to do it in your contract, then you may be required to have the case resolved in that manner if either side decides to enforce this contract right, and there is plenty of case law that says if you agreed to this method of dispute resolution you're stuck with that process and can't run right to court instead.

If you use independent arbitration outside of the court system, the finding of the arbitrator is called an *award* or a *decision*.

If you want to challenge the award of an independent arbitrator, you may have to bring a civil action to either enforce the award if you won or vacate the arbitration ruling if you lost.

Arbitration through the court system

In many states, arbitrators are lawyers who volunteer their time to help in small claims court. The arbitrator conducts a trial, referred to as a *hearing*.

To use arbitration provided in the court system, both sides must agree to participate. If they don't a judge decides the case.

One advantage of using arbitration is that the rules of evidence are even more relaxed than in a small claims trial before a judge.

The decision of an arbitrator may or may not be subject to appeal depending on the state. In New York City there is no appeal from an arbitrator's award because there is no record made of the hearing.

"No record" means that there was no stenographer present taking down the testimony, nor were there tape or video recordings made of the proceeding before the arbitrator. In that case, an appellate court would have nothing to review. This means if the arbitrator makes a mistake as to the law or the facts, the parties are stuck with the decision. It cannot be appealed.

Using a court-provided arbitrator is generally voluntary, so if you think you're well prepared to prove your case and want to have the option of appealing if you lose, you may not want to use the arbitrator; you'll want to select the judge.

One advantage of using arbitration is that your case will probably be heard the day or night it's scheduled, because there are usually many arbitrators present to assist but only one judge. So if you're in a hurry, the arbitrator is the quicker avenue.

Arbitration by contract

Numerous private entities provide arbitration services. These companies work primarily in business disputes. You and your opponent may voluntarily seek out an arbitration company and submit the dispute to be decided under the terms and procedures of that company. In some cases, having signed a contract commits you to settle any dispute through arbitration.

You can have the case submitted to a single arbitrator or a panel of arbitrators, usually made up of an odd number of people to avoid stalemates.

The two types of contractual arbitration are:

- ✔ **Binding arbitration** means that you agree in advance to accept the ruling of the arbitrator and not go to court.

- ✔ **Non-binding arbitration** allows the losing side to go to court and have a trial on the very same issues that were before the arbitrator.

If an arbitration decision goes against you, you may opt for a trial after-ward, despite the substantial costs involved. You may feel that you know why you lost and be confident that you can convince a judge that your position is correct and the arbitrator is wrong. But going to trial sort of defeats the idea of arbitration — to keep out of the court system.

If the arbitrator awards you money and the losing party refuses to pay, in most states, the winning party can go to court and have the arbitration award upheld as if it were a court order by bringing a new action in court to convert the arbitration award into an enforceable judgment.

In most states, this action to enforce the arbitration award won't be heard in small claims court. It is a special type of lawsuit heard in the regular civil court. This will be true even if the money awarded in the arbitration fits into the small claims monetary limits.

You don't have to go to trial to enforce an arbitrator's decision. Generally the winner only has to establish that the process was fair and that the arbitra-tion forum's rules were followed. Because you used private arbitration, the procedural and evidentiary rules of your state don't have to be followed. The rules applied are those of the private arbitration forum, which you and your opponent agreed to before you used that process.

Because you agreed to the procedure, it's very difficult to convince a court to reverse an arbitration award even if there were mistakes of law or fact by the arbitrator.

Arbitration allowed by statute

Each state has certain laws that give people the right to arbitrate disputes rather than go to court. A law in your state may allow you to file a complaint with the state agency that regulates the business you plan to sue, for example. Instead of going to court, you have a hearing with a regulatory agency.

A common example of statutory arbitration is with *lemon laws,* which give new and used-car buyers recourse in the event the cars they buy are defective. In many states, lemon laws govern the sale of motor vehicles and provide a forum for the resolution of disputes without the use of the courts.

You may have an advantage if you have a dispute with someone subject to mandated arbitration. A licensed professional may want to resolve your claim rather than have the licensing agency investigate your claim, conduct a hearing, and possibly suspend or revoke his license.

Arbitration clauses

You may not know it, but you may have agreed to have certain disputes resolved by arbitration when you signed a contract. Unless you actually read the fine print in every contract you sign or accept by clicking on a box on your computer (most people don't), the arbitration clause may have escaped your notice.

Arbitration clauses are common in consumer credit agreements and Internet purchase contracts. If the contract you signed has an arbitration clause, you'll end up in arbitration rather than in the courtroom if you have a dispute with whomever you signed the contract with.

If you start your small claims action and the defendant produces a contract showing that you agreed to private arbitration to resolve all disputes, almost all courts honor such an agreement because you accepted the terms of the contract containing that language.

Only if you can somehow show that the arbitration process is really unfair or would violate some of your constitutional rights would a court even consider voiding the arbitration clause and letting you stay in small claims court.

Some of the arbitration forums selected by the businesses seeking to enforce the clause are really inconvenient. For example, the arbitration may take place in another state or have fees that are far in excess of those of the small claims court.

Some courts find that such clauses violate the plaintiff's rights because they discourage the unrepresented consumer from participating in the process, leading to the business winning many claims on default — which, of course, is the business's intent all along. On the other hand, if you agreed to submit your disputes to private arbitration, and you don't participate, the defendant can still submit his side to the arbitrator, resulting in an award against you, which he can seek to enforce in court.

If, after you file your small claims case, the defendant produces a contract with a mandatory arbitration clause and your state rules allow court review of arbitration awards, you should ask the judge to adjourn your case pending a determination by the arbitration forum. This may save you the expense of having to file a new action if you want to challenge the arbitrator's ruling in court.

You can't count on defeating an application for private arbitration by the defendant when you agreed to this well before the dispute arose. Not reading the contract is never a good excuse.

Participating in a preliminary conference

Some courts have a mandatory preliminary conference between the parties and the judge or a member of the judge's staff. The intent of this is to hopefully have the parties reach a settlement of the case without the need to go to trial. If you fail to find a solution during the settlement conference, you then proceed with your case in small claims court.

You may be asked informally how you intend to prove your case and the defendant asked what his defense is. Based on this information, the person conducting the conference may point out the weaknesses in each side's case in an attempt to foster a settlement.

Settling Rather Than Going to Trial

At some point the defendant may contact you and offer to settle the case. You can settle a case at any point before you actually walk through the courtroom doors, and you have several very good reasons to do so:

- ✔ There's a big difference between winning a case and getting paid the money you're owed. (I discuss this further in Chapter 21.) Settling the case in theory eliminates the problem of trying to collect money from someone who doesn't want to give it to you.

- ✔ Settling guarantees timely payment of the money the defendant owes you, because he'll want to pay up before you change your mind and file the case.

- ✔ You don't need to go to trial to prove your case, and you don't run the risk of losing.

As I repeat throughout this book, to win at trial you must prove both that the defendant caused the damages you claim you sustained and that you have actual damages that can be quantified as a monetary loss as a result of the defendant's actions. Plaintiffs in small claims cases often lose cases because they fail to prove these points.

Failure to prove the case usually occurs because of lack of preparation or experience in court. Small claims cases also fail because plaintiffs don't understand the statutes that often relieve the defendant of liability in a case.

Because the stipulation is an agreement settling the dispute, you may be accepting less money than you sued for. As the plaintiff, you're trading the risk of proving your case at trial and perhaps collecting nothing for a guaranteed payment from the defendant in a timely manner. As the defendant, you're paying less that the amount the plaintiff is asking for but agreeing to make payments voluntarily without requiring the plaintiff to take steps to enforce a judgment.

Often court personnel or volunteer mediators can help you prepare a settlement agreement. Some courts even have simplified forms for this purpose. If you decide to settle the case, spend some time preparing the settlement agreement. A badly drafted agreement is worse than no agreement at all.

Deciding where to settle

Often, it makes sense to settle the case when you and the defendant appear at the courthouse for the trial. Although this may seem a bit last minute, settling in the courtroom allows the settlement agreement to be *allocated,* which means that the judge swears you and the defendant in and then reviews the settlement with the two of you to make sure you each understand the terms of the settlement.

The judge may then so order the settlement agreement. By *so ordering* the agreement, it becomes an order of the court subject to enforcement by either party if the terms are not met.

A settlement agreement is usually called a *stipulation.* If the stipulation is so ordered and then the terms are violated — for instance, the defendant doesn't make the payment as agreed — the party violating the terms of the agreement may be subject to sanctions for being in contempt of a court order.

If the stipulation is not so ordered, and the defendant breaks the contract between the two of you by not paying as agreed, you may have to take steps to have the case restored to the trial calendar to determine liability, damages, or both.

This obviously means more work and anguish for you. Having the stipulation so ordered prevents the defendant from coming in and saying he didn't understand the terms of the agreement when it was signed.

If the judge asks you if you understand the terms of the agreement when he allocutes it with you and you don't, say so. Ask any questions you have. This is not one of those occasions when silence is golden. Judges generally don't like to have the parties before them six months later with one of them saying, "Judge, I didn't understand the agreement," when the stipulation clearly shows it was allocated before a judge. This is especially true if you're before the same judge.

A typical allocution goes something like this:

> Do you swear or affirm to tell the truth and nothing but the truth?
>
> You're appearing without an attorney?
>
> You've agreed to settle this matter?
>
> You've entered into a stipulation settling your dispute with the aid of the mediator?
>
> You've read the stipulation I'm showing you?

You understand it?

You signed it voluntarily?

You understand by settling the case in this manner you give up any right you may have to have a trial on the underlying issues?

Entering into an oral agreement

Never enter into an oral settlement agreement, for all the obvious reasons. If you do so, you basically have nothing to back you up if the defendant decides to back out of the arrangement, and you'll be back in court trying to prove your case. In the meantime, the defendant may have taken the time to make himself *judgment proof* by disposing of or transferring his assets, making it impossible for you to collect if you win the case at trial.

There is an exception to "never" enter into an oral agreement — if the oral agreement is recited on the record either by a stenographer or a system that records everything being said in court. This is an exception because even though the agreement was oral, it can be reduced to a printed transcript relatively easily to show that everyone swore or affirmed on the record to accept the settlement terms.

Spelling out the terms

Like all agreements you enter into, the agreement that settles your case without a trial should clearly spell out what happens if either party fails to live up to the terms of the agreement. For example:

- If the defendant doesn't pay what he agreed to pay, do you have to notify the court and reschedule the matter for a *trial on the merits,* that is a trial at which you'll have to prove all the essential elements of your case and the defendant can assert all of his defenses, or can you *enter a judgment* against him? In other words, the defendant has waived any right to defend the case and has agreed that if he doesn't live up to the terms of the agreement there is no trial, and you can get a monetary judgment against the defendant.

- Do you have to give the defendant a *notice to cure,* which is the opportunity to correct any default before entering the judgment? In other words, you have to send a letter to the defendant saying that you didn't receive the scheduled payment he agreed to make and if he doesn't correct this default — failure to perform — you'll enforce your right to enter a judgment against him with the clerk of the court.

There is a good reason to send a notice to cure because sometimes believe it or not the check is really in the mail or has been lost. This gives the defendant who was acting in good faith the opportunity to make good on his word and live up to the terms of the agreement.

It also may save you one or more trips back to the court. For example, if the defendant finds out about the judgment being entered when the sheriff freezes his bank account, he may file an application in court to unfreeze his account and shows the court that the payment was made but lost in the mail.

✔ If the defendant pays you what he owes and you're supposed to return the item that was the subject of the dispute to him upon payment, what happens if you don't deliver the item? Can the defendant restore the case to the trial calendar, or does he now have to bring a new lawsuit against you to either get his money back or compel you to deliver the goods?

✔ If the defendant doesn't pay, can you enter a judgment for the amount you sued for or only for the amount that you settled for?

✔ If the defendant doesn't pay can you get interest and costs that you may have waived in the settlement agreement?

Often court personnel or volunteer mediators can help you prepare a settlement agreement. If you decide to settle the case, spend some time preparing the settlement agreement. A badly drafted agreement is worse than no agreement at all.

Chapter 10

In Your Defense: Advice for the Defendant

· ·

In This Chapter

▶ Finding out you're being served

▶ Answering a summons

▶ Responding in court

· ·

A lot of this book is focused on how to file a claim, and how to decide what course of action is best to take if you are wronged in some way and are seeking retribution in small claims court. But it takes two to tango. For every plaintiff in court, there must also be a defendant — the person being sued.

If you're on the receiving end of a court summons, you need advice just as much as the person suing does. In this chapter, I step over to the other side and discuss what to do if you're entering small claims court as the defendant.

Taking Action when Served with a Claim

If you're the defendant, it's wise to read all the advice given to your adversary, the plaintiff, so you understand how small claims court works. For that reason, the content in this book is definitely relevant to you no matter what side of the court battle you find yourself on.

Knowing what the opposition is up to may also give you some ideas on how to defend your case. At minimum, keep the following in mind:

✔ **Rule #1:** Never ignore a summons and complaint!

✔ **Rule #2:** There is no Rule #2. And Rule #1 applies to all court proceedings, not just small claims court.

Legal papers can be delivered to you in a number of ways; you may receive a summons and complaint via

- ✔ Actual in-hand delivery
- ✔ Delivery to a person where you live or work
- ✔ Affixing them to the door of where you live
- ✔ In the mail, the most common delivery method in small claims court

The law only requires that the method used to serve papers is reasonably likely to get them to you. It doesn't require verification that you actually received the complaint or that you thought it was delivered in a reasonable way. (Chapter 8 talks about the specifics of each method.)

Ignoring a summons at your peril

If you get served with any legal documents do not — do *not* — ignore them.

It doesn't matter that you've never heard of the person suing you. It doesn't matter that you never had any contact with the plaintiff. It doesn't matter that you have no idea who in the world the plaintiff is. The plaintiff thinks she has a problem with you that needs to be resolved in court.

Even if you receive the complaint by a very odd means — carrier pigeon, smoke signal, or singing telegram — you can't ignore it. The plaintiff may have asked the court to approve some sort of alternate method of service on you and that may be it.

Don't think that you can decide that because the papers weren't properly served, you can ignore them. Only the court can determine if the summons and complaint was served in accordance with the law. Remember that you are not a judge — and even if you are, you are not the judge in this circumstance.

If you think that you weren't served with papers properly, put this information in your answer, either when you first show up in court or, if your state permits, in a written answer filed with the court before your trial date.

At the time you receive the summons and complaint, make a note somewhere of how you received it and document the event in your records. If the issue of service comes up, it will be helpful to you if you can show you actually were in Timbuktu at the time the process server claims she was handing the papers to you on your front steps.

Because plaintiffs sometimes wait awhile before suing, and people tend to move, if you claim you no longer live at the address where the plaintiff alleges you were served at, it helps if you come to court with a copy of your new lease or a utility bill showing where you really lived on the date of service.

If you ignore legal papers you receive, a default judgment will be entered against you. This is not a good thing. It may sit on the court records for years, but eventually you will find out about it, and usually at the worst possible time. You go to borrow money or rent an apartment and a judgment shows up on your credit report. Your bank account will be restrained. Your wages will be garnished. Perhaps you go to sell your house and discover there is a judgment lien against the property. You then have to run around trying to resolve a case that's several years old.

The problem can get worse especially if the plaintiff is dead or has moved and you can't locate her.

It can get very expensive to have a judgment removed from the court and your record and you will need a lawyer to do it.

Refusing certified mail isn't a good strategy

Most states permit serving a small claims summons and complaint by mail. A summons usually arrives via certified mail return receipt or some other method that requires you to sign for it.

Don't think you can avoid dealing with a summons by not accepting it. Unclaimed certified mail often doesn't get returned to the courthouse until sometime after the scheduled court appearance date. So if you don't pick up the certified mail, it's possible the court will hear the case without you being there to tell your side of the story, and a default judgment will be entered against you.

If you don't accept delivery of a complaint, the person suing you will get a default judgment. To fight the judgment, you have to take steps to vacate your default and to convince the court to put the case on the calendar for a trial on the merits. Having notices sent to you marked "unclaimed" rather than "undeliverable" is not the best way to convince the judge that you deserve to have a second chance to have your day in court.

Unclaimed means service was attempted and you never contacted the post office to pick up the mail. *Undeliverable* or similar notations means that the plaintiff did not have an accurate address and therefore it was impossible for you to get the notice.

Pleading for mercy: Reading the plaintiff's documents

The documents used in a lawsuit are called *pleadings*. You may have thought that pleading is what you hear from your kids when you won't let them do something they want to do. That is a different kind of pleading, but no less annoying.

Every lawsuit begins with two pleadings — the summons and the complaint:

✔ **The summons** is the notice the court issues; it doesn't come directly from the person suing you. It basically says, "You're being sued. If you don't respond, the plaintiff will get a judgment against you and you will have to pay her." The summons tells you when you have to respond by.

The summons should also tell you how you have to respond — in person or in writing. If you don't understand what to do, the best thing to do is show up at court as soon as you get the summons and ask the clerk what you have to do or stop in at the help center if your court has one.

Your response is called an *answer*. You either have to file your answer with the court by a particular date or show up at the courthouse on a particular date and present your response to the court at trial.

✔ **The complaint** is the plaintiff's statement as to why she's suing you. In small claims cases it should be short, usually just a single sentence, but specific enough for you to prepare to respond to it. In regular civil cases it will be more detailed and tell the plaintiff's story as to why you're being sued.

Considering settlement

If you get served a summons, your first reaction may be to tear it up, which you know not to do. A second option may be to shave your head, start wearing a Groucho nose and glasses, and leave town on a freight train, but this isn't wise either. A third equally unwise option is to storm the clerk's office in a rage and threaten to feed the summons to the clerk one letter at a time.

A more sensible alternative is to call up the plaintiff, settle the problem out of court, and go back to your normal life without worrying about going to court. This is not a bad idea, especially if you know there's a good chance you may lose in court.

By settling the case out of court, I don't mean going to the plaintiff's house and calling her out into the street to settle it like a dispute in a Western. Settlement means trying to resolve the matter amicably without going to court. (I discuss some of the ways to mediate a settlement in Chapter 9.)

When you settle something outside of court, each side generally has to give in a little. So if your neighbor has been asking you to cut down the dead tree that can fall on either house, rather than ignoring her, offering to split the cost may be a solution.

When I say "settle the matter," I mean sit down and write out an agreement for the two of you to sign. It's not that you shouldn't trust each other to act in good faith, but by writing everything down you both know what you've agreed to, when things are going to get done, and who's paying for what.

I can't tell you how often I receive applications from defendants trying to have the default judgment set aside who tell me, "I settled this with the plaintiff. She told me not to worry; I don't have to go to court." Only later does the defendant find out that the plaintiff basically gave her the equivalent of a sucker punch. The plaintiff convinced the defendant not to show up so she could get a default judgment.

Preparing Your Response

Unless you're the type of person who gets sued on a regular basis, getting served papers can really ruin your day. It can cause a range of emotions from rage to anxiety, and none of these emotions is useful or productive. You may be chomping at the bit to point out what a liar the plaintiff is and what the real facts are. But you have to be prepared to respond in a reasonable and rational way.

Although it's upsetting to think that someone is unhappy enough with you to sue you, don't brood about it. Taking action to deal with the problem is the best response to a summons. Take a breath, keep calm, and get a strategy in place. Remember this is America where people sue other people for just about anything imaginable.

Considering getting a lawyer

The first thing to do after you read the papers is to check with the small claims court to see if the rules permit you to have a lawyer.

Some small claims courts permit both the plaintiff and defendant to have a lawyer. Others don't allow either side to have legal counsel. Most, however, allow defendants to be represented by an attorney, even if the plaintiff is barred from doing so. The reasoning is that the plaintiff selected small claims court and agreed to not be represented under the rules, but as the defendant, you didn't participate in that decision, so it's only fair to let you have counsel if you want it.

If you're a corporation or some other business created under the law of a state, you may actually be legally required to be represented by counsel. So find out as soon as you can.

Preparing your answer

You have to answer a summons in one of two ways: oral or written. The two require different responses:

- ✔ If the court permits only oral answers, you just show up on the date of trial prepared to defend yourself.

- ✔ If you can file a written answer, you generally must file before the court date with a copy sent to the plaintiff and the original filed with the court.

An oral answer isn't a speech you memorize before your court date. It just means that you don't file a written answer with the court before the trial date.

Prepare what you're going to say when you get before the judge by writing it down. For one thing, it helps you get your facts straight in your head. For another, it will be helpful if the court decides to ask for a written answer after your hearing or the judge permits you to hand in a written summary of your response to the plaintiff's allegations.

A written answer to a summons can include several options:

- ✔ **Denial:** You can deny the allegations of the plaintiff's complaint. The plaintiff has to prove everything you deny.

- ✔ **Admission:** You can admit certain information. Anything admitted is not in dispute and the plaintiff does not have to prove it at trial.

- ✔ **Affirmative defenses:** You can also assert an affirmative defense, which is a legal defense to the plaintiff's complaint that basically says that even if you did what the plaintiff said you did, you have good legally recognized reasons that relieve you from responsibility. (See the next section, "Answering in the affirmative," for more information on this defense.)

- **Counterclaim:** You assert a counterclaim in which you allege that the plaintiff is really the person responsible for the incident. You can even assert a counterclaim for other disputes between you and the plaintiff.

- **Cross-claim:** You can serve a cross-claim in which you allege that you're not responsible for the incident but some other defendant is.

- **Third-party action:** You can bring a third-party action against another person who the plaintiff did not name as a defendant in the suit, but who you claim is really the person responsible.

Answering in the affirmative

If there's no way to deny what you did, an affirmative defense may be your best defense. Affirmative defenses are arguments such as the following:

- You already paid the plaintiff everything she was due.

- The plaintiff waited too long to sue and the statute of limitations has run out.

- The contract had to be in writing to be enforceable in court and it wasn't.

- The plaintiff isn't licensed and is legally required to be to bring a claim or collect money.

- The complaint fails to state a cause of action — a set of facts that gives the plaintiff a right to sue you.

These all are defenses that, if you establish them satisfactorily in court, can have the compliant dismissed.

This list is not exhaustive and your state may have some other ones they permit. Preparing an affirmative defense may be one of those things to talk to an attorney about or people at a help center. You may have one and not even know it.

Making a motion

Another avenue available to you as a defendant in some small claims courts is making a motion. (This is dealt with in some detail in Chapter 14 as something the plaintiff may receive from a defendant.) A *motion* is a request to the court for some *interim relief,* which is a request to the court to take some action in the case before the trial.

In some small claims courts, motions are either not permitted at all or can only be made with the permission of the court. In other words, you have to make a motion to get permission to make a motion.

If you're represented by an attorney, and your lawyer believes you have an affirmative defense — you know a legal reason why the case should be dismissed (see the preceding section, "Answering in the affirmative") — you or your lawyer can say to the judge, "Your honor, there is no legal reason to continue this case. Please dismiss it," and forestall a trial altogether.

Say the plaintiff loaned you, her no-account sister-in-law, $1,000 ten years ago to use as bail money. You never paid her a dime in return. She recently divorced your brother, so she has no compunction suing you now. The case would be barred by the statute of limitations in most states, because as a contract claim the plaintiff only had six years to sue.

As the defendant, you can make a motion to dismiss on that basis. It would be successful even if the plaintiff produced proof of the payment to you and a promissory note from you.

Going to Court

You received the summons and complaint and read it carefully. It tells you to appear for a trial on a certain date, give an oral answer, and be ready to try the case on the merits.

If you've read the rest of this book so you can get into the plaintiff's mind and anticipate her every move, you know that you have to prepare and be ready to go. You're not going to assume that the case will be adjourned. In fact, you know exactly what this case is about.

It was only a question of who was going to go to court and start the suit — you or the plaintiff. In any situation where you are the defendant, you have to know what the plaintiff must do to prove her case and what you must do to defend against the claim.

Keeping quiet as a trial strategy

The plaintiff has the burden of proof, so it's possible that you can sit there and not say anything and hope that the plaintiff doesn't present a convincing case. That's right. You can clam up just like some defendant in a film noir legal drama.

Don't confuse not speaking at your small claims trial with the criminal law's standard of not having to testify against yourself. Although it has the same result — the defendant not testifying — there is no constitutional reason for this procedural stance in small claims court. This is a trial strategy to use when the plaintiff fails to properly present her case.

The term for this burden is that the plaintiff must prove her *prima facie* case. This is just the Latin term for presenting legally sufficient proof to establish a claim.

The problem with this "sit down and shut up" strategy is that the rules of evidence are relaxed in small claims court.

The standard is only *substantial justice,* which means that evidence, which would not be enough to win a case in a regular civil part of the court, may be enough in small claims court.

Although the issues may seem really important to you, in the great scheme of the law, the amount of money involved generally does not have a life-altering effect on the parties. The judge may give the plaintiff a great deal of leeway and let the plaintiff meet the standard of proof with less evidence.

As the defendant, you don't want to take that chance. So as a practical matter, it behooves you to present evidence in the form of testimony and exhibits that contradict the plaintiff's case to prevent her from winning.

If you raise a counterclaim or an affirmative defense, you have the burden of establishing those claims, with the plaintiff having to rebut your allegations. The same substantial justice rule applies to you on these matters as it did to the plaintiff on her case.

Having your say

You can avoid having to pay the plaintiff if you can convince the court that either you didn't do what the plaintiff says you did or that you were justified in your actions. You can do this in several ways:

- ✔ Presenting evidence that shows you're not legally responsible.
- ✔ Filing a counterclaim, which is basically turning around and suing the person suing you.
- ✔ Mounting an affirmative defense, which says you did what you're being accused of, but there was a good reason for it.

If you file a counterclaim or an affirmative defense, you have to present evidence on your behalf.

Part III
Presenting Your Case in Court

Courtroom lingo you ought to know

- **Burden of proof** — The idea that the plaintiff has to produce the evidence to establish the case.

- **Liability** — One of two essential parts of any trial — proving the defendant is really at fault.

- **Damages** — The other essential part of any trial — proving that money can fix the problem the defendant caused.

- **Subpoena** — A legal paper that compels someone to testify as a witness or to produce some required records.

- **Credibility** — How believable are you? The defendant? In a case where which story makes the most sense, credibility may be more important than the law.

Find tips for doing legal research at www.dummies.com/extras/filingand winningsmallclaims.

In this part . . .

✔ See how not to let your wardrobe, appearance, demeanor, and manner of speaking lose your case for you; prepare yourself to make a winning first impression in court.

✔ Arm yourself with proof and evidence that is valid and effective in supporting and proving your claim; speculative or inconclusive evidence won't cut it in small claims court

✔ Weigh the pros and cons of bringing live witnesses to court, or even taking the stand yourself, and look at what kinds of questions to ask your witness and what questions to avoid.

✔ Look at ways to best sound like an actual lawyer in the courtroom, and not just like an actor who plays on television.

✔ Understand how—and how soon—you can expect to receive your judgement, and what to do if you are not satisfied with the outcome.

✔ Check out `www.dummies.com/extras/filingand winningsmallclaims` online for information on things you should think about after you've been to court.

Chapter 11

Mastering Courtroom Etiquette

*Y*ou can prepare your case, make friends with the clerk, do everything right and still blow it by walking into court dressed like a street urchin from a Dickens novel or by addressing the judge as, "Hey, dude (or dudette)." If you want to make the right impression (which, for better or worse, can influence your case), this chapter helps you look good in the courtroom, both figuratively and literally. In this chapter, I also give you some tips to help you feel more at ease in the courtroom.

Mastering First Impressions in Court

First impressions are, well, just that. You can't get a do-over on a first impression, no matter how hard you try. When you stand in front of your closet on court day to pick out an outfit, don't automatically reach for the nearest hanger. What you wear in court can — very well may — be used against you.

Dressing for success: Your appearance at your appearance

How do you dress for important stuff in your life? If you said shorts, tank top, and sandals, I suggest you stop watching reality-based television shows and check out 1950s legal drama reruns. Although dress codes have been liberalized over the last few years, you can still make a good impression by dressing to demonstrate that the event is important to you.

Judging your clothes

Judges like to think that you believe coming to court is an important event in your life. More than likely, you've never been to court before and the judge has never met you, so one subtle way to influence the judge is to look like court is important to you. How you dress creates an impression of the type of person you are in the judge's mind.

As silly as it sounds, the impression you make may assist you in proving your case. This is especially important if credibility is an issue, such as a case that has little or no written proof and no independent witnesses to establish what occurred. The judge relies solely on the oral testimony of the parties and decides which party's version of the story sounds more believable. The person who comes across as more credible or more truthful often gets the benefit of the doubt and prevails. So looking credible and respectable can influence the judge.

On the other hand, if the judge is your next-door neighbor, it won't matter as much how you dress, because the judge knows you well enough so that your appearance won't change his already established opinion much.

Clothes to leave home include:

- **Ripped, torn, stained, or otherwise disreputable-looking clothing:** Even if you want to look poor and needy, wearing old, tattered clothes isn't the way to do it. And it doesn't matter that those ripped jeans cost over $100. No jeans, period.

    Don't go to the other extreme and rent a tux or buy a gown to wear to court, either; overdoing your attire can make it look as if you're mocking the court.

- **Shirts with sayings on them:** Whether it's the name of your favorite sports team, alcoholic beverage, or a shirt with a religious or political statement, leave it at home.

- **Sneakers:** Unless you have a foot problem that requires orthopedic shoes, invest in a pair of dress shoes if you're a guy. If you're a woman, wear a low heel; stilettos don't create the right impression.

- **Baggy pants:** It doesn't matter if they're in style. Most judges find looking at three inches of your underwear offensive.

- **Hats:** Most courts don't permit litigants to wear hats unless it is for religious purposes, so be prepared to remove yours when you enter the courtroom.

- **Distracting clothing:** Dress conservatively. If you're female, there's no reason to emphasize the fact in court. You want the judge looking at your evidence, not your cleavage. If you're male, leave the muscle shirt at home. You want to impress the judge with the strength of your evidence, not your physical strength.

Be aware that judges have refused to hear cases when the judge felt a litigant was improperly dressed for his courtroom. In all likelihood, a judge won't dismiss your case, but he may postpone your trial whether you want him to or not.

When you file your case, you can ask the court if there is an official dress code by court rule or an unofficial dress code by judge rule. Rumor has it a colleague of mine asked a female attorney who was wearing fishnet stockings to leave his courtroom.

If court personnel ask you to remove your hat or put away reading material, just do it. Asserting your First Amendment rights in a shouting match isn't the best way to start the session. And if you get too argumentative with court personnel, you can find yourself with a desk appearance summons issued by the court officers for you to show up in the criminal court and explain your behavior or cooling your heels overnight in the local hoosegow. If you wear a hat or other garment for religious purposes, calmly ask to explain the situation to the court officer who asks you to remove it.

Another reason not to act up is that sometimes the court security get curious and run your name through the outstanding warrant files from the criminal court. If they find you're wanted somewhere, your case will be postponed while you are in custody for an unscheduled appearance in criminal court.

Leaving some things behind

Court personnel frown on people reading newspapers, magazines, and books while the court is in session. Your focus should be on what's happening in the courtroom. Besides, by watching what is going on in other cases, you can get a sense of how the judge treats litigants and conducts the trial.

Likewise, cellphones, video equipment, and other recording devices are generally not permitted and have to be checked with the courthouse security people, so if you were planning on recording your 15 minutes of fame with the intent to broadcast your case on the Internet, forget it.

It goes without saying that bringing a weapon to the courthouse is not allowed. In many places litigants forget this and stash weapons in bushes and other places outside the courthouse. This often results in the court security conducting their version of an Easter egg hunt — patrolling the grounds and confiscating the abandoned weapons.

True story: I'm conducting a trial over the quality of some kitchen cabinet doors the plaintiff had ordered from the defendant. The plaintiff, wanting me to see the poor quality, had actually brought the doors to court as an exhibit. He had them tied together to make transporting them easier. When he presented the doors, they were still tied, and I asked if there was a way to untie them so I could see them. At this point, the plaintiff took out a knife to cut the sting. This led me to inquire of the courtroom staff if the knife was permitted through security because it could only wound me and not inflict a fatal injury. (At the time, the question seemed somewhat humorous, but in the current climate, I'm not so sure.)

Don't bring food and drink into the courtroom. Most places won't even permit food and drink in the courthouse, let along the courtroom, unless they have a food service area in the building. This isn't a picnic, so don't act like it is.

Knowing what to expect when you show up

One of the most important things you can do to get in good with the court is be on time. Better still, get there early! Getting there early means you have time to find a place to park and to look for where your case is on the calendar without worrying about missing it. If you have to take public transportation, make sure you know where you're going and how to get there and leave yourself enough time to get there.

Looking for your case

In all likelihood, there will be a list of cases posted outside the courtroom door. This is called the *calendar* or *docket*. The calendar usually has the cases listed in numerical order. Your case is given a number when you file it, so look for the number on the calendar.

After the case number, the docket usually lists the name of the plaintiff and the name of the defendant. In some places the cases are listed alphabetically by the name of the plaintiff. This of course makes it much easier to find your case.

If you're the defendant, look for the plaintiff's name.

Large cities like New York can have more than a hundred cases scheduled for each small claims session. This makes it crowded at the courthouse. You don't want to be in the hall looking for your case on the calendar when the clerk is calling it — another reason to get to the court early.

A large number of people can make for a noisy courtroom, so it's important to pay attention. Telling the clerk you missed the case because you didn't hear it is not a good way to start things off, especially if the clerk has a side job hawking beers at your local ballpark and the voice to prove it.

Entering the court

After you find your case on the calendar, go to the courtroom and pay attention to what's going on. In less populated places, you may be asked to check in with the clerk. This means you give the clerk your name or the number of your case, and tell the clerk whether you're the plaintiff or the defendant. For instance, go to the clerk and say, "Number ten on the calendar, plaintiff present."

In places with many cases on the calendar, a clerk will *call the calendar,* meaning he starts at the top of the docket and announces each case. For instance, the clerk may yell, "Penn A. Pasta against Duncan Doughnutt." If you brought the case, you would respond "plaintiff" or "plaintiff present." Or if you're being sued, "defendant" or "defendant present." If you have a very common name, make sure there aren't two of you on the docket for the same session.

In all likelihood, the clerk will call out the entire calendar to see how many cases have both sides ready for trial, which ones have someone asking for an adjournment, and those where one or both parties didn't show up. In courts with smaller calendars, where you check in with the clerk when you get there rather than having the clerk call the case docket, the clerk may start by calling the cases and send them right to the judge for trial.

Yelling "Yo" or "Yup" like you're at a storage auction isn't a good idea. Court personnel consider it disrespectful, and such a response doesn't identify who you are in the case.

Don't just wave your hand or just stand up. You must announce who you are. Why, you ask? Because if you're the plaintiff and the defendant doesn't show up, you'll either be given a judgment on default or proceed to inquest. An *inquest* is a trial where the plaintiff presents his evidence without the defendant being present. If, when you heard the word inquest, you immediately thought about coroners and forensic work, you're watching way too many crime dramas on the tube.

After instructing people to please answer plaintiff or defendant, I'll call the case and one or both parties either just waves his hand or starts walking toward me on the bench. Please don't do this. Tell the judge who you are. The judge is not psychic.

If the plaintiff is suing a bunch of different people, including you, make sure you answer to your name and not to the first one for that plaintiff. If you answer to the wrong name, you may be running around later trying to get a default judgment cleared up. If you respond to the wrong name, the lawsuit gets resolved under that name. Then, when your name actually is called, you may be long gone from the courtroom, so you don't respond, and the plaintiff can likely get a default judgment because you weren't there for the trial! Remember a default judgment is just as valid as a judgment after a trial and it's awarded in situations where the defendant doesn't show up.

If you're the defendant, and the plaintiff doesn't respond, the case will be dismissed because the plaintiff failed to appear. You don't want to be looking for the clerk after the calendar call trying to explain that you were on time and in the courtroom but either didn't hear your name or didn't know you had to tell anyone you were there.

Minding your manners

If you want to know how to behave in court, here it is in a nutshell: Be polite, be courteous, and be respectful. Clearly, it's not that complicated, but many people miss the mark and hurt their case.

Treat the court — meaning not only the judge, but all of the court personnel — as well as your opponent with respect. Don't get into an argument with your opponent. And don't get into an argument with the judge — a really bad idea.

The judge or the clerk tells each party where to sit or stand. Traditionally, the plaintiff sits closest to the jury box even when there is no jury.

In some courtrooms you get to sit at the counsel tables; you may even have a microphone. Generally you can just speak in a normal voice into the microphone; you don't have to lean forward as if you're at a Congressional hearing.

In other courthouses you stand at the bench in front of the judge in close proximity to your opponent. The judge may or may not have people step into the witness box to testify. More likely, people will testify from where they're standing.

Only one person can speak at a time. If the trial is being recorded, it becomes difficult to have an accurate transcript if everyone speaks at once. The judge decides who speaks when and will give each person a chance to speak.

Don't interrupt the testimony of your opponent or a witness. Even if the nose on the person speaking is growing at a rate to make Pinocchio look like the "before" picture in a cosmetic surgery ad, let him finish. The judge usually asks for your responses, and if he doesn't ask specifically, you can ask the judge if you can say something that contradicts what the speaker said. Most judges will say something to the effect of, "Let him finish speaking, then I'll give you a chance to ask questions" or "Tell me what you want to say."

If you were a first-class jerk in dealing with the clerk and other court personnel before the trial started, you can be sure that your reputation has preceded you, which is not a good thing. The judge already has an impression of you and will be less likely to tolerate any discourteous actions.

One thing all judges dislike is litigants thinking that small claims court is like small claims court on television. Save the dramatics for the stage, not the courthouse. After all, if your case were that interesting, there's a good chance the producers of one of those shows would have tried to convince you to have your lawsuit heard on television.

Dealing with the Judge

All judges take their jobs very seriously. They realize how they treat you as a litigant affects how you'll view the law and the fairness of the judicial system. Because the judge takes his job seriously, you would be wise to do the same, even if the judge is someone you know personally.

Discovering who will hear your case

Who will hear your case, a judge or someone else? As with many things in court, the answer is, "It depends." The answer varies from state to state. There are several possibilities, including:

- **A judge:** In most states, an actual judge presides over small claims court. This is good, because a judge knows the law. This also is not good, because the judge knows the law. So the judge can analyze the case based on the law and may be less likely to abandon legal rules of evidence and prior case law. This assumes that the judge has not only been trained as a lawyer but is a judge in his regular job.

  I say this because in some places the judge doesn't have to be a lawyer or to have had any legal training, or the extent of his training is what he received from the court system when he was elected or appointed as a local judge.

- **A lawyer:** In some courts, the small claims judge is actually a lawyer volunteering his services to the court system so that the small claims court runs efficiently. This person will have knowledge of the law but may not be up on all the niceties and nuances that the full-time judge would have.

  The fact that someone is a lawyer doesn't mean he has any courtroom experience. A lawyer whose practice is patent law may never set foot in a courtroom except to volunteer to help out in small claims court.

- **A citizen trained by the court:** In some places, the small-claims judge may be plain old Joe Citizen with no legal training other than what was provided by the court system as the minimum training for judges. A citizen-judge is more likely to apply good old common sense to your case and very little law — which may or may not be to your benefit.

A person acting as a judge, but who isn't a judge by profession, may be called a *magistrate* or *arbitrator* or something similar. Unless the official presiding tells you something different, you can say "judge" or "your honor" or even just "sir" or "ma'am" no matter who the judge is. Ask the clerk or a court employee how you should address the judge if you're not sure.

Even if you know the person from outside of the court setting, respect his position and call him by his title.

Who actually hears your case affects your right to appeal should you lose; I address this in Chapter 22.

Requesting a judge

In places where there is an option to have the small claims cases heard either by a professional judge or by an arbitrator or magistrate who is not a professional judge, each party has the opportunity and right to request that the professional judge hear the case. So long as one of you wants a judge, that's who will preside over your trial.

You may be able to designate that you want an actual judge to hear your case when you file your complaint or, if you're the defendant, when you file your answer.

It's important to check your local rules, because in some places you only get to see a judge after you've had a hearing before some other court-appointed person and lost. You then have to file for a new trial before the judge and start all over again, assuming the facts of your case permit it.

In those places where you can't designate a trial before a judge prior to the trial date, yell "By the Court" or "By the Judge" when your case is called. Your case will then be directed to the judge to be heard.

Asking for a judge comes with one distinct disadvantage: Your case may not be heard at that small claims session. The judge can only hear a certain amount of cases each small claims session and that number is not known until the calendar is called. In addition, no one knows how long each case will take. A case can be as short as five minutes or as long as several hours. Trials don't run according to a clock. They're not sporting events, although they do have many similarities.

A case takes as long as is necessary for the judge to insure both parties have presented their respective cases. So if the cases before yours take a while, your case may be adjourned by the court and you'll have to come back another day.

You may be annoyed at this, but think about it: Don't you want the judge to give you as much time as you need to present your case? Also, do you really want to have the judge starting to hear your case three or four hours after he took the bench to start hearing cases? What do you think the judge's attention span will be by that time? So if court personnel ask if you're willing to come back on a new date, it may not be such a bad idea to agree to that.

On the plus side, because you have an older case, you should be further up the calendar on the next trial date with a better chance of getting your trial — plus, you'll have a feel for the court and the procedures having spent some time observing the process on your first appearance date.

Asking for a judge to be removed

The situation may arise in which either you or the defendant knows the judge from outside the court.

If you or the defendant feel you can't get a fair trial you can ask the judge to *recuse* himself, or voluntarily step down and not hear the case. Although the words sound similar, *excuse* and *recuse* are different things.

Listing reasons for recusal

Some of the reasons you may think the judge should recuse himself include:

- ✔ The fact that the judge ruled against you in another case.
- ✔ The fact that you just heard the judge decide a case similar to yours in favor of the defendant.
- ✔ The fact that the judge has some personal connection with you or the defendant. Perhaps your kids go to the same school or play on the same team. You all attend the same religious institution. You see each other at the local pizzeria. You run the only shoe store in town and the defendant the only auto repair shop.

But guess what, none of these reasons requires the judge to step down. Absent certain limited circumstances, in most states the decision to stay on the case is left solely to the discretion of the judge. So if the judge says he can be fair in your case, you're stuck with him. Like so many other court contests, the decision of the judge is final.

In some situations, the judge automatically has to recuse himself from the case. If either party before the judge includes one of the following relationships, the judge must step down:

> ✓ Blood relative
>
> ✓ Former client
>
> ✓ Former or current law partner or business associate

In these rather obvious cases, the judge should automatically speak up and send the case somewhere else. But these exceptions are rare.

Refusing recusal

In many cases, you can ask the judge to recuse himself, but your request will be denied. The idea is to prevent litigants from judge shopping. If you could get a judge to recuse himself just for the asking, anytime you didn't like the judge, you'd ask him to step down. A system like that would cause chaos.

Besides, what are you going to do in a small community where everyone knows each other? There may not be another judge available locally which would mean you're schlepping to the next county for trial.

If you genuinely feel you have a legitimate issue with the judge and that the judge should step down, notify the clerk of the court and your opponent in advance so that the case can be reassigned to another judge, if there's more than one, or transferred to another location. Getting the case reassigned in advance saves you the trouble of asking for a recusal when your case is called.

State your reasons for recusal in a calm, nonconfrontational manner. If the judge denies your request, accept the ruling and move on. Complaining will get you nowhere and can hurt your case. If you get too rude in regard to any ruling from a judge, you can find yourself being held in *contempt of court,* which means you've refused to obey the rules of the court or the ruling of the judge. At the minimum, a contempt citation usually delays your trial. It can also result in a fine, or if you're really obnoxious, having a court officer restrain or remove you from the court.

Although judges are used to being asked to recuse themselves on occasion, no one wants to be accused of being unfair, especially in the courtroom. Raising the issue with the clerk or some other court staff, rather than the judge, prevents the request from becoming an incident.

Getting Over the Courtroom Jitters

It's normal to be a little nervous the first time you're in court. If you aren't a little nervous, the judge may wonder how many times you've been there in the past.

One way to control your jitters is to watch a few other small claims court sessions before your own. For some people, writing out what they need to say in court also helps them get through the experience.

Going to court before you go to court

Can you watch some trials before you do yours? Yes, you can, and it's a good idea. Small claims courts, like most civil courts, are open to the public. Watching a few cases can help you get familiar with the procedures the court follows so you aren't confused by what's going on when your trial comes up.

Take the chance to watch the judge in action. You can get a feel for whether the judge lets all of the parties talk and present their cases uninterrupted or takes charge of the proceedings and asks all of the questions himself.

One thing you won't see is the judge insulting the litigants like some of the judges do on television. The behavior of judges and how they interact with litigants is scrutinized. If a judge is being rude or insulting, that judge will get a call from a supervisor suggesting that maybe it's time for a vacation.

Another thing you probably won't see is the judge using a gavel. I know on television and in movies judges always use gavels, but real judges don't. They control the courtroom by their demeanor and attitude. If everyone respects each other and lets each party have his turn, there is no need for a gavel.

If the judge is using a gavel, it means everything is already out of control. (Judges do have use for a gavel on occasion. Sometimes in chambers they find it hard to crack a walnut or lobster claw and a gavel comes in handy.)

Putting your case on paper and preparing exhibits

Writing down all the facts in your case so you don't leave anything out is a good way to feel prepared for your day in court. Make an outline of the facts or write out a statement explaining your relationship to the defendant, the events that took place, and why you think the defendant should compensate you.

If you have pictures or documents you want to use, pick out the best of them, identify what's in them, and put down when they were taken. Be able to explain why they're important. No judge wants to receive a stack of photographs containing shots of the same item from 360 different angles, nor pictures of parts of your house or car totally irrelevant to your case. Sometimes less is more.

Because you've read this book and have prepared your case, you won't be one of those litigants who hands the judge a pile of papers and asks "which ones do you want, judge?" or "which ones do you think I need?" The judge isn't there to try your case for you.

It's better to just talk and tell your story, but if you're more comfortable reading it, most judges allow you to do that. One thing you can't do is just submit your statement into evidence. The defendant has the right to have you put under oath, to hear the events from your mouth, and to ask you questions. A piece of paper cannot answer questions.

Likewise when the defendant puts on his case, you have the right to ask him questions.

If you're submitting documents or photos to the judge, give another set to your opponent. This saves the time of having the court personnel give your opponent a chance to look at the document before the judge sees it, in case he wants to object to your using it. It also saves time shuffling papers between you, your opponent, and the judge. Most importantly, it prevents evidence from inadvertently finding its way into your opponent's file and remaining there rather than with the judge.

Preparing to interview witnesses

When you're writing down questions to ask witnesses, remember an old saying that trial lawyers follow: "Never ask a question unless you know what the answer is going to be."

What this means is, if you don't know what the other person is going to say, don't ask the question. Many cases are lost because a person, who is now under oath, says something different than what was expected or suddenly can't remember something critical to the case. If you need the defendant's testimony to prove your case, this could be a problem.

If there's no independent evidence to support your claim, and the entire case relies on the credibility of each party, don't expect to get any help from the defendant. Another old saying in the legal world is, "No one lies in court; everyone just has his own version of the truth." If you remember this, you can avoid surprises at trial.

Protecting Your Case by Making a Record

Whenever you're dealing with the judge, there's a good chance that whatever you say is being recorded. In legal speak this is called *making a record*. In some courts, as soon as the clerk begins calling the calendar, recording devices are turned on. If your court is one where the recording starts when the clerk comes out, then nothing you say in court, whether you're sworn in or not, is off the record. Everything is capable of being reviewed by another court.

Only the court's recordings become part of the record; you can't bring your own recording devices into court so you can't make your own record.

Recognizing what constitutes a record

In court proceedings, a *record* means one of several types of documentation. The record can be

- ✔ Written by a stenographer
- ✔ Taped with a recorder
- ✔ Recorded using a computer
- ✔ Captured on camera, if the court permits cameras in the courtroom

Having a record makes it possible for you to appeal if you lose the case, whether you're the plaintiff or the defendant. If there's no record, you can't appeal because an appellate court can't determine what occurred at the first trial.

Although everything said from when the doors open may be recorded, not everything that happened is considered part of the official record for use on appeal. It also should be noted that the record will include all exhibits and documents placed into evidence should you appeal, so it's important that they remain with the court. However, in this section, I refer to the record as documentation as to what was said in the court.

In some places, like New York City, there's a record only if the case is heard by a judge. If the case is determined by an arbitrator, there is no record and hence no appeal.

Knowing that you're being recorded at all times makes it easier to understand why it's important to follow court protocol and let one person talk at a time. You wouldn't want to have words put in your mouth that you didn't say because the person preparing the transcript couldn't figure out who was talking on the tape.

If you lose the case and decide to appeal, you need to obtain a copy of the record. Jot down the approximate time your case was heard so you can properly order the transcript, although court personnel or the computer system usually keeps a log of the cases in the order they were heard.

If you need a transcript of the record to appeal the judge's decision, there usually is a fee involved. You'll be given a written transcript rather than a copy of the tape; the transcript will contain everything said at the trial.

Going off the record

Even if someone asks to go off the record and is granted permission to do so, all the conversation will still be recorded if electronic devices are used. A stenographer generally stops taking notes when the judge goes off the record.

If either side appeals, you may want to challenge something that was said off the record, which led to an adverse ruling on your case. If there are no lawyers involved in a case, it's unlikely that anything will be off the record because non-lawyers generally don't really know what should or should not be on the record.

Most judges prefer to keep everything on the record, meaning that the recording is continuous even if someone asks to go off the record. This protects the integrity of the system and prevents litigants from claiming that the judge said or did something when the recording was off that favored the other side.

In just about every theatrical courtroom drama, at some point one of the lawyers objects and asks that a question and answer be stricken from the record. If the judge grants that request, the stenographer doesn't delete the question and answer from the formal record; it just means that the question and answer are marked as being stricken from the record.

This is done in case the judge was wrong to exclude the question and answer and the appellate court wants to examine that ruling and perhaps overrule the trial judge. If the question and answer were actually removed from the record, then such review would be impossible.

Getting a Postponement

Because life often doesn't play out exactly how you plan it, you may find yourself having prepared for your day in court only to have some unexpected event occur that requires you to ask for a postponement of your trial. There's a simple answer to the question "Can I postpone my case?" — that answer is "maybe."

Having to rearrange your socks drawer or put your paper clip collection in size and color order are generally not grounds for a postponement. Such a request should be reserved for serious events such as illness, death, or the like.

One of the purposes of small claims court is to have a case decided quickly and at a reduced cost to the parties. A postponement really defeats these purposes, because it delays resolution of the dispute and increases the expenses of the parties such as taking additional time off from work or having to pay witness fees.

The request to postpone your case is called a *request for an adjournment* or a *request for a continuance*. Some people believe that each side has a right to one automatic adjournment. This is a myth. The decision as whether or not to grant an adjournment may be in the hands of the clerk or a judge. Don't presume you will get an adjournment just because you ask for it.

Asking for an adjournment or continuance

As with everything else in the legal world, there's a proper protocol to follow when asking for an adjournment, and not following the rules can hurt your case.

Letting your opponent know

If you make the request before the scheduled trial date, the request probably goes to the clerk of the small claims court. In the interest of fairness, you also have to notify your opponent. So whether you're the plaintiff or the defendant, you have to send a copy of the written request to the other side.

Courts often reject written requests that lack any indication that a copy was sent to the other side without even reading them. So if you send a letter to the court or the judge, indicate that you also sent a copy to your opponent.

If the court thinks you haven't let your opponent know you're asking for a change to the court date, you may receive your request back stamped with the words "*ex parte* communication" and no other explanation. *Ex parte* means only one side is participating.

If you're more fortunate, the court will send your request back to you explaining how to make the request or suggesting you speak to the clerk about what to do to get an adjournment.

Asking properly and for a good reason

You can send a written request to the court and to your opponent asking for a postponement, or you can appear at the scheduled time and request the adjournment from the judge or the clerk. In either case, you better have a really good reason to ask for an adjournment.

If you're requesting an adjournment in writing, make sure you send it far enough in advance so your letter can be received by the court and reviewed and sent to the clerk or the judge so as to have time to act on it. Sending something by fax may seem like a good idea because of the speed involved. But this is really a bad idea for several reasons:

- The court rules may prohibit fax communications.
- The fax may not be sent to the correct person at the courthouse.
- The fax will not establish that you gave notice to the other side of your request.

Some reasons that won't fly when asking for an adjournment include:

- **You're not ready.** If you aren't prepared and don't have all your proof or witnesses available, then why did you bring the case in the first place?
- **You want to harass the other party.** If you can't present a good reason for adjournment, the court will suspect you just want to aggravate your opponent and won't look favorably on it.

One of the more common reasons a person requests an adjournment is to either consult with or to retain an attorney. Even if the rules of your small claims court prohibit the use of lawyers at trial, they don't prevent you from speaking with a lawyer before your court date. Most judges will grant an adjournment to permit either party to speak with or actually retain an attorney, especially if it is the first time the case is on the calendar.

The reason that judges grant adjournments in these cases is that the failure to do so creates an appealable issue should you lose your case after the judge denied your request for counsel. You may have to explain why you had this epiphany about needing a lawyer now instead of anytime prior to your case being called. Such a request will usually be granted because court systems, unlike street punch-ball games, don't like do-overs.

Sometimes the court grants an adjournment if both sides agree in advance and notify the court in writing of the agreement. If you and the defendant agree to adjourn your case, it's especially important to notify the court as soon as possible especially in situations where an interpreter has been ordered by the court at public expense.

If you request an adjournment when you appear before the judge, have several alternative dates available when you can come back. Asking for a postponement and then having no idea when you can come back is not a good idea. You may end up with the next available date from the court, which may not be convenient for you. Because you're asking for the delay, some judges give your opponent the first choice as to a new date.

If you receive a copy of a request for an adjournment from your opponent, don't assume it's going to be granted and stay home on the scheduled date. Unless you receive written notice from the court that the case has been adjourned, it's much better to show up at court on the scheduled date prepared to go forward. If you're the defendant and don't show up, the plaintiff may go ahead and get a judgment against you. If you're the plaintiff and don't show up, the case will be dismissed.

I have read countless requests from defendants to vacate a default judgment or from a plaintiff to restore the case to the calendar that contain the words "my opponent told me he was getting the case adjourned, and I didn't have to come." Please do not fall for such things.

Marking the case as final

If the judge grants your request and gives you an adjournment, your case may be marked in the court file as "final." Having a *final* marking essentially means that you're given an adjournment and a new court date, but you won't get another one beyond that.

If it's not marked final then the court will entertain another request for an adjournment in the future if the situation warrants it. Remember, the general rule in small claims court is to have cases decided on the merits by giving the parties their day in court, so unless one of the parties is abusing the system, it's likely an adjournment will be granted. But that's never a certainty — it's discretionary with the judge.

The three final markings that can affect what happens on your new court date are as follows:

- ✔ **Final versus both parties:** If either side is not ready the next time you come to court, the other side can go forward and present all of their evidence. A final marking against both parties can be granted even if only one side requested the adjournment.

- ✔ **Final versus plaintiff:** If you're the plaintiff and not ready on your new court date, the court will dismiss the case. This is usually granted when the plaintiff is making the request for the adjournment and the defendant insists he's ready for trial.

✔ **Final versus defendant:** If the defendant isn't ready at the new court date, you can go ahead with your case whether or not the defendant is prepared. This is the situation when the defendant is asking for the continuance and the plaintiff insists he's ready for trial.

A final marking is final against you and the defendant, but it's not final against the court. So, if the court can't get to your case, the court can give you another date. It's not a good idea to get into an argument with the judge when he tells you that your case won't be reached that night even though it was marked final.

Say your case is called and the defendant asks for an adjournment. You ask the judge to mark the case "final." The judge agrees, gives you a new date and the case is marked final. Then on the new trial date, you need the adjournment, but the case was marked final. If the defendant now wants to play hardball, you could find your case dismissed. So be careful what you ask for.

Chapter 12

Providing the Proof You Need to Make Your Case

*A*s the plaintiff, you have the burden of proving the allegations of your case. The *allegations* of the case are the essential elements you set out in your complaint. In a small claims court complaint, the allegations may be some general statement such as "breach of contract" or "damage from car accident" but your proof has to be something more than that. It has to consist of evidence in the form of documents, pictures, or witnesses that back up what you say. (I deal with witnesses in Chapter 13.)

Evidence can either be *documentary,* as in papers or photographs, or *testimonial,* as in what someone — you or your witnesses, including an expert witness — says. It can't be speculative or inconclusive. You need to have actual proof that supports your claim.

For example, handing the judge a photo of a damaged car and telling the judge, "Here look at this; the defendant did it; please award me money for repairs," would be speculative. You've not given the judge any evidence such as paid repair bills or estimates from a mechanic from which the judge can even guess at what it'll cost to fix your car. In fact, because there is no testimony as to how the accident happened, it would be mere speculation that the defendant caused it.

The Proof Is in the Pudding: Gathering Evidence

You prove your case by introducing evidence. *Evidence* is testimony of what a person saw, heard, or did; it's also documents, photographs, and objects. The problem is that not all evidence is admissible at trial.

Documents lacking authentication or reliability or unqualified persons claiming to be experts are examples of inadmissible evidence. These issues are dealt with in this chapter and Chapter 13.

One of the advantages of small claims court is that the technical aspects of the rules of evidence are relaxed. This doesn't mean that the rules of evidence are totally eliminated; it means that the person hearing the case has the authority to allow into evidence testimony or objects that may be inadmissible in a regular civil trial.

Because not all evidence is admissible, each state has developed "rules of evidence" to be followed at trials. Most of these rules are found in statutes or state evidence codes. Other rules of evidence have developed from case law. As you can see, presenting evidence at a trial can be a challenging task. Even experienced lawyers sometimes have problems proving their case because they can't get some information into evidence, usually because there is no way to verify its reliability.

Small claims court recognizes that evidence can be a tricky area of the law, so to make the court more user-friendly, the rules of evidence are relaxed. When preparing your case, ask yourself how you convince the court that what you're saying is valid or that the document you want to submit is reliable or believable.

Put yourself in the position of the judge. Consider seriously whether you would accept a photo as accurate or a statement as being true without some other verification.

For instance, you want to use a photo of the damage to your car; however, not only is the license plate not visible in the photo but neither is the make of the vehicle. And the photo is in black and white. So trying to convince a judge that this is your Toyota Camry and not one of several million other Camrys produced may be a stretch.

I strongly suggest that you always focus on what you want to accomplish, how to accomplish it, and how to document what you're trying to prove before you actually do any of it. In other words, be prepared. If you do your homework as you go along, having your evidence ready for trial shouldn't be a big deal.

On the other hand, if it's so easy to gather evidence to make out a case, why do they need so many detectives on television law shows? In the next sections, I explain the types of evidence you need to gather and how to use them to prove your case.

Carrying the burden of proof

The plaintiff — the person bringing the case against a defendant — always has the burden of proof.

This means that you have the responsibility to establish what happened and have enough evidence that the defendant is responsible for the damages that resulted to convince the judge your story is the more believable one. The term often used is that you have to establish your *prima facie* case in order to prevail at trial. *Prima facie* is Latin that means "at first appearance," so, essentially, you have to prove that your case is what it seems to be.

What this means is that after the judge hears what you've said, the judge can say, "You've told me enough, so let me hear what the defendant has to say." If, after you present your case, the judge takes out a bugle and plays Taps, there's a good chance you've failed to prove the essential elements of your claim. If that happens, your case can be dismissed without the defendant having to say anything.

An example of failing to make out a *prima facie* case would be a car accident where you're looking to have the defendant pay for the damage to your car. You just have the picture of your car. The judge asks, do you have a receipt for the repairs or two estimates of the cost of the repairs? If you answer no, it shows that you're totally unprepared for your trial. Your case will be dismissed because you failed to make out a *prima facie* case. You lacked an essential element: proof of your damages.

Evidence is proof that what you say is true. When I refer to "proof" I don't mean using your older siblings ID to get into a bar. I mean the testimony and documents that substantiate your claim. The stronger yours is, the stronger your case will be.

The law recognizes three different burdens of proof, best illustrated by picturing Lady Justice with the scales:

- **Beyond a reasonable doubt** means the scale is totally out of balance on your side because you've piled up a great deal of credible evidence.
- **Clear and convincing evidence** means the scales are substantially tipping over in your direction.
- **Preponderance of the evidence** means that the scales are only slightly tipped in your favor, just enough to get the scale out of balance. It's more likely than not that your presentation of the facts is true.

Most people are familiar with the burden of proof in a criminal case — the standard of "beyond a reasonable doubt." This does not mean 100 percent certainty. And it doesn't mean no doubt at all. But it's the most difficult proof standard recognized in the law.

The person bringing a criminal case has a heavy burden to meet in order to convict someone and send her to jail. The "beyond a reasonable doubt" standard is not used in civil cases, so you don't have to worry about it in small claims court.

Civil cases occasionally use the "clear and convincing evidence" standard, which is somewhere between by a preponderance of evidence and beyond a reasonable doubt. It's a higher standard to prove than by a preponderance of evidence but is less stringent than the criminal standard of beyond a reasonable doubt.

Clear and convincing evidence is the standard used in civil cases that may have some criminal implications as well such as a fraud, or a usury based contract claim, that is where the defendant loaned you money at a rate of interest that exceeds the legal limit in your state. The situations in which clear and convincing evidence is the standard in civil cases are so few that as a practical matter you don't have to worry about it for most small claims cases.

As a plaintiff, the burden of proof you must meet in a typical civil case is preponderance of the credible evidence. This generally means that it's more likely than not that the facts are what you claim they are and not those claimed by the defendant. If you don't meet the burden of proof, the case will be dismissed.

Looking at direct versus circumstantial evidence

Evidence is divided into two categories:

- ✔ **Direct evidence** is a conclusion drawn from a fact. What a person says, hears, or does — if it's believed to be true — can prove a fact.

- ✔ **Circumstantial evidence** is a conclusion inferred from the circumstances. Circumstantial evidence is a reasonable conclusion drawn from the available facts.

These examples help clarify the differences:

- ✔ **Direct Evidence:** You walk out of your house, and water is pouring down from the sky. You're quickly soaked to the bone. If you testified to these facts, a reasonable person would conclude that you had established that it was raining.

  Direct evidence from every gangster movie script ever written: The bad guy is about to get off because his slick lawyer has bamboozled the court. The wife of the poor slob he rubbed out jumps out of the crowd and shoots the bad guy and his lawyer. This is direct evidence because everyone sees the wife pull the trigger and shoot the ne'er-do-well.

- ✔ **Circumstantial evidence:** You walk out of your house in the morning; there are puddles of water on the ground, your newspaper is soaked, the grass is wet, and when you get in your car, you need to use the wipers to clean the windshield. Although you don't have any direct evidence or experience that it rained at night, the circumstantial evidence of what you observed would allow a reasonable person to conclude that it had rained.

  Circumstantial evidence isn't always true. If you live in a pineapple under the sea with a trouser-wearing sponge and a starfish who walks on two of his five points, there's an alternate reason for the exterior moisture.

  Another example from every murder mystery script ever written: The accused is heard to say to her nemesis "I'll kill you." Five minutes later, everyone at the party hears a shot. They come into the room, and the accused is standing there holding a gun and her nemesis dead on the floor. No one saw the shooting, but the circumstantial evidence leads to the arrest of the accused.

  Of course, the lawyer of the accused proves that someone else did it, and the accused just happened to walk into the room immediately after the shooting and picked up the gun, just because people in these scripts do dumb things like that.

Knowing your enemy: Discovery of the facts

If you're the defendant, you may be puzzled as to why you're being sued. You may not recognize the name of the plaintiff or, if you do, you may not remember any dispute. (Although obviously, if you were in an accident, you probably remember the plaintiff.)

Because the plaintiff doesn't have to bring a lawsuit immediately, a year or more may elapse between the date of the incident and the date you're sued. The complaint in small claims court often is such a brief statement and so lacking in detail that the defendant may have trouble figuring out why she's being sued.

In regular civil court, the procedure for either the plaintiff or the defendant to find out more about the other side's case is called *discovery*. It's a fact-finding exercise so that each side can learn more about the case and perhaps get it resolved without going to trial when all the details are known to both sides.

Discovery is not a procedure readily available in small claims court — but read on, because in some instances, the procedure is used for small claims cases. First, take a look at why discovery is not always appropriate for small claims cases, and how it can actually defeat the purpose of a small claims case:

- ✔ **Discovery delays the litigation.** Discovery devices such as oral depositions, written interrogatories, and demands for production of documents aren't permitted without the consent of the court, and it takes time to get that permission.

- ✔ **Discovery can be costly.** For all of the same reasons that it causes delays — taking depositions, soliciting written answers, producing or copying documents — discovery costs money.

- ✔ **Discovery may require the court to get involved.** The court may need to make sure that both sides comply with any requests for discovery.

- ✔ **Discovery is usually conducted by attorneys.** Discovery requires familiarity with the rules of evidence (which I discuss at the start of this chapter). Because there are no attorneys in most small claims cases, conducting discovery becomes a complicated procedure.

The bottom line is that discovery defeats the purpose of small claims court.

Although discovery is rare in small claims court, I explain some of the more common discovery procedures just in case you show up and the defendant's lawyer starts asking the judge to let her do it.

One of the more common discovery devices is an *oral deposition:* A witness is put under oath and asked questions about the case with a reporter or recording device taking down the questions and answers. Taken before the actual court date, depositions are expensive because you have to hire a court-certified stenographer, and you have to produce a transcript, which may be used at trial.

Lawyers like to use this discovery device in most civil litigation because not only do they obtain information about the case, but they get to see the witnesses while they're being questioned. Is the witness nervous? Is the witness evasive? Does the witness have the memory of an amnesiac or does she spit out answers with the accuracy of a computer? All of this is information a lawyer can put to good use during a trial.

Because small claims cases generally move quickly through the legal system and the issues involved don't usually require the need to preserve testimony and gather such additional information that discovery provides, discovery is rarely necessary.

However, there are legitimate reasons for doing a deposition in small claims court. You probably want to take a deposition of a witness if

- The person is leaving the state.
- The person is ill or possibly dying.
- The person is going to be unavailable to testify at trial for any reason.

Other common discovery devices are called *written interrogatories.* These are questions about the case one side sends to the other that have to be answered in writing, and the answers must be sworn to before a notary. This is a time-consuming process and would only be used in small claims court on a very limited basis.

If you get served with a set of written interrogatories, and the small claims court hasn't issued an order permitting them, you may want to notify the court of the situation. If there is a court order, then you'll have to answer them. In any case, don't ignore them.

If you're served with written interrogatories, you may want to have a lawyer review your answers before you send them back to the other side. Nothing prevents you from seeking legal advice for your small claims case even if lawyers aren't permitted in court.

The reason to have a lawyer review your answers is so you don't admit something in your response that will get your case thrown out of court or give the defendant a defense she is unaware of.

Other common discovery devices include the following:

- ✔ **Notice to admit:** A demand served on you where your opponent asks you to concede certain facts. Anything admitted then doesn't have to be proven at trial. For instance the landlord sends you a copy of the written lease and asks that you admit that it's the lease between the two of you.

- ✔ **Notice to produce:** A demand that you give the defendant copies of documents and exhibits you plan to use at trial so that she's not surprised when you present them to the judge. It may be that you may have documents in your possession that your opponent needs to properly prepare her case. For example, you don't have a copy of the written lease with the landlord, but you're sure that it says you can have pets in the apartment. You may ask that the lease be produced before the trial so you can prepare your case.

  A notice to produce is not the same as a subpoena, which I describe in the next section.

- ✔ **Demand for a physical examination:** In any personal injury claim, the defendant has the right to have you, the plaintiff, examined by a doctor of the defendant's choosing. Because personal injury claims are rarely brought in small claims court, the odds are you won't have to deal with this issue. But if you are given such a demand, you either have to comply or ask the court to void the demand.

Subpoenaing information

The closest thing to discovery in most small claims court cases is the use of the subpoena. A *subpoena* is a legal document that directs a person to come to court and either bring evidence needed for the case or testify as to the facts of the case.

Subpoenas are used to produce witnesses at the trial. For example, if you want a police officer to testify about the accident you're suing the defendant about, a subpoena is necessary to get her to come to court. In fact, any time you need a witness who is a governmental employee, such as a police officer, the proper procedure is to subpoena the person to ensure that she shows up.

Although you may subpoena some records from a governmental agency for trial and ask that someone come from the agency to testify about the contents of the records, don't be surprised if that person has no information about your case and is only the custodian of the records.

You may also want to subpoena someone who witnessed the event and is not a party in the lawsuit. If you need a witness and that person won't appear voluntarily, a subpoena is needed to make her show up at the trial.

In civil litigation other than small claims court, your lawyer issues any subpoenas and makes sure they're served. Because this is small claims court, you as either the plaintiff or the defendant needing the witness or documents ask the court to issue the subpoena.

Although the court issues the subpoena, you have to fill out the subpoena form and provide the information. The clerk or a judge may review the document before it's served, depending on the practice in your small claims court. In many states, if you want someone from the government to appear, a judge has to sign, or *so order,* the subpoena. This may not be necessary for other subpoenas.

Sometimes you get before the judge and discover that you really need to subpoena some record to prove or defend your case. The judge, wanting to have the case decided on the merits and not on a party's inexperience with the process, may tell you to go see the clerk and subpoena some particular record.

Listen to what the judge is saying to you — and write it down. Make sure you understand what you're being asked to do. Judges don't particularly like to have the clerk pop up 15 minutes later saying, "Judge, there's a guy downstairs who says you told him to get a subpoena. He has no idea what you said."

In some states, the *litigant* — the plaintiff or the defendant — who wants to subpoena records needed to prove her case or needs a witness to appear at the trial to testify is responsible for having the subpoena served. Check with the clerk as to the proper method to serve a subpoena in your small claims court. It may or may not be the same way the summons and complaints are served. (Refer to Chapter 8 for tips on serving summons and complaints.)

If you're responsible for having the subpoena served, keep some notes on how you did it and if necessary you may have to fill out an affidavit of service. As pointed out in the section on service of the summons and complaints, it's never a good idea to serve something yourself because if there is a dispute as to what you did as a party you're presumed to be biased.

If you don't serve the subpoena properly, two things may happen:

- ✔ You now have to ask for an adjournment to properly serve the subpoena, which, of course, delays your case.
- ✔ The judge tells you it's too bad; the trial is now and you have to go forward. Without the information you need to prove your case, you substantially reduce your chance of winning.

Say, for example, that after you move into your new house, a dispute arises as to some personal property the seller was supposed to leave and didn't. You want the lawyer who represented you at the purchase to testify as to what was agreed to with the seller at the closing. Although your lawyer wants to testify, in many states, the ethical rules require that she be subpoenaed to testify.

If you need certain records, you also need a subpoena, especially if the records are from a governmental agency. For example, you keep having sewage backups in your basement from the municipal sewer line. You need to subpoena the local sewer department records to establish whether they have been maintaining the sewers and whether other customers have made complaints about the problem to them.

If you have to subpoena records, make sure you have the subpoena served far enough in advance so that the person has enough notice to show up and the person who keeps the records you want has time to get them. This is especially true of governmental agencies, which sometimes are a little bit slow in responding.

If you subpoena records there may be a charge for photocopying, or if you subpoena a witness there may be a fee fixed by the rules to compensate the person testifying, such as a mileage charge. You can avoid any surprise fees if you prepare your case in advance and discuss charges with the clerk or the help center if there is one. You can also check the court rules online or read any information the court provides to assist you in preparing.

Submitted for Your Approval: Presenting Evidence

Sometimes what you need to prove your case is not testimony from other people but hard evidence in the form of documents or photographs that graphically prove your point. It's your job to gather and present this evidence to the court.

Of course, as with everything in small claims court, there's a right way and a wrong way to present evidence, which I cover in the next sections.

Placing photographs into evidence

One of the ways to prove the extent of damage you suffered as a result of the defendant's actions is to bring photographs to the trial. Photographs of the location of the accident, how the car looked after the accident, what your apartment looked like after the flood, or your yard looked like after your neighbor's tree fell in it are all helpful in proving your case.

You just can't hand in the photographs and ask the court to use them as evidence — or, actually, you can if the judge lets you. But there's a proper way to submit photos as evidence. The accuracy of the photograph must be established or authenticated, especially because technology makes it so easy to alter photos today.

When introducing photographs, follow these guidelines:

- ✔ **Make copies before the trial date.** You should even send copies to your opponent so she isn't surprised at the time of the trial. If the evidence in the photos is overwhelming enough, the defendant may decide to settle rather than fight.

- ✔ **Submit only a few photos.** Generally there is no need to have 100 pictures of the couch damaged by the sewer backup. Sometimes overkill makes the judge's eyes glaze over and reduces the impact of the evidence.

- ✔ **Label the photos.** Include pertinent information so that the judge knows what she's looking at when she reviews the pictures. Keep the labels as short as possible. It's not necessary to have all the facts attached to the photograph. Your testimony will provide all the details needed. A label should be something like: living room floor, 123 Main St., with the date of the photo and either the case number or names of the parties.

If you're taking photos to be used as evidence, follow these guidelines:

- ✔ In taking a picture of an intersection, try to include a street sign, house number, or some other recognizable landmark that establishes the location.

- ✔ If you're trying to establish the condition of an apartment on the date you vacated, including a daily newspaper with a readable date can help, especially if your camera doesn't date the photograph.

- ✔ Judging the size of something from a photograph can sometimes be difficult. If the size of a hole or the distance one thing is from another is important to your case, use a ruler or yardstick or some other item to give a general idea of the size.

A picture may be worth a thousand words, but a bad picture is useless.

If you took the pictures, state when you took them, what you think the pictures show, and that the pictures fairly and accurately show the location or the item at the time of the occurrence or immediately after the occurrence. It helps if you have a camera that records the date a picture is taken. If you didn't take the pictures, you have to get that information from the person who did and they probably will have to testify as to those facts.

If you have the photos on your cellphone or some other electronic device, make copies of them. Otherwise, your phone will have to be put into evidence. And if the court doesn't make a decision right away, your phone will be staying with the judge until the case is decided. Judges really don't like taking items of personal property into evidence and then having to be responsible for their return. And for many people today, being without their cellphones for more than five minutes produces hyperventilation and general panic.

For security reasons, many courts don't allow any electronic devices, including cellphones, into the courtroom. This means you either have to leave it in your car or check it with security.

So when your case is called, you have to go and retrieve the device if you have photographic evidence on it, go through security again, explain to security that the judge told you to retrieve the phone, have the security officer call the clerk to ask the judge if she wants to let you bring in the phone. This delays the case because rather than wait for you to return, the court may move on to the next case that's ready. So a word to the wise: Print out any photos you have on an electronic device before court.

One way to get a photograph into evidence is to show it to the defendant and ask her to identify the location in the photograph or the condition of the item or premises shown. However, the danger with doing that is that if the defendant says the photo doesn't reflect the conditions, you may be stuck with the defendant's answer because you called her as your witness. You then have to introduce evidence to contradict what the defendant said. Or you have to ask the defendant why it doesn't fairly and accurately depict the scene of the incident, which may act to your advantage if you can get the defendant to bring out information helpful to your case.

If your case involves an incident that required either party to notify an insurance carrier, there's a good chance that the insurance company took pictures. If you want the defendant's insurance company to bring the pictures to court, you may have to subpoena them in advance of the trial.

The danger with relying on the defendant or the defendant's insurance company's pictures and not on your own photographs is that if they don't have them at the trial, you have a problem. And relying on something you haven't seen to prove your case can be very dangerous. It has the same risk as asking a question that you don't know the answer to. If you put the defendant's photos into evidence, you're vouching for the accuracy of them because they become an exhibit offered by you, the plaintiff. You're then stuck with the contents of the exhibit as part of your case.

Whether you're a landlord or a tenant, it's a good idea to take photos of the apartment before the tenant moves in and after the tenant vacates. These pictures help establish the condition of the apartment on both occasions.

Putting documents into evidence

In order to get a document into evidence, you have to explain where it came from, who produced it, why you have it, and what it shows about your case.

A big problem litigants have is with bills and receipts that don't identify the source; that is, they're written on a receipt paper that can be purchased at any stationary store, and for all a court knows, you could have bought a receipt pad and created your own receipt.

A receipt also rarely says who the purchaser is. If you're submitting a document from a store containing what you allege are all the items purchased to correct the improperly performed work of the defendant, and the receipt doesn't have your name on it or the address where the materials were delivered, the receipt is practically useless. It may have been acquired by anyone for use at any location.

Another mistake you can make is to submit a receipt that contains items purchased for another purpose and not arising from the issues of the case.

If you know you're buying things for a particular purpose, especially if you're considering a lawsuit, separate them at the checkout counter and get a separate receipt. Otherwise you'll be drawing circles around items and making notations on the receipt to convince the judge that these purchases are related to the litigation.

Another problem is that the bill is not marked "paid" or if it is marked, it doesn't say how it was paid — cash, check, or credit card. If you used a credit card to pay the bill, you'll have to bring the monthly statement from the card issuer showing that it's your charge card and the item was purchased.

If you're purchasing materials to correct damage you allege resulted from the defendant's actions, try to make sure that the receipt identifies the source, designates who is the purchaser, and how payment was made. The failure to have such documentation often means that the receipt cannot come into evidence and you're stuck trying to prove your case using other means.

Submitting evidence when you're the defendant

All of the rules concerning how evidence is presented apply to the defendant just as well as the plaintiff. The difference is that the defendant doesn't have to present any evidence initially. The plaintiff has the burden of proof.

However, if you, as the defendant, have asserted an affirmative defense, a counterclaim or cross-claim (all of which I explain in Chapter 8), you have the burden of proof on those issues and have to present evidence in support of those contentions. The same rules and warnings apply to you just as if you were the plaintiff.

Because you're the defendant and may not know exactly why you are being sued by the plaintiff when you receive the summons and complaint initially, you may have to request an adjournment at the first court appearance to better prepare your case. If you can give a good reason, the court will generally allow a short adjournment.

Chapter 13

Handling Live Witnesses Well

· ·

In This Chapter

▶ Deciding whether to testify

▶ Calling the defendant to the stand

▶ Dealing with live witnesses

▶ Submitting testimony on paper

▶ Questioning witness credibility

▶ Calling in the experts

▶ Staying calm when a witness "misremembers"

▶ Adjourning for a lost witness

· ·

*L*ive witnesses are much harder to handle in court than documents. Documents don't forget key facts, get tongue-tied in court, and have a hard time remembering their own names, much less what happened. And, documents don't tell so many lies that, a la Pinocchio, their noses grow past the courtroom door.

But witnesses do have a positive side. Bringing in people who can substantiate your story cuts down on bringing in so many affidavits and documents that your side of the courtroom looks more like a scene from a hoarders' show than a trial.

In this chapter, I review the advantages and disadvantages of using live witnesses. I walk you through the questioning process and give you guidelines on what to ask and what not to.

Choosing Not to Be Your Own Witness

If you're filing your case in small claims court, you're probably willing — if not downright eager — to get into the courtroom and tell your side of the story. In most cases, it goes without saying that you're going to serve as one of your own witnesses. However, if you have *agoraphobia,* a fear of public places (not to be confused with angora-phobia, fear of wool sweaters), are worried that the judge will remember you from a traffic violation in 1977 where you concluded your case by calling the judge a fascist pig and exhorting all present to "free the Indianapolis 500," or are afraid that you'll blow your own case simply by opening your mouth, you may consider having someone else with knowledge of the facts testify in your place.

Having someone testify in your place really isn't a good idea in most cases. I explain why in the next sections, but if you're not deterred, I also tell you how to do it legally.

Sending someone to court in your stead

In most cases, whether you're the plaintiff or the defendant in the case, you need to be the one standing in court if you want to win. You can't give someone an affidavit or a power of attorney and have him stand in for you for the following reasons:

✔ You're the one who was there; you're the one who knows the facts. It's in your best interest to be the one presenting them.

✔ Your opponent is legally entitled to cross-examine you in court. It's impossible to cross-examine someone who doesn't show up.

One exception to this rule is a situation in which you're the owner of a car claiming property damages after a car crash. However, your spouse — not you — was the driver of the car, so you don't have information as to how the accident happened and have no reason to testify. The driver of each vehicle and any passengers or witnesses would be the ones to testify. You as the owner should attend the trial but you won't get a speaking part in the production. Ownership can be established by producing the vehicle registration information.

Here's another exception: Say you bought your son a new computer for school, but when he received it in the mail it didn't work. Although you paid for it, he would be the person to testify as to what was wrong with the computer.

Using a power of attorney

Most people have heard of a power of attorney, but few people understand exactly what it means. A *power of attorney* is a document in which one person, the *principal,* appoints another person, the *agent,* to act in the principal's place. In court, the agent is the *attorney-in-fact* for the principal.

So if you appoint your brother-in-law by using a power of attorney to stand in your place and make decisions for you in court, you've made him attorney-in-fact for the specific case. And you'd better have a lot of faith in his judgment, because his judgment, not yours, will determine how your case goes.

You can use a power of attorney for a specific event or transaction or give a general power of attorney to govern all of your affairs. You may want to use a power of attorney in small claims court if you can't attend the trial yourself.

Suppose both you and your spouse are the plaintiffs, have an equal amount of information about the case, and both have an equal stake in the outcome. The day of the trial, one of your kids is sick, so one of you has to stay home. Your spouse gives you a power of attorney and with it, the authority to settle the case by a written agreement with the defendant rather than go to trial. You can sign any stipulation for both you and your spouse.

Because both of you are plaintiffs with knowledge of the event, you wouldn't need the power of attorney to participate in the trial. If you lack any knowledge of the event, having a power of attorney won't help at the trial, because you're basically window dressing and can't testify as to the facts.

One situation in which a power of attorney can come in handy even if you have no knowledge of the case is if there are other witnesses to testify on your case. For example, your spouse owns the car your daughter was driving at the time of the accident. The property damage claim is brought in your spouse's name as the owner, but she's away on business. The power of attorney would allow you to participate in the trial and not have the case dismissed because the actual plaintiff is unavailable.

The decision of the judge is binding on the principal who issued the power of attorney.

Obtaining a power-of-attorney form

You must put a power of attorney in writing; an oral power of attorney is useless. Each state has its own preferred form for creating a power of attorney. If the form isn't properly filled out, it's ineffective.

Power-of-attorney forms are available in legal supply stores, office-supply stores, and even convenience stores. They also may be available online. The problem with buying a form at a place other than a legal supply store is that the state legislature sometimes changes the requirements for a valid power of attorney. If you use an old, undated form, then the attorney-in-fact is not properly established, making the form useless. For example, New York went from having the principal, the person creating the power of attorney, initialing a list of things the agent can't do to having the principal initial a list of things the agent can do.

Sometimes banks and other such institutions have their own power-of-attorney forms. These may or may not comply with the statutory form in your state and the form preferred by the court system. The form from the bank may be designed for use in many different states. Your best bet is to get a form from a local lawyer or a legal supply store.

The same problem exists with a power of attorney you find online; because the forms aren't universally accepted, an online version may not pass muster in your local court.

Determining whether you can use a power of attorney

Can you use a power of attorney in small claims court? Guess what. The answer is, as in so many other things in court, maybe. Some states don't allow anyone to act as an attorney-in-fact; other states allow them, and some states allow them only in certain circumstances.

Even if your state permits you to use an attorney-in-fact, the small claims court may require you to submit your paperwork in advance of the trial so that the court can review the form and determine whether it's properly executed.

If, for some reason, the court won't accept the power-of-attorney forms for review before your trial date, it probably makes sense for you to have a lawyer either prepare the form for you or review it before you try to use it.

If you send someone to the trial with a power of attorney that's not filled out properly, it will be deemed defective and may be fatal to your case. If you're the plaintiff, your case will be dismissed. If you're the defendant, the court may declare you in default and enter a judgment against you.

Calling the Defendant as Your Witness

As you're preparing for trial, you may wonder whether you should call the defendant to the witness stand as part of your case. In certain situations you do, but generally, unless you're an experienced trial lawyer in real life, it isn't a good idea.

Differentiating an attorney at law and an attorney-in-fact

An attorney at law is not an attorney-in-fact. An attorney at law provides legal services and is a member of the bar. An attorney-in-fact is your agent and is authorized to represent you only for the specific purposes set forth in the power-of-attorney form.

It's generally not a good idea to have your attorney at law be your attorney-in-fact because you're asking one person to do two different things. The attorney at law is there to protect your legal rights, but the attorney-in-fact is there to stand in for you — be you, in other words.

If you ask your attorney to serve as your attorney-in-fact, you're asking your legal representative to give advice to himself. Also, legal rules say lawyers shouldn't be both an advocate and a witness in a case, which is what you would be asking your lawyer to do in this situation.

The lawyer is also asking for trouble down the line. In the event something happens in the transaction, the first thing the principal is going to say to the lawyer is, "who told you to do that?" At which point the lawyer better hope his malpractice insurance carrier is on speed-dial.

Calling the opponent to testify is fairly common in car-accident cases when lawyers are representing the parties involved. The lawyer who calls the opposing party as a witness knows what questions to ask and what responses to expect from the opposing party because the questions will be limited to obtain certain specific facts. Questions won't be asked that allow your opponent to tell his entire life story complete with 8-x-10-inch glossy photos.

The danger of calling your opponent to testify is that calling a person as witness on your case means that you're vouching for that person's truthfulness, and therefore, you're stuck with the answers that person gives to the questions you ask. As any lawyer will tell you, if you don't know what the answer will be, don't ask a question in court.

It's not a good idea to call the defendant as your witness in a small claims case because you won't know how he will answer your questions. Prepare your case under the assumption that the defendant is going to contradict everything you say.

If you do call your opponent as a witness, ask limited questions such as "Is this your signature on the lease?" or "Is this a picture of my car after the accident?" or other questions to which the answer is not in dispute.

That being said, if your case is one of the rare small claims cases in which discovery was conducted (see Chapter 12 for a discussion of discovery) and you have sworn depositions of your opponent's testimony or sworn answers to written interrogatories, you'll have a really good idea as to what the defendant has previously said under oath. You can then ask the same questions if the answers help your case and get the information before the court. If the defendant changes his story you can use the sworn statements to contradict the testimony and question his credibility. But to do this takes a lot of preparation. So unless you know what you're doing it's probably better not to try it.

Questioning Witnesses

Questioning witnesses isn't really rocket science, but it does take preparation and considerable thought. You want your questions to elicit the testimony you want to help your case and not aid the defendant in proving his defense or destroying your case. Think about what you want each witness to prove and then write down the questions you think will get the witness to say that information on the record for the judge to hear.

You have a couple reasons to always write out the questions you want to ask and the points you want to make from each witness before you start your trial:

- ✔ You may not get a chance to ask a question you forgot to pose the first time around; even if the court allows you to ask questions on redirect testimony, there are limits on what you can ask — a concept I talk about in the next section.

- ✔ You can and should consult your written notes. This will keep you focused in the event there is an objection to the question you asked and the court decides you can't ask the question. For instance, if the court was allowing you to ask some leading questions and now says you can't continue to do that, you can figure out a different way to get at the information you want to get on the record, and the judge's ruling won't push the question right out of your mind. I explain leading questions in the next section.

You don't want to be scribbling follow-up questions when you should be asking them.

I explain the different types of questions you can ask if the person you're questioning is your witness or the defendant's witness in the following section. The section after that tackles leading questions, a term you may be familiar with from television lawyer shows but really have no idea what it means, in the next section.

What not to do

It's never a good idea to call the defendant as your witness, then slowly walk away from the witness stand, whirl, charge back to the witness stand wagging your finger in his face and shouting, "And where were you on the night of the murder?" It may be emotionally satisfying, and the stupefied looks on the faces of the judge and the other people in the courtroom may be amusing, but having to come up with bail after you get thrown in jail for contempt of court will probably be less amusing. Stick to the questions relevant to your case.

Explaining question categories

If you've watched any legal show on television, you probably know the two categories of witness questioning:

- **Direct examination:** The person who calls the witness asks the questions first.

- **Cross-examination:** The opposing side questions the witness after he testifies under direct examination.

If you call the defendant as your first witness, when you ask the defendant questions, it's called direct examination. Likewise, if the defendant called you as his witness, it would still be direct examination. The key is who called the witness not whose side the witness is on.

After your opponent concludes his cross-examination, the court usually permits redirect and re-cross-examination. Redirect questions are permitted for you to respond to new information that came out on the cross-examination of the witness. It's not supposed to be used to elicit testimony you forgot to get on direct examination or questions you forgot to ask. Re-cross-examination is to be limited to any issues that were raised with the witness on redirect examination.

That said, because this is small claims court, the judge may be inclined to be lenient and let you ask things that you forgot to ask on direct examination. But if you prepared and wrote out your questions and the points you wanted to make with the witness, you won't find yourself in that position.

In a case involving a car accident at an intersection, situations in which you can and cannot ask questions on redirect or re-cross-examination include:

✔ **No redirect allowed:** After the witness testifies, you realize that you never asked him whether there was a stop sign in the direction the defendant came from. If neither you nor the defendant asked any questions about stop signs on direct or cross-examination, you can't ask about it on redirect.

✔ **Redirect is allowed:** On cross-examination, the witness states that you had a stop sign in your direction, implying that you didn't stop. Because the stop sign is a new issue raised on cross-examination, on redirect you can ask either, "Did you see me stop at the sign?" or "Isn't it true that the defendant also had a stop sign?"

Because this is small claims court and most litigants don't have lawyers, the court usually lets you ask additional questions that you forgot to ask. Remember, though, that this procedure is at the judge's discretion. The judge can also refuse to let you add evidence or ask questions you forgot to ask, so get it right the first time.

Someone once said insanity is when you keep doing the same thing over and over thinking you'll get a different result. This is especially true when you question a witness: You can't keep asking the same question over and over again because you didn't like the answer you got.

The judge may not think that you fit the definition of insane, but if you keep doing this you'll drive him and everyone else in earshot crazy. After the judge tells you to move on and ask another question, do it. But if you prepared your case you won't have this problem.

Asking leading questions

If you've ever seen a movie or television show with a trial scene, you probably recall a moment when a lawyer jumps up during a witness's testimony and yells, "Objection, your honor! Counsel is leading the witness."

A *leading question* is a question that contains the answer in it so that the witness only has to answer "yes" or "no." For example, in a landlord-tenant case asking the tenant, "the rent was $500 a month and you stopped paying it in June because the roof was leaking?" If a leading question is improper because the question already contains the answer, it follows that a proper question — one that is not leading — makes the witness provide the information.

Generally, you can't ask leading questions when you're presenting your direct case. During direct examination, the testimony is supposed to come from the witness testifying and not the person asking the questions.

However, courts permit leading questions to be used during direct examination in certain situations:

- ✔ When the information isn't in dispute and using leading questions will save time.

- ✔ To help jog the memory of the witness without putting words in his mouth.

- ✔ If the witness is a child or someone with a disability who may have trouble expressing himself.

- ✔ If the witness is *hostile,* meaning the witness is reluctant to testify. (Fortunately, this isn't the hostile that means "I'm going to punch your lights out next time I see you.")

Also, because this is small claims court, the strict rules of evidence aren't necessarily applied, and the court may permit more leading questions than it would in a civil trial. This is done to expedite matters, and because there is no jury, the judge can better control the pace of the trial and the information he wants to get from the witnesses.

But the general rule is that leading questions can't be used on a direct case to prove your case or the defendant's defense.

You're allowed to ask leading questions to get the answers you need during cross-examination.

An example of a leading question that is permitted on direct examination would be something like this where all of the information in the question isn't in dispute:

> Question: "Are you the owner of a 2010 Toyota Camry, New York license plate number 123-ABC and were you driving that car on May 1, 2012, at 8:00 a.m. easterly on Main Street, in Springfield, when you were involved in an accident with the defendant who was driving a 1999 Chevy Malibu bearing New York license plate number 789-XYZ westerly on Main Street?
>
> Answer: "Yes."

If the court didn't permit leading questions, the testimony would have to be given as follows:

> Q: Do you own a car?
>
> A: Yes.
>
> Q: What kind of car?
>
> A: A 2010 Toyota Camry.

Q: Is that vehicle registered?

A: Yes.

Q: In what state is it registered?

A: New York.

Q: Do know the license plate number?

A: Yes.

Q: And what is that plate number?

A: 123-ABC.

Q: Were you driving that car on May 1, 2012?

A: Yes.

Q: Where were you driving?

A: I was on Main Street in Springfield.

Q: In what direction were you going?

A: I was heading easterly on Main Street.

Q: Did anything happen on Main Street while you were driving your car?

A: I was involved in an accident.

Q: At what time was the accident?

A: 8:00 a.m.

Get the idea? There are probably another half dozen questions to ask before all of the information in the leading question has been elicited from the witness. Pretty boring, right? This is why the court often allows leading questions to establish information not in dispute.

Because your case is in small claims court, you probably won't have to figure out how not to ask a leading question, because you can almost always ask leading questions in small claims court.

However, if the judge doesn't allow you to ask a leading question and you don't know how to ask a non-leading question, then you have a problem. You have to be prepared to ask the questions so that the information you need comes from the witness and not you. Which is why you should write down the questions you want to ask and the order in which you want to ask them.

If your opponent has a lawyer, there's a good chance the lawyer will object to your questions as being leading. In all likelihood, the judge will overrule the objection and let you ask the question because he wants the case to be over in his lifetime. The lawyer knows this, but will make the objection in an attempt to throw you off your game. Forewarned is forearmed! But if you wrote down your questions you'll move on and not lose your train of thought.

If you call the defendant as your witness, the court presumes that the defendant is not going to volunteer information that can hurt him, and he is considered a hostile witness, so you're permitted to ask leading questions.

Presenting Affidavits in Place of Live Witnesses

Whether you're the plaintiff or the defendant, relying on a witness to prove your case is always a problem, especially if the witness is not a family member or friend and doesn't have a vested interest in the outcome. But when you go to court, the general rule is that all persons who have knowledge of the event or incident should be available to testify.

Different people see different things and interpret the same event differently, which is why, in major cases, investigators gather as many witness statements as possible. And people experienced in trying cases will tell you eyewitness testimony tends to be unreliable because of how people see the same thing differently.

But suppose that at the last minute, you find out your key witness can't make the trial. Can you use an *affidavit* — a written statement in which the witness swears to the truth of the contents before a notary public — if your witness can't appear at the trial? This is another one of those maybe answers, depending on which state you're in.

Most courts won't allow a case to be proven by an affidavit, because the other side cannot *cross-examine,* or ask questions, of a piece of paper. Well, they can, but they won't get much of an answer in return. It's a fundamental aspect of any trial that the other side has the opportunity to question a witness.

You may be able to use an affidavit to establish a peripheral issue involved in the case, but not to prove the essential elements of the case, especially if the witness is the only person with the necessary knowledge.

That being said, an affidavit is better than nothing and you may get a judge to accept it in certain circumstances.

If you really need the witness who can't appear for some reason, your best option is to ask for an adjournment, especially if an emergency is preventing the witness from appearing. If your witness just didn't show up, check out the upcoming section, "What to Do When Your Witness Doesn't Show Up."

One thing a judge doesn't want to hear halfway through your trial is, "Well, I have some witnesses, but I didn't think I needed them, can I come back?" This tactic will in all likelihood result in something you won't want to hear from the judge, "I'm sorry, your trial is right now."

Impeaching a Witness

No, I'm not talking about removing a president from office — *U.S. Constitution For Dummies* by Michael Arnheim covers that. Witness *impeaching* means calling a witness's credibility into question, and trying to cast doubt that what a witness says is accurate or truthful.

Because of the relaxed rules of evidence in small claims court, credibility often becomes a major issue in the case.

You can impeach someone's testimony in a couple ways:

✔ **Show that a previous statement or action is inconsistent with trial testimony.**

For example:

- In a suit by a tenant to recover a security deposit from the landlord, the landlord claims that there never was any security deposit given so there's nothing to return. If the tenant produces a receipt given by the landlord when the tenant first entered into occupancy of the apartment, the receipt can be used to impeach the landlord's testimony.

- In a car accident case, the defendant says that you ran the stop sign and hit him. You show him a picture of your car with the right side smashed in and his car with the front damaged. The photos impeach his testimony because they lead to the conclusion that he hit you.

✔ **Use a rule of law called *falsus in uno*.** This isn't a specialty pizza at a national pizza chain. *Falsus in uno* is a Latin term for the idea that if a person lies or misstates one thing, the judge or the jury can disregard that person's entire testimony. So if you can establish that the witness is misstating a material fact about the case, the judge doesn't have to believe any of that person's testimony. A *material fact* is one that is important and if accepted by the judge as true would help prove the plaintiff's case or the defendant's defense.

✔ **Produce a statement the witness gave under oath — such as in an affidavit, a deposition, or even testimony at another trial — that contradicts his statement at your trial.**

If you're lucky enough to produce such a previously sworn to statement, you get to have your own "Perry Mason" moment during the trial when you confront the witness and ask: "You were under oath when you made that prior statement and you're under oath now. Please, tell this court were you lying then or are you lying now?" At which point, you may be inclined to bow to the audience and receive a standing ovation. . . . You may be inclined to do that, but it's a really bad idea and probably wouldn't go over too well with the judge.

Don't get carried away with the idea of being able to impeach a witness for any misstatement. The misstatement or changed testimony generally has to be about an important, or *material,* fact or element of the case. Getting the details wrong isn't enough, as in these examples:

✔ You're suing your neighbor who killed your tree when he trimmed off branches that hung over the fence onto his property. In your complaint you said the tree was a maple but it was actually an oak. This was a mistake, but it would be unlikely to be able to be used to impeach your testimony because the kind of tree that was trimmed was not material to the case.

✔ In a car accident case, the police report states you said you were going between 15 and 20 miles per hour. At trial, you say you were going around 15 mph. This is not a material variation of the facts, which will lead to the impeachment of your testimony.

(As I and my judicial colleagues know based on the testimony of numerous litigants, no one in America ever drives over the speed limit.)

If you have one of the rare small claims case where discovery was conducted, the deposition transcript or answers to the written interrogatories often provide a gold mine of information that can be used to impeach a witness because those statements like those made at trial are under oath.

Another place to obtain inconsistent statements used to impeach may be in witness statements given to the police, insurance companies, and other persons investigating an accident.

Bringing in an Expert Witness

Even in small claims cases, you may need the testimony of a witness who possesses some special knowledge or skill in order to prove your case. In the legal profession, such a person is known as an *expert.* (It's important that you realize there's a difference between an expert and a know-it-all.)

In most small claims cases, in fact in most civil cases, you have no need for an expert witness. The events and incidents that make up most of the small claims court calendar are common, everyday occurrences, which the judge hearing your case will have some knowledge about.

In certain situations, an expert witness is recommended; in the following situations, an expert is required:

> ✔ If your case involves some knowledge, skill, or training beyond that possessed by the average person. As the plaintiff, you need someone with training in the defendant's business or profession to give an opinion as to the standard of skill for that profession in your community and whether or not the defendant lived up to the standard of care and expertise.
>
> For example, you claim that the defendant failed to properly repair your car's transmission. You get another mechanic to look at your car, and he tells you that the defendant didn't do the repair properly. You need the second mechanic to testify as an expert on the issue of whether the defendant made the repairs properly. The mere fact that the car isn't working properly does not mean the defendant did something wrong. The expert can testify as to what the defendant did and what should have been done to fix the problem.
>
> You can't testify yourself about what the second mechanic told you. This is considered hearsay and isn't proper evidence. *Hearsay* is dealt with in Chapter 14.
>
> ✔ If you're suing for *malpractice,* which is negligence of a professional such as a doctor, dentist, veterinarian, lawyer, or accountant. These professions require special skill and training beyond that of the average person, and the legislature of each state sets forth standards for education and training to practice that profession
>
> Only an expert can give an opinion as to whether the defendant professional performed services that meet the community standard for that business.
>
> ✔ If you need some unusual evidence to prove your case, you need an expert. For instance, to establish that it's the defendant's signature on the contract or to set the value of the baseball cards lost in the flooded basement .

If you're using an expert to testify, you have the burden of establishing the credentials of the witness so he qualifies as an expert. You need to establish any schooling or training he's had, whether he's published articles in professional journals, lectured or taught in his subject, been doing the job for a number of years, is licensed by any governmental agency, or is a member of recognized professional associations.

Sometimes this issue is easily eliminated if your opponent concedes that the witness is an expert, or if the judge asks the witness some questions and satisfies himself that the witness is an expert. After all, the judge is the person hearing the case and weighing the witness's testimony.

If the rules of your state require it, you may also have to let your opponent know in advance the name of the expert you intend to call so that he can challenge that person's credentials or call his own expert to contradict yours.

Before you hire an expert, you may want to find out if he's ever testified in court. A well-trained lawyer often can devastate the creditability and testimony of an inexperienced expert.

Locating an expert isn't easy. There are some services that provide this information to lawyers. So you may want to contact a lawyer who does litigation for some names. Or you probably can locate such persons online now.

If you do locate an expert, make sure the expert has knowledge of your particular problem. Hiring a tax lawyer to testify as an expert in a legal malpractice case where you claim your lawyer screwed up at your medical malpractice trial is a waste of money. Likewise, trying to use a chiropractor to contradict an orthopedist is the legal equivalent of mixing apples and oranges.

Recognizing the economics of paying an expert

The need to have an expert witness causes problems because the expert generally won't testify for free, and you're the one who has to pay him. In most cases, payment has to be made before the trial starts.

The problem with cases where expert testimony is required is that the cost of having an expert come to court to testify often exceeds the amount of damages you're seeking or reduces your award so substantially that it won't be worth it for you to even bring the suit. This is especially true in small claims court where the amount you can sue for is limited.

The cost of the expert is not recoverable by you as part of your damages. It's a cost of the litigation that each side must absorb as part of their respective cases.

Also, you can't just submit the report of the expert into evidence at the trial in an effort to save money. In effect, you're trying to make the piece of paper become the witness. This isn't allowed because your opponent has the right to cross-examine the expert not only on his credentials but also on his conclusions.

Establishing a witness as an expert

Can anyone be an expert? Surprise, surprise, the answer is "maybe." It's possible to have someone who is not professionally trained in a particular area be classified as an expert.

However, you have to ask certain questions of that person so as to convince the judge of the person's expertise, such as

- ✔ How long the person has been doing a particular job
- ✔ How many times the person has encountered the situation being discussed
- ✔ What training, if any, the person has had in that area

If the city or state where you live requires certain professionals to be licensed in order to perform the work you are claiming was not done properly, the expert you call must also be licensed.

If you need an expert and the person is not properly qualified, the person will not be permitted to testify or if he testifies, the court can ignore what he says. You can have your next-door neighbor who likes to tinker with car engines come in and challenge the testimony of a licensed mechanic, but the court will probably not deem him to be an expert and can disregard his entire testimony.

On the other hand, if your neighbor worked for 40 years as the in-house mechanic for a national car-rental company and was exempt from licensing because of that fact, there's a good chance you can make him an expert by asking the right questions about his training and experience.

For example, you allege that your local Maserati dealer screwed up your engine when you took your Maserati in for servicing. Unable to find another Maserati mechanic within a thousand miles, you call Hans the mechanic who used to work at the local Edsel dealership to testify as your expert. Unfortunately, Hans may know about Edsel engines but lacks the skill and expertise to testify about repairs on a Maserati. You probably should have been tipped off when he referred to it as a "dang infernal machine."

Any expert must be able to establish what the standard is in your community for performing the particular service in question. If the expert doesn't know the standard then he cannot testify.

In most states, professionals and artisans are held only to a community standard; that is, they can be evaluated only against the skill and expertise of persons performing that work in the local area.

A common example is that a local doctor in the middle of nowhere shouldn't be judged by the same standards as a doctor at a major university medical center. The Internet, however, has started to erode this distinction, because it makes a vast variety of information available not only to the professional but to everyone, thereby expanding the definition of the level of skill and knowledge expected of the professional or artisan.

If your opponent is calling in an expert to testify, the Internet also gives you the opportunity to bone up on the latest information on the issue the expert is going to testify about. This gives you the opportunity to ask the expert questions and attack his credibility by showing that maybe he's not such an expert because he's not aware of the latest information on the subject.

Unfortunately, in small claims court, you probably will have no idea if your opponent is calling an expert witness and who he's calling as that expert because there is no requirement to disclose the names of witnesses in small claims court proceedings. But if you're the plaintiff, you should know what kind of case you're bringing and if you're claiming the defendant didn't do properly what you paid him for.

The fact that you're challenging the skill level of the services the defendant performed should cause you to ask yourself when you're preparing the case, "Self, how will I prove the defendant messed up? I need someone who knows that business to help me prove my case." And because you know you have to prepare your case before you go to trial, you'll have thought about whether you need an expert and if you do where you'll get one and what you'll ask.

Conversely, the defendant knows why you're suing him and knows he'll need an expert to prove he did the work as agreed and up to the community standard.

Don't ask a question unless you know what the answer is. You can actually make the expert look better by having him answer your questions accurately, thereby raising his stature with the court. So if you ask a question hoping for a "deer in the headlights" response from the witness and instead get a recitation that sounds like the expert did his dissertation on that very subject — back off on any further questions.

Say you live in Naples, Florida. You're suing the local artisan who installed the sunroom on your house. The person you hired to be an expert is your next-door neighbor who is a snowbird from Montana who builds ski lodges. Although an expert on ski lodges, he is probably not going to have sufficient knowledge of local standards and practices to testify as an expert on the requirement for the construction and the costs of a sunroom in Florida.

So if your neighbor is a Jack of all trades and you want him to testify as an expert, just remember the end of that quote: "Jack of all trades. Master of none."

Keeping Your Cool When Your Witness is Lying

You just called your neighbor to testify as to how many times you complained to the defendant about his dead tree hanging over your property. On the witness stand, your neighbor suddenly has no recollection of ever hearing you complain. In fact, he now says that on more than one occasion the defendant offered to split the cost of removing the tree and you responded, "It's your tree; you pay."

One thing that you don't do is to pop up out of your chair and yell "Liar, liar, pants on fire." Or "Your honor, the witness speaks with a forked tongue."

It is of course very upsetting to have to listen to someone not tell the truth. But remember that person may not be lying; he may actually believe what he's saying. Just because the witness's recollection of the events differs from yours doesn't mean he's lying. To keep your cool, keep these points in mind:

✔ Each side has the right to examine or cross-examine every witness. This means you'll get a chance to question the person who made the statement you think is false. If you called the witness and are now surprised by the response, you can ask the court to declare your witness a hostile witness so that you can ask leading questions, which I explain earlier in the chapter.

✔ If you have documents or other evidence that contradict a witness's statement, you can use those items to question the person or ask the court to take them into evidence.

✔ You can testify yourself or call a witness to *rebut,* or contradict, the testimony.

✔ You can and should politely object to the testimony. If you believe that someone is testifying improperly or is not following the rules, the proper procedure is to object to what is going on. The judge may ask you why you are objecting and give you a chance to explain what you feel is wrong. In some instances, it's obvious that there's a problem with the testimony and the judge won't ask you to explain why you are interrupting because he agrees with your objection. (Chapter 14 deals with objections in more detail.)

In any case, remain calm and polite. If you have an experienced judge and it's obvious that a witness's testimony is completely contrary to what you were expecting, there's a good chance that judge will take over the questioning so as to get a better sense as to whether the witness is having a credibility problem or a memory problem.

What to Do When Your Witness Doesn't Show Up

If your witness fails to appear as scheduled, without giving you any explanation, you have several alternatives:

✔ **Ask for an adjournment.** This is the easiest way to go. If you can't get the defendant to agree to a short adjournment, you'll have to ask the court. The decision to reschedule the case is left to the judge's discretion, so you better have a good explanation. If you can document that some unforeseen event occurred such as illness of the witness or death in his family, bring that information with you. Also be prepared to propose several alternative trial dates.

✔ **Ask for the court to issue a subpoena.** Because a *subpoena* is a legal document, if a person receives a subpoena and still decides not to show up for court, you can ask the court to hold that person in contempt. (I give you information about subpoenas in Chapter 12.)

But if you compel someone to come to court when he really doesn't want to, you may not get the favorable testimony you're expecting. The recalcitrant witness can kill your case once he gets on the stand. Unless you can't prove your case at all without the subpoenaed witness, it may be better to prepare to go forward without that person and get that evidence in through some other means.

Just to emphasize the point: In every trial I've overseen, when an expected witness fails to show, I invariably offer to either subpoena the witness, or if the witness is under subpoena, have the court officers go get the witness, take him into custody and bring him into court to testify. No lawyer has ever taken me up on that offer. Any capable lawyer much prefers to work around the missing witness and get the information before the court by some other means. So a word to the wise.

✔ **Substitute a sworn statement or oral deposition, if you have one.** If you can establish that the witness is truly unavailable as in dead, moved away, in the military, or such, and you have a transcript from an oral deposition or some other sworn statement from the witness taken when the defendant was present and able to ask the witness questions, most states allow you to read that testimony into the record at trial as if the witness were present.

The problem with this is that small claims actions rarely include oral depositions before trial and they often aren't even permitted. You may get lucky though, in the following situations:

- You're suing for property damage to your car from an accident. A passenger in your car is also making a personal injury claim against both you and the defendant. You can use a deposition taken in that case in your small claims case.

- You're suing a tenant who has vacated an apartment for damages. You want to use the testimony of the real estate broker who helped you find a new tenant and saw the apartment in its damaged state. If the broker testified at the eviction trial in another part of the court, that testimony can be used if the broker isn't available.

Chapter 14

Sounding Like a Lawyer in the Courtroom

Sounding like a lawyer is easy — after all, actors master the lingo in the time it takes to memorize a script. But understanding what lawyer lingo actually means and how it's used in the courtroom takes years of practice. Trust me, there's more to it than wagging your finger and shouting, "Objection!"

I assume you don't have years to attend law school and learn all there is to know about arguing a case effectively, so in this chapter, I give you a crash course on the common terms used in court and tell you when, where, how, and why to use them to your best advantage, whether you're the plaintiff or the defendant.

Understanding and Making Motions

You hear it in every courtroom drama: Someone makes a motion to dismiss the case, to allow a witness to speak, or to strike a witness's testimony from the record.

A *motion* is nothing more than a request for the court to intervene in some way. Although you generally see motions made in the courtroom in the movies, you can make a motion before, during, or even after your case goes to court.

The next sections explain when to make a motion (if ever) and what it can do for you.

Understanding what a motion is

In legal terms, a *motion,* sometimes called an *application,* is a request for interim relief that is asking the judge to address some legal issue relating to the case. Motions can be made by either side.

Because I am talking about small claims court where cases are supposed to move quickly and motions can delay the process, you should check with the clerk of your court to see if motions are permitted, and if they are, if there are any restrictions on when and how the motion can made.

If you are making a motion before your trial date, there is a good chance the motion will have to be in writing. You will have to file the original motion papers including affidavits and exhibits you want the court to consider and mail a copy to your opponent. A copy of every written motion has to be delivered to your opponent with the original to the court.

You must submit some proof that you served (delivered) a copy of the motion papers to your opponent or else the court can't grant the relief you're asking for if your opponent doesn't show up. Why? Because if you can't prove you gave your opponent notice, how would she know you were making a motion in the first place?

Each court has certain time limits for submitting a motion on papers. If you just hand your motion papers to your opponent in court two things can happen:

- ✔ The court can reject the papers because you never gave your opponent any notice and you waited until the trial date to serve a copy on her.

- ✔ The more likely scenario is that the court will grant your opponent an adjournment to respond to your application. This of course will delay the case. The delay may be substantial, with the judge asking your opponent how long she needs to respond in writing to your written motion.

Your opponent may ask for time to respond in writing to your motion, which is referred to as filing "opposition" to the motion. You will want to ask the judge to direct your opponent to serve her response to you a few days before the motion will be heard by the judge so that you can address your opponent's response in a document called a reply.

You may not want to or have to submit a reply but it's important to ask for the right to do so. Otherwise you'll show up in court, get handed your opponent's papers, be surprised by what she's saying, and then be asking the judge for a chance to reply to the contents. This will again delay your case.

Also, don't be surprised if after you've served your motion papers, your opponent makes her own motion, called a *cross-motion,* which requires that you file opposition papers.

Motions can get complicated and delay a trial for a substantial amount of time, which is why many small claims courts limit when and whether motions can be made — they defeat the purpose of small claims court.

There is more of a likelihood that a motion will be made if the defendant has a lawyer. The fact that you don't have a lawyer won't relieve you of the obligation to properly respond to those papers, but the judge may give you a little more slack in how you respond. A trip to the help center if your court has one may be well worth your time in this situation.

Motions are important and should never be ignored. A motion may not seem as important to you as the trial, but failure to respond to a motion can lead to your case being dismissed and you not getting your day in court.

Motions may be made:

- ✔ **Pre-trial:** Often these motions seek to dismiss for some legal reason such as the statute of limitations has run, you're not the proper party, or the case doesn't belong in small claims court at all, or to postpone the case — that is, you need an adjournment.

- ✔ **During trial:** These can also be made to dismiss the case. For example, after you present your case, the defendant asks that the case be dismissed because you failed to prove anything. Other motions commonly made during trial are to prevent a witness from testifying for some reason, exclude an exhibit that isn't properly authenticated, or strike a witness's testimony for a reason such as it's hearsay.

- ✔ **Post-trial:** A post-trial motion usually has to do with changing the outcome of the judgment in some way. Post-trial motions are usually made to the judge who heard the case after you receive her decision. It may be to ask the judge to reconsider some evidence presented during the trial which you believe she misinterpreted or misunderstood, or to submit new evidence that recently came to light and was unavailable to you at the time of trial.

  It's very difficult to successfully ask a judge to consider new evidence after the trial because you have to explain why you didn't have that evidence beforehand. If you knew about it — such as a witness who wasn't available at the time of trial or documents you requested from the government or a bank that weren't delivered on time — then why didn't you ask for an adjournment?

  It's not a successful trial strategy to withhold part of your case hoping you can get by with the minimum amount of evidence and then ask for a new trial later on to present your entire case. In fact, it's a really bad strategy.

Motions can be made more than once. The defendant can make a motion before your trial starts to dismiss your case on some technical ground. She can then make the same motion after you present your case and also after she presents hers. Motions can also be made after a judgment is rendered.

Usually, if the defendant is making a motion, she's seeking to either delay the case or have it dismissed on some legal or technical ground. If the plaintiff is making the motion, it generally means that she has a problem — such as getting witnesses or documents for the scheduled trial date — or wants the judge to restore the case to the calendar. The plaintiff may have missed the original trial date and wants the case to come to trial or is trying to stop the defendant from engaging in tactics to delay the case.

Because small claims court is designed to have cases tried quickly, and motions delay the process while the judge decides on them, the rules of your state may either prohibit the use of motions or limit their use to specific circumstances.

In courts where there are judges and arbitrators, the rules usually require all motions to be addressed to judge and not to an arbitrator. So, if you want to make a motion, notify the clerk of that fact either before the case is called or when your case is called.

Getting a flavor of pre-trial motions

In a small claims case, the person most likely to seek a pre-trial motion is the defendant. The most common pre-trial motion is to ask for an adjournment because the defendant just received the notice, needs more time to prepare, and is not ready to proceed.

Examples of typical pre-trial motions a plaintiff may make include the following:

- ✔ Your tenant hasn't paid rent for three months — April, May, and June. By the time the case comes to trial, July rent is also overdue. The proper action is to ask the court to add July's rent to the claim before the trial starts so that you don't have to bring a new lawsuit for it.

- ✔ You sued the defendant as John's Car Repair. However, you now know that the correct name of the shop is the Bang the Dent Out Service Center, Inc. You make a motion to amend the caption—that is, change the name of the defendant to the correct name—before the trial starts so that if you win, you can collect on your judgment.

✔ In small claims courts where the defendant has to file a written answer, examining that answer may give you grounds to ask for a judgment because the defendant doesn't raise any legal defense to your complaint.

For example, you're suing your deadbeat brother-in-law for the money he owes you. His written answer admits he borrowed the money and he never paid you a cent. His defense is that he lost his job and has no money. In the law that is known as "Too bad. We all feel sorry for you. But you owe the money." It's not a legal defense that requires a trial. You can file a motion and ask the court for a judgment because there is no legal defense.

In this situation you may want to see if your court has mediation services so you can enter into an agreement where you get a judgment and you enter into a payment schedule with the defendant.

Asking for postponement

When your opponent asks for an *adjournment* — a postponement — before the trial starts and has a legitimate reason such as an illness, a family emergency, or the inability of a witness to attend, you have a strategic decision to make.

Even if you don't consent to your opponent's request for an adjournment, the court is likely to grant a motion if the reason seems valid and there haven't been any prior requests for a postponement..

Beware of being treated as you treat your opponent. If you're inflexible or difficult when your opponent requests a change, when the next trial date comes along and it's you who needs an adjournment, your opponent may consider turnabout fair play and contest your application. And if the judge remembers the incident and thinks you were unreasonable, she may deny your application, in which case, you'll have to go to trial even if you're not ready. So be reasonable.

It's a myth that each side is "entitled" to one adjournment. The court has sole discretion in determining whether to grant a motion to adjourn. Always be prepared to go forward.

Asking for dismissal

A pre-trial motion that's much more serious than asking to postpone a trial is a motion to by the defendant to dismiss your case. In making a motion to dismiss, the defendant is saying that some legal reason exists that makes your claim unenforceable.

Some common pre-trial motions for dismissal are:

- ✔ **Wrong court:** In other words, you are not dealing with a court that handles cases such as yours.

- ✔ **Case filed too late:** The defendant is saying that the statute of limitations has run and the case can no longer be brought.

- ✔ **Wrong party:** The defendant may claim that you sued her as an individual when you should be suing some other party — for example, the driver who ran into her and forced her car into yours.

- ✔ **Case has already been heard:** The defendant may claim that you already sued for the same matter and lost.

The thought of your case being dismissed without even being heard may seem a little frightening. In reality, it's unlikely that a defendant without a lawyer will know to raise these issues. A motion to dismiss the case may be a problem only if the defendant has an attorney.

Delaying for discovery

As a general rule, *discovery* is prohibited in small claims court — you need to get the consent of the court. The way you get consent is to make a motion before a judge. Discovery is the legal process where each side tries to find our more information about their opponent's case. I discuss discovery in Chapter 12.

If discovery was granted and the other party did not comply, this could lead to another pre-trial motion to compel the discovery to be completed.

A typical discovery motion may be in a car accident case where the defendant's insurance company got statements from the witnesses to the incident. So as not to be surprised at trial by a courtroom of witnesses claiming you ran the red light, got out of the car and yelled, "I knew I shouldn't have had those last ten beers; it always makes me sleepy" you may make a motion to see those statements before the trial date.

Making motions during trial

You can make a motion during trial. Of course, if both sides are representing themselves without the assistance of counsel, there's little likelihood that either side will have the expertise to make any motions, but if your opponent has a lawyer, you probably will be faced with at least one motion during your trial.

The most common motion is one by the defendant to dismiss for failure to prove the case. A motion to dismiss is made by the defendant after the plaintiff presents her case.

A defendant's lawyer may say you failed to prove your *prima facie* case, meaning that even giving the best possible interpretation to all of your evidence, you've failed to make a legally enforceable claim against the defendant. If you have a case in which the testimony of an expert is needed, and you don't have that expert, you can bet that a motion to dismiss will be made and granted.

Several things can happen if the defendant's lawyer makes a motion to dismiss the case on *prima facie* grounds:

- **The motion is granted.** Your case is over, dismissed on the merits.

- **The motion is denied.** The defendant has to present her case.

- **The judge responds** *decision reserved.* In the interest of time, the judge decides to wait to decide the motion until after the defendant has presented her case.

  Technically, the judge is supposed to rule on the motion when it's made, and if necessary, take a recess to make the decision. In reality, reserving a decision gives the judge the ability to hear the whole case before deciding on the motion. Reserving the decision allows the case to move forward. Because there is no jury, there's really no prejudice to either side.

A common motion that may arise during the trial and one the judge may generate herself is to adjourn the case when it becomes apparent a party or a witness needs an interpreter. If the judge thinks an interpreter is needed, don't even waste your time objecting. Because if the case goes ahead, and the loser appeals alleging she didn't understand English, the appeals court will most certainly order a new trial.

Finishing up with a post-trial motion

Post-trial motions may be made immediately after both sides present their respective cases, or they can be made after the case is over and the judge has rendered a decision.

The losing party may make a motion to the judge requesting a new trial. This is not the same as an appeal. An *appeal* is an application to a higher court to review what happened at the trial.

A post-trial motion for a new trial is addressed to the trial judge and basically says "Hey judge, you misinterpreted some of the evidence" or "Hey judge, I just learned some facts about the case that I couldn't have possibly known before, and I think I should have a new trial."

The problem with post-trial motions is the *substantial justice* standard, which holds that as long as the trial was fair and each side had an opportunity to present its case, substantial justice has been achieved. In that case, no new trial will be granted.

Another type of post-trial motion is one made if either party missed the trial date: This is one where the party that missed the court date asks that the case be restored to the court calendar for a trial on the merits. Because it's small claims court where the policy it to try to give the parties their day in court and receive a decision on the merits, these motions generally are granted.

Like all motions, a motion to restore the case rests in the sole discretion of the judge. Most states require any such request be accompanied by a reasonable excuse for why you missed the date and a meritorious claim or defense, meaning that there is some legal basis to support your complaint or if you're the defendant to defeat the plaintiff's complaint.

- ✔ If you're the plaintiff and don't show up, your case would be dismissed. You can make a motion to have the case restored to the trial calendar so you can have your day in court.
- ✔ If the defendant fails to appear for the trial and a default judgment was entered against her, the defendant would have to show some sort of reasonable excuse as to why the case should be restored, basically re-tried with the defendant present.

In some places, a reasonable excuse for missing the trial is "I forgot" or "I missed the bus." If you have a legitimate reason, such as you were out of town, never got notice, or had a medical problem, present any proof you have when you make the motion. If you just screwed up, it's probably better to just admit that and throw yourself on the mercy of the court.

The essence of small claims court is to give both parties an opportunity to have their case heard and get their day in court. As a practical matter, most courts grant these applications and restore cases to the calendar. However, don't count on getting your case restored if you missed the trial.

If you know in advance that you're going to have a problem with a scheduled trial date, it's better to notify your opponent and the clerk of the court beforehand rather than trying to get your case restored after the fact.

Raising Objections

Anytime you see a trial on television or in a movie, you can bet at some point one of the lawyer characters will jump up and yell, "I object." In a movie, it's very important that you jump up and yell either "Objection" or "I object" at the same time, because it accentuates the drama. If the actor is really feeling it, she may even "strenuously object."

The only reason the actor makes an objection is because it's in the script. You shouldn't raise an objection unless you have a valid point, because judges don't necessarily respond well to theatrics for theatrics' sake.

Allegedly, trial lawyers are trained so that if they happen to nod off during the trial, the first thing they do when they wake up is yell, "Objection." At a minimum, it gets everybody to stop and gives the lawyer a chance to get her wits back. If the judge asks what's the objection, lawyers are trained to respond either "hearsay" or "relevance," because those are types of objections that everyone has to stop and think about.

If both you and the defendant in your trial are unrepresented, it's unlikely that an objection will be made to your case. On the other hand, if the defendant has a lawyer, there's a good chance you will hear objections being made. The lawyer may actually be raising a legal point or may be doing it to spook you and get you off your game.

On the other hand, if you think something doesn't sound right, don't just sit there and say nothing. Politely say something like, "Your Honor, that's not right" or, "She wasn't there, so how can she say that?" If you do it in the right way, you're really making an objection without calling it one.

Going to court and watching some small claims trials before your own can help prepare you for these types of encounters on your own day in court.

Looking at what an objection is

So when should you raise an objection? Basically, you make an objection when you believe that the evidence being presented to the court shouldn't be heard or considered for some reason.

Sometimes lawyers object just because something doesn't sound right. They may not know why the evidence should be questioned but have a gut feeling or a flashback to their trial practice class in law school that the evidence being offered is objectionable. When there's an objection, the judge may ask the person making it to explain what the basis for the objection is. This is a good time to listen to what is going on.

You will have no idea what you did wrong, if anything, but if the judge asks the lawyer to explain the objection, you may learn what you did wrong and be able to correct it yourself. For example, say the defendant's lawyer objects saying that you're leading the witness. Chapter 13 explains what a leading question is, and by incorporating the information in that chapter, you can revise your question so that you don't lead the witness.

If you don't understand the explanation, you can ask the judge to explain what's going on. The problem with this is that the judge has to balance her role between being the person who decides the case and providing legal assistance to either side, so you may not get an answer from the judge that will help you if she agrees to answer at all.

When the other side raises an objection, keep your cool. This is one of those times when having a serious and respectful demeanor can help you out. If you don't go into hothead mode and fly off the handle, the judge in ruling on the objection may tell you what's wrong so you can correct your error.

If you make a scene, the judge may not tell you what's wrong. If you can't figure it out, you may find yourself trying to correct something you don't understand and make things worse or not get a key piece of your evidence into the record.

On the other hand, if you look completely befuddled, the judge may actually ask the necessary questions for you to get your evidence into the court record and move the case along, especially if the issue is something the judge needs to know about in order to decide the case fairly.

Raising common objections

Certain objections are commonly raised in court. Some common objections you may hear include:

- ✔ **No foundation:** This means you haven't established the authenticity or accuracy of a piece of evidence. For example:
  - You offer a photograph as evidence without saying what's in it, who took it, and when it was taken.
  - A witness starts testifying without explaining how or why she knows anything about the matter at hand.
  - You have a person testifying as an expert without asking questions to establish her expertise.

✔ **Relevancy:** The legal term for "Who cares?" or "What's that got to do with this?" For example, in your fender-bender trial, you testify that you were coming from your favorite restaurant before the accident, and include testimony as to who was at the restaurant, why you like it, and what you ate. All this information may encourage everyone in the courtroom to try the place for dinner but isn't relevant in establishing whether you or the other driver had a green light.

On the other hand, information about your behavior in the restaurant may well be relevant if the issue is whether you were intoxicated and if there are witnesses to that.

✔ **Asked and answered:** You already asked the witness that question and got an answer. You may want to ask the same question either to make sure the judge got the point or because you didn't like the answer from the witness. The other side will object because they don't want the judge to hear the answer again because it hurts their case or because they don't want the witness to change what was a favorable answer.

Generally, if the judge didn't understand an answer, the judge will ask the witness to clarify the response. Remember, though, if you asked a question and didn't get the answer you wanted, it's unlikely you're going to get a better answer by asking the question again and again — it may only reinforce the issue.

Ruling on objections

When an objection is made, the judge has to make a ruling. The judge may:

✔ **Sustain the objection:** The judge agrees that the objection is valid. You will be required to ask the question a different way or to try to get the information or document into the record in some other way. In small claims court, the judge may not use the word *sustain;* she may say something like, "Don't answer that question" or "You can't use that document."

✔ **Overrule the objection:** Overruling the objection means that the question is proper and the witness can answer it or that the document can come into the record. The judge may not say "overruled" but say something like, "I'll allow it" or "I'll let it in."

✔ **Allow the answer or document into the record over the objection:** Allowing the answer in over an objection is common in small claims court. It's not really the same as overruling the objection, but it has the same effect.

The judge is really saying, "Yes, your objection is technically valid, but this is small claims court where substantial justice applies and the strict rules of evidence don't have to be followed and I'm not going to keep us here all night while the plaintiff tries to figure out how to get the document or statement into evidence."

The judge may say she's allowing it into the record but will take the objection into account when deciding what weight or influence to give to it.

Dialogue around a typical objection may go like this:

> You: Judge, I have a picture of my car here.
>
> Defendant's lawyer: Objection.
>
> You: Why's she objecting, judge? She knows it's a picture of my car after the defendant hit it.

Now what do you do? You have no idea why you can't use the picture, do you? If the judge sustains the objection, you look like a deer caught in headlights before you figure out what's going on.

If the judge says, "Counselor, what's the nature of your objection?" and the lawyer answers, "No foundation," you still may not know what you did wrong but may be able to figure out that you should have asked something else first to establish the reliability of the evidence being offered. (I discuss the ins and outs of evidence in Chapter 12.)

In all likelihood, when you produce any tangible evidence, the judge will ask you the questions necessary to establish a foundation for the evidence. Sometimes, in the interest of moving the case forward, the defendant's lawyer will ask the appropriate questions such as: "Who took the picture?" "When was it taken?" "Does it fairly and accurately represent the condition of your car after the accident?"

Introducing Evidence

Evidence is the way you prove your case. Sometimes you have concrete evidence, such as a traffic-camera recording of your accident, which occurred right in front of the annual policeman's ball. Other times, you don't have concrete evidence and have to rely on what other people say to prove your case.

The next sections describe types of evidence that may or may not help you prove your case.

Handling hearsay

Raise your hand if you've heard the term "hearsay." Everyone has. Most people know that there's something wrong with hearsay evidence, but have no idea what the term really means.

In fact, a lot of lawyers don't exactly know what it means either. Part of the reason for this is that there are so many exceptions to the hearsay rule that the rule has lost its effect.

What hearsay is

The hearsay rule developed to keep certain types of evidence out of the court record because they were thought to be unreliable. *Hearsay* is defined as an out of court statement, either written or oral, offered in court by a witness and not the person who made the statement to prove the truth of the matter being made in the statement. (If you're thinking you should have bought *Brain Surgery For Dummies* instead of this book, fear not. You're not too different from the thousands of lawyers who decided to become tax attorneys because they couldn't grasp the hearsay evidence rule.)

Breaking the hearsay rule down to its parts makes it easier to understand. The hearsay rule is:

- ✔ **An out of court statement:** The statement was not made in court, on the record, during the trial.

- ✔ **Either written or oral:** The statement may be something someone said, wrote down, or did.

- ✔ **Offered in court:** A party to the lawsuit is trying to get the statement into evidence.

- ✔ **By a witness and not the person who made the statement:** Someone other than the person who made the statement, produced the document, or did the action is testifying as to the contents of the statement.

- ✔ **To prove the truth of the matter being made in the statement:** The statement is being offered to the court as containing information that's true and accurate.

What makes hearsay inadmissible is that the person who originally made it is not in court repeating it and is not subject to cross-examination. In other words, no one can question the person who originally made the statement as to its truth, reliability, or accuracy.

A document people commonly try to use at a trial is a police accident report. But guess what, the police report is hearsay. Suppose the police report is prepared by an officer who arrives at the scene an hour after the accident. The police officer finds a witness and the witness says that a passenger in the defendant's car got out of the car after the accident and says "I told Demolition Dora, the driver of the car, not to speed up and run the red light, but she never listens, especially when she has been drinking and talking on her cellphone."

The officer, who did not see the accident, interviews the witness and puts that statement in the police report. You, the plaintiff, want the police report to be put into evidence as proof that the defendant, Demolition Dora, ran the red light. Neither the passenger who made the statement, the witness who heard it, or the police officer is in court to testify, but you want to use the statement to prove your case.

This is classic hearsay that consists of:

- ✔ **An out of court statement:** What the passenger said.

- ✔ **Either written or oral:** The original statement was oral. The fact that the police report is in writing does not make the statement written. It would be written if the passenger had given a written statement to someone.

- ✔ **Offered in court:** You're trying to have the written police report put into evidence.

- ✔ **By a witness and not the person who made the statement:** Not only is the passenger who made the statement not present, neither is the witness who heard it, nor the police officer who recorded it.

- ✔ **To prove the truth of the matter being made in the statement:** You want the statement to be used as proof that the defendant ran the red light and maybe even that she was speeding, drunk, and on her cellphone.

What makes this hearsay is that the person who made the statement is not present in court and available for cross-examination. In fact, it's double hearsay, because neither the witness nor the police officer is present and subject to cross-examination.

Even if you can get the police officer in to testify, it's still hearsay because she didn't make the statement and in fact didn't hear it originally. If you get the witness to testify, the statement is still hearsay because the witness didn't make the original statement, but the passenger did.

This is one reason affidavits — notarized written statements by someone with information who's not present in court — are not permitted. The content of an affidavit is hearsay. The person who made it is not present in court to be cross-examined.

Because this is small claims court and the rules of evidence are relaxed, sometimes you can use an affidavit or police report even though it is hearsay.

You won't be able to use the police report to prove the truth of what someone told the police officer, but if the report shows the location of the cars after the accident, which is something the officer observed, you can use it for that limited purpose. If you can't produce the actual witness, try to get an affidavit and give it your best shot.

Exceptions to the hearsay rule

The hearsay rule has so many exceptions that a great deal of hearsay evidence is permitted at small claims court trials.

The first exception is an *admission,* which is a statement by the defendant admitting responsibility for some fact important to the case.

For example, you loaned your spouse's deadbeat brother $2,000 just because he asked. You put nothing in writing. Although he promised to pay you back, he hasn't.

After a year, he sends you a cocktail-stained postcard from a resort in Tahiti, saying that he knows that he owes you the money but he just doesn't have it at the moment.

If you sue him, you can use the letter as an admission that he owes the debt. It's an exception to the hearsay rule because people generally don't lie about facts that create some liability.

In the same situation, but the postcard says only, "Thanks for the money" without acknowledging a loan. He could admit you gave him the money but could claim that it was a gift. In this case, you would still need to prove it was a loan.

A second exception is referred to as a *prior inconsistent statement.* The witness is present at trial and now is asserting different facts than given at prior time.

For example, say the passenger in Demolition Dora's car gave a sworn statement to Dora's insurance company saying that Dora sped up and ran the red light. The passenger is now at the trial and says on the witness stand that Dora was going 25 mph and had the green light. You can use the prior inconsistent statement to show that the trial testimony has been manufactured.

A third, very common exception involves business records. The records a business keeps in the regular course of its business can be used in evidence. Business records are considered reliable because the business needs accurate records to supply and bill its customers. In some states, you need someone to testify as to how the records are kept to establish that the records are truly a business record that can be used at trial.

Many states now permit medical records to be certified by the hospital and used as evidence at a trial without bringing in a person from medical records or billing to testify. Say that after the accident with Demolition Dora you were taken to the Cannonball Adderly Emergency Room at Mercy, Mercy, Mercy Hospital. You didn't have insurance, so the hospital sues you for the medical services rendered. The hospital does not have to bring in the ER staff to testify as to what services were rendered.

Someone from billing can come in and testify how the billing records are kept and qualify them for the business record exception as to what services were rendered. The billing person would come in to testify as to the fair and reasonable value of the services. On the other hand, if the issue was what injuries you received in your lawsuit against the driver, the certified hospital record would be admissible without parading in all of the hospital staff to testify as to treatment.

In some states, the hospital can just send copies of everything with a certification or affidavit that the records are true and accurate and kept in the regular course of the hospital's business.

Other exceptions to the hearsay rule are:

- **Dying declaration:** A favorite in movies, this is when the dying evildoer confesses to the crime so the wrongfully accused can be released from jail.

- **Excited utterance:** A statement made by someone without any time to think about what she's saying such as, "Oh my gosh, that guy just ran the red light!"

- **Declaration against interest:** Similar to the admission exception that applies to all facts but limited to acknowledging a criminal act or monetary obligation.

To further confuse the issue, another hearsay exception can be made if the hearsay statement isn't being offered to prove the truth of its content but to show the state of mind of the person who made the statement.

Looking at the best evidence rule

The *best evidence rule* is really self-explanatory. It requires that you produce the original and not a copy when it comes to documents and exhibits. If you only have a copy and your opponent charges that it's not best evidence, you have to explain what happened to the original document.

The existence of the original document can be extremely important in a case, especially if you and the defendant each only have copies and the copies aren't the same. Yes, I know you're shocked that this can actually occur — by the way, "there's gambling at Rick's." Courts generally don't like to hear, "The dog ate my evidence" as an excuse, so just fess up if you have no idea where you put the original paperwork.

Invariably, when there's a dispute about the terms of a written agreement, when you get to court your copy and the defendant's aren't the same. This doesn't necessarily mean that someone *tampered* with the evidence such as altering her copy to make it fit their version of the facts. It means that, as in most situations that start out on a friendly footing, no one bothered to see that all the copies were identical when they were signed, because it seemed inconceivable that things could end badly.

Take the case of your deadbeat brother-in-law who borrowed money he hasn't repaid. He actually signed a promissory note acknowledging that you loaned him the money. Unfortunately, when it gets to the trial you can't find the original; you only have a photocopy.

Deadbeat is going to claim that he paid you and that's why there's no original. You have to explain what happened to the original document. If you can explain it to the judge's satisfaction, then you can use the copy to prove the terms of the agreement. Fortunately, if Deadbeat claims payment, he may have to prove it. Of course being wilier than you, he'll claim he gave you cash and he asked for a receipt but you refused to give it, saying, "Come on, we're relatives."

The best evidence rule is an evidence rule undergoing change in this modern digital age. What exactly is the original when taking about electronically created and stored documents becomes an important issue at trial. Most judges really don't want to keep your cellphone, laptop, or other communication device. So bringing hard copies to court and authenticating them can become a problem.

Understanding the parol evidence rule

The parol evidence rule has nothing to do with working in the prison library so you can get out early on good behavior. That word is "parole." *Parol evidence* refers to oral or spoken evidence. Remember your French: "Parlez-vous français?" (Do you speak French?) Same root word. Parol evidence means that a court will not admit oral testimony to alter the terms of what appears to be a complete written agreement.

A *complete written agreement* is one that has all the essential terms. Anyone one reading it can figure out what each party agreed to do without looking to extrinsic evidence such as other documents.

In other words, you produce a signed written contract showing that you were going to paint the defendant's house and she was going to pay you $5,000. The defendant now says that wasn't the agreement at all. She says the price was only $3,000, and you agreed to install vinyl siding, replace the windows, and repoint the chimney. The defendant is trying to use oral evidence to contradict the terms of a complete written agreement.

In these cases, the law says basically, "So, Ms. Defendant, if that wasn't the agreement, why did you sign it?" The parol evidence rule prevents one party from claiming that a written agreement *complete on its face,* meaning it makes sense and looks legal and reasonable, was not actually the contract between the parties.

Like most rules in the law, there are exceptions, such as fraud, duress, or anything that would establish that there was no intention to enter into the agreement. Saying you didn't read it before you signed it may be true, but is generally not a legal defense.

That said, oral testimony is admissible to show that after the contract was signed, the parties agreed to certain changes. The problem with these cases is the same problem with every case where oral testimony is the key — the court has to decide whose story is more believable, the plaintiff's or the defendant's.

Chapter 15

Understanding the Judge's Decision

Most likely, you laid out your hard-earned money for this book because you were intrigued by the word "winning" in the title. You have a claim to make and obviously it's one you want to win.

After days, weeks, or months of preparing your case, waiting for the judge's decision seems like added torture. Win or lose, you need to know what the judgment you receive means. In this chapter, I run down the different ways of getting a judgment and how they affect you, whether you're the winner or loser in court.

Receiving Your Judgment

On television reality shows, where only the winners move on to the next stage, contestants know their fate pretty speedily — the judges render a decision as soon as the contestants finish or the audience votes whether to keep them or not.

It doesn't work that way in court, except on television. In most cases, the judge won't make a ruling until long after you've left the courthouse, although most judges prepare a decision within a day or so. There are several reasons for the delay:

✔ The judge wants to get to all the other people who have cases on that night's calendar.

✔ If the judge decides the case immediately, either you or your opponent is going to be dissatisfied — sometimes both parties leave unhappy. And although most people accept the decision graciously, others don't and may publicly question the judge's parentage and his mother's pedigree or announce he knows where the judge lives or what kind of car he drives.

Judges don't particularly like these situations and neither do court personnel assigned to protect the judge. So not rendering a decision from the bench avoids this.

✔ Sometimes the judge just wants to think about the case, to take time to consider the evidence presented and to check the applicable law.

You presumably put a lot of time into preparing your case, so it's a good thing when the judge takes the opportunity to quietly consider the evidence.

If the judge rules from the bench, and you lose, are you going to think the judge put enough effort into considering your case? What message does instant decision-making send to the public about the seriousness of the process?

When you do finally receive a decision, it may be a very short statement on a preprinted form, and it may or may not state the judge's reasons for deciding as he did.

There's no legal requirement that the judge explain his decision. You and the defendant may just get a statement that says "judgment for plaintiff" and then indicates the amount of money awarded. If interest is also to be added to the judgment, the date from which interest will run will be included. If it says "judgment for defendant," the case is over. You lost.

Understanding a Loss

The fact that you don't prevail on your case can be the result of several factors:

✔ **The law is against you.** If there's a statute or case law that governs the issues of your case, no matter how great the facts are in your favor, the judge is required to rule against you. For instance, say you just completed the Taj Mahal of home renovations for the defendant. Your state requires contractors be licensed, and you're not, so you have no legal basis to collect the money you're owed because you lack a license.

✔ **The facts are against you.** You have a really bad factual case and even though the law is in your favor, you can't recover. For instance, you're in an accident with a driver who is drunk, driving 100 mph, backwards, at night, without lights, on the wrong side of the road. He hits your car and you spin off the road into a pile of hay.

You have no physical injuries and the only damage to the car is that your bumper fell off. Great liability. But no injury, so no actual damages suffered and no monetary recovery. Unless you try to recover for the bump on your head you got when you sneezed from the hay and hit your head on your steering wheel.

✔ **Both the law and the facts are against you.** In other words, you have a really lousy case but you don't know it.

✔ **The defendant has a better case than you.** For instance, the statute of limitations has run. Or you're in the wrong court. Or you're the guy driving drunk on the wrong side of the road.

✔ **Your case is bogus and you know it.** You're a loudmouth and a liar, and the judge catches you on both.

✔ **The judge isn't trained as a judge.** The elected judge's full-time job is running the local pet-grooming parlor. He either doesn't understand the legal issues in your case or the facts are so technical that he has no idea what you're talking about.

✔ **You're totally unprepared to present your case.** You thought all you had to do was show up, tell your story, and bowl the court over with your charm. You believe proof is for math majors and distilleries and not you.

Any of these reasons, or some combination of them, can lead to a finding against you.

As Mick Jagger sings, "You can't always get what you want," and even if you win your small claims case, you may not get the amount of money you asked for. So when I say both parties may be unhappy with the decision, I mean it: You may win the case, which means the defendant lost so he's angry, but if the judge only gave you half the money you were looking for, you're not too thrilled either.

In situations where the plaintiff wins but is awarded less money than he asked for, both the plaintiff and defendant may decide to appeal the case. Make sure you pay close attention to all the notices you receive from the court. You wouldn't want to miss a deadline because you're focusing only on your appeal and not paying attention to notices that say the defendant has also challenged the judge's ruling.

Getting the Brush-Off: Being Dismissed

Back when you were in high school, you looked forward to the ringing of the bell and dismissal for the day. That's one of the few times you probably looked favorably at dismissal. When it comes to courts, a dismissal isn't a good thing. Having your case dismissed at any time during the proceedings usually creates problems you may not be able to fix.

However, in some situations, you can lose your case and still not be knocked out of the box. If the judge rules against you after a trial, an inquest, or a motion, you still may be able to rise like a phoenix and come back. It depends on whether your case is dismissed with or without prejudice:

- ✔ **With prejudice:** A dismissal with prejudice is not a good result. In fact, it's a bad result. It means your case is over for good; you can't come back. The judge is saying that based on the law, you have no case at all.

  For example, a plaintiff is in a profession that requires licensing. The plaintiff doesn't have his license at the trial because it was revoked for violating the license law based on complaints from this defendant and others. This case would call for a dismissal with prejudice because the plaintiff could never comply with the law.

- ✔ **Without prejudice:** A dismissal without prejudice, although not as good as a win, does permit you to bring your case again, assuming the statute of limitations hasn't run or some other legal impediment doesn't arise between the date of dismissal and the date you bring a new case. A dismissal without prejudice is usually done when you've made some technical error and the judge wants to give you a chance to correct it.

  If the error was minor, and subject to a quick remedy, the court may just grant an adjournment and make everyone come back at a later date. If the error was more serious, the court may dismiss the case without prejudice to renew. This means you can bring it again by starting a new lawsuit or, in some situations, by a motion to restore the case to the calendar.

  For example, say the plaintiff is a licensed businessperson, but left his license at home. The court may adjourn the case to give the plaintiff a chance to bring in his license. Or, at trial, the plaintiff produces his license but when the judge looks at the license, he sees that it expired the day before the trial. Because the law requires the plaintiff to be licensed to bring his case, the court may dismiss the complaint without prejudice to renew when the plaintiff gets a new license.

In many states, if there's a dismissal without prejudice, you don't have forever to refile your case. Your state may limit the time you have so as not to prejudice the rights of the defendant and his ability to defend the case. After all, you're the one who can't go forward. Many states limit this to one year or less.

Dealing with Defaults

Sometimes you can win your case without having to go to trial through a *default judgment.* There are several ways to get a default judgment and they can arise at different points in the litigation. I cover them in the following sections.

Winning because the defendant never answered

The first opportunity for a default judgment occurs when the defendant doesn't answer your complaint. In some states, if the defendant was required to file a written answer to your complaint and doesn't do so, you can get a judgment against him for the amount you sued for. (Chapter 8 explains how to serve a complaint.)

Of course, you must establish that the defendant was served with the summons and complaint. If that was done, then the allegations of your complaint are presumed to be true. Because the defendant didn't answer, the court presumes he isn't contesting the allegations and grants you a default judgment, which means that you don't have to show up in court at all.

In many states, this process isn't available in small claims court because the defendant isn't required to file an answer. He's supposed to show up at court on the trial date and orally answer your allegations.

Although some states may give you a default judgment without requiring you to prove your case, in most states you need to present your evidence before a judge through the process of an inquest.

Winning because the defendant didn't respond to a motion

A second opportunity for a default judgment occurs if your small claims court allows motions to be made. This situation isn't that common because many small claims courts don't allow motions at all or permit them only with the consent of the court.

You as the plaintiff may make a motion for summary judgment when you put forth your evidence based on affidavits and documents and say to the court, "Judge, look at my proof here; there's no way the defendant can win, so give me a judgment."

If the defendant fails to respond to the motion after having been given notice of it and the court believes you have enough evidence, you may be awarded a default judgment based on the motion alone. If the defendant responds to the motion and the judge rules in your favor, you still win , but it isn't a default motion.

Likewise, if the defendant makes a motion to dismiss your complaint based on an affirmative defense, such as the statute of limitations having passed or the defendant proves payment, and you don't respond, the defendant gets a default judgment dismissing the complaint.

Seeing Inquest Judgments

An *inquest* is essentially a trial without the defendant being present. But it's important to understand that you can lose an inquest. You don't just win because you showed up.

For example, if you're suing a tenant for owing rent after the tenant moved out but don't bring the lease or something else to prove that the defendant was your tenant and actually owed rent or owed the amount you claim was due, you could lose your inquest for lack of proof.

The three categories of inquests are:

✔ **Inquest clerk:** The plaintiff is suing for a fixed sum, such as the amount on a promissory note, and the defendant doesn't answer. If the defendant doesn't answer, the clerk can enter a judgment for the amount sued for in the complaint because it's a sum of money that can be calculated from reading the complaint. (I talk about monetary options in Chapter 5.)

✔ **Inquest on papers:** The defendant doesn't answer, but the court requires something more than just the complaint. You may have to submit affidavits as well as other documents to support the claims in your complaint.

An inquest on papers may involve a defendant who rams his car into a utility pole and the utility sues for the cost of replacing the pole. Proof is needed to establish the accident took place as well as the cost of replacing the pole.

✔ **Inquest by the court:** The defendant doesn't show up, and you have to go ahead with your case. You have to testify and place your evidence before the judge. It's a trial without the defendant.

In small claims court, the most common inquest is an inquest by the court because the summons and complaint in small claims court generally does not have to include much detail, so the court wants to see what proof you have to support your claim before it grants you a judgment against anyone.

Part IV
Dealing with Specific Problems

Small stuff you should sweat

- ✔ "I could've sworn I had that right here in this shoe box!" Always keep organized records of landlord/tenant agreements.

- ✔ "Hey Honey! Any idea where that thick book is they gave us when we bought the condo?" Know your rights and obligations as a unit owner.

- ✔ "License? We don't need no stinkin' license." If your business requires a license, producing it is an essential element of every claim involving the business.

- ✔ "Wow! I just got this great deal online from some guy in Timbuktu!" The Internet makes buying and selling easy, but litigation hard.

Read up on the basics of contract law when negotiating with businesses at www.dummies.com/extras/filingandwinningsmallclaims.

In this part . . .

- ✔ Get tips for handling disputes about rental properties with your landlord, your tenant, or your condominium or homeowner's association.

- ✔ Prepare yourself for bringing claims against moving companies, car rental agencies, and the airline industries, and how to deal with unlicensed versus licensed businesses.

- ✔ Find out the best approaches to suing the people closest to you, including your neighbors, family, friends, and partner (or ex-partner).

- ✔ Check out www.dummies.com/extras/filingand winningsmallclaims online for information on the laws for small claims court in different states.

Chapter 16

Getting Hit Where You Live: Contract Cases Involving Your Home

In This Chapter

▶ Handling landlord/tenant disputes from either side

▶ Fighting the condominium or homeowner's association

▶ Dealing with home-purchase down payment disputes

*E*veryone needs a place to live, and having a place to live usually involves money changing hands, unless you're living with your mom and dad — and sometimes even then.

Real estate transactions involving either rental or purchased properties are common. Disputes between a tenant and landlord, between a home association and owner, and between a buyer and seller often end up in small claims court.

In this chapter, I take a look at the types of small claims lawsuits that can hit you where you live and help you develop a strong case against your opponent.

Looking at Disputes between Landlords and Tenants

The landlord-tenant relationship, although not starting out that way, often ends up being an adversarial one. Whether you're renting a house, an apartment, a room over a garage, or a palace, places to live are loaded with things that break; the landlord accuses you of breaking them, you accuse the landlord of not fixing them. She accuses you of not paying your rent, and you accuse her of not returning your security deposit. In the next sections, I discuss the different ways a landlord-tenant relationship can end up in court.

Suing over the security deposit

The most common reason for landlords and tenants to end up in small claims court is the landlord's refusal to return the tenant's security deposit. The purpose of a security deposit is to ensure that the landlord is compensated if the tenant wrecks the apartment before leaving or if she skips town without paying the last month's rent. It's hard to get blood out of a stone or rent out of someone you can't find, so the security deposit, usually collected when the tenant first signs a lease, is designed to cover those costs.

Many states require a landlord to place the security deposit in an interest-bearing account and to surrender the interest to the tenant when the security deposit is returned. This may not apply in one- or two-family homes where the landlord shares the premises with you. If the landlord is a professional landlord, which means she doesn't live in the other half of the house, she may have to comply with the deposit law.

In some states, the landlord must deposit each tenant's money in a separate account and not commingle different tenants' deposits. Check your state's rules on this. It's an issue often overlooked, and if the landlord was required to do so and didn't, it can help the tenant establish greater credibility if the dispute goes to trial.

Some landlords wrongfully take the concept of the security deposit and turn it into bonus money for themselves. After the tenant leaves the property — either voluntarily or involuntarily after a court-ordered eviction — some landlords just keep the security deposit, even if the apartment needed no repairs or no rent is owed. A devious landlord worries about returning the money to the former tenant only if the tenant goes to the trouble of suing her for it.

Equally devious, some tenants attempt to trick their landlords out of the security deposit by simply skipping out on the last month's rent and announcing that they are "living out their security deposit." So, if the landlord wants to collect the last month's rent after the tenant moves out, she has to locate the tenant and sue for it. Although no one gets hurt by this practice as long as the apartment isn't damaged when the tenant moves out, it isn't the purpose of the security deposit and isn't really legal, either.

The best way to avoid a small claims suit involving a security deposit is simply to use the money for the purpose it's intended, and be sure that everything is handled in a fair and transparent manner.

As a tenant, the best practice is to inspect the apartment with the landlord present the day you move out, hand her the keys, and get your security deposit back right then. If the landlord refuses to give you your deposit back that day, have her sign a paper stating that she received the keys, that the apartment was in good shape when you left, and that you will receive your security deposit within one week — or whatever date you agree to. It's always a good idea for both sides to have a third person present to verify what occurred. (Of course, if you're leaving in the middle of the night without telling anyone because you have more creditors chasing you than villagers chasing a Transylvanian count, this isn't a viable option.)

One simple but common error tenants make gives the landlord the legal right to keep the security deposit — not surrendering the keys to the landlord when they move out. The common law rule is that the tenant is still in legal possession of the apartment so long as she has a set of keys.

So, leaving the keys on the kitchen table, in the mailbox, or mailing them back may not count as a valid surrender of the keys and allows the landlord to legally keep your security deposit or charge another month's rent if you move on the last day of the month and the landlord doesn't get the keys until the next day. This means returning all of the sets of keys you have, not just one of them.

Getting your security deposit back

Getting your security deposit back is much easier if you follow a few rules, starting with when you first move into a new rental. You'll have an easier time getting your deposit back if your case goes to small claims court if you:

- ✔ **Can prove that you gave the landlord a security deposit:** It's amazing how many people use only cash to pay the security deposit or to pay their rent each month. If you give the landlord cash, be sure to get a receipt each time.

  It's always better to use a check for any type of deposit. If you're the tenant, it gives you proof of payment. If you're the landlord, it gives you a bank account in the tenant's name so that if you get a judgment, you have some place to look for money to enforce it.

- ✔ **Take photographs when you move into an apartment and again when you move out.** This advice is important for both landlords and tenants. It s also a good idea to take pictures of every wall in every room. It's amazing how different the condition of an apartment becomes depending on which party took the pictures. Establish the date the photos were taken, either by including a newspaper in the picture or using a camera that dates the photos. If there is damage, use a ruler or some other common item to establish the size. Remember the size difference between the item you bought from an infomercial and its actual size? The same discrepancies can happen in damage disputes.

✔ **Inspect the apartment with the landlord when you're leaving. Both you and the landlord should sign a statement as to the condition of the apartment.** You can also get a third party, not connected to the transaction, to inspect the property when you leave. If a real estate broker was involved when you rented, ask a representative from that office to do an inspection when you leave.

✔ **Keep your rent and security deposit receipts.** Many states require a landlord to keep a log of tenant rent payments and to give the tenant a receipt for rent paid each month. If the landlord is required to do so, this can shift the burden of proof to the landlord to prove that she complied with this rule. The failure to comply can lead the court to conclude that the landlord is the party to bear the loss because she didn't follow the law.

✔ **Bring a copy of your written lease to court.** The written lease establishes whether a security deposit was required and in what amount.

If there's no written lease, the tenant is forced to prove the security deposit with checks or receipts. Put them in a safe place!

Keeping the security deposit as a landlord

If you're a landlord who wants to keep the tenant's security deposit, you face some of the same problems as the tenant who wants it back. Taking some of the same steps the tenant does at the beginning of your relationship makes it easier to keep what you're owed later. (See the preceding section, "Getting your security deposit back.")

Three reasons a landlord legally would not return a security deposit are

✔ The tenant hasn't paid the rent and owes money.

✔ The tenant left the apartment in a damaged condition.

✔ The tenant didn't return the keys, which means that legally she hasn't surrendered possession of the dwelling and still owes rent.

As a landlord, be sure to record who actually paid the security deposit at the time of the lease signing. Tenants have been known to try to claim the security deposit even though it was posted by a governmental agency or charitable organization as part of a housing assistance program. If the tenant didn't post the deposit, she can't ask for it when she leaves, unless she actually paid back the agency that put up the money and can prove it.

Maintaining accurate records

One of the best ways to prove your case in court is to keep good records. The landlord is the person who prepares the lease agreement and controls the terms and conditions, and as such, the law expects the landlord to set the rules for the tenancy and keep the records needed to prove that the terms and conditions have been either kept or broken.

In addition to the lease, a landlord should be able to produce a rent payment log for the tenant or a receipt book indicating when rent was received. In some states, the landlord is required by law to maintain these records and the failure to do so can be used against you at trial.

As the landlord, you should be able to produce

- A signed copy of the lease
- Signed copies of any amendments or extensions of the lease
- Rent records
- Security deposit records

If state law requires you to keep a security deposit in an interest-bearing account, you better do so. The failure to do so can create a legal defense for the tenant and at a minimum undercut your credibility at trial.

It's amazing the number of times the landlord and the tenant each produce a copy of the lease, and as if by wizardry, the two aren't the same. This usually isn't the result of either party trying to trick the other one, but more often than not, is caused by the social nature of signing a self-prepared lease at someone's kitchen table rather than having one prepared by an attorney or the real estate broker or rental agent. No matter where the lease is signed, make sure you check all of the copies to ensure they're the same. If changes are made, everyone should initial the changes and date them as well.

Because landlord-tenant relationships are the source of a great deal of litigation, many states have passed laws setting forth certain terms that are to be included in a written lease. The burden to make sure the lease complies with the law is on the party who prepares the lease — generally the landlord. Whether you're the landlord or the tenant, it's a good idea to check to see if there are any required clauses to be included in the lease. The failure to do so can in some situations make the entire lease void or in other situations make the non-complying clause unenforceable. In either case, you'll have created an unnecessary complication in your case and getting the court to rule in your favor.

Check with an attorney, real estate broker, or advocacy group to find out what clauses are needed. It may be dangerous to buy a form lease at the candy store or download one from the Internet because they will be generic in nature and may not comply with your state law. The cost of having a professional prepare the lease at the start of the tenancy will outweigh the cost you'll incur in going to court to enforce the terms of a defective agreement.

Keeping the deposit if you don't get the keys

If the tenant never surrenders the keys, you may have to bring an action in the appropriate court to have possession awarded to you, because the tenant still has not technically surrendered possession. You can't just go in and change the locks and throw out the personal property left behind.

The tenant remains liable for paying rent until the court orders possession to be given to the landlord. If the court hearing the case awards the landlord just the possession of the apartment and doesn't give her a money judgment for past-due rent, the landlord has to bring a separate action for that amount either in small claims court or regular civil court — unless the court issued an order finding no rent was due.

It's a far better practice to resolve all of these issues in your first trip to the courthouse. All too often the landlord and the tenant enter into an agreement where the tenant surrenders the premises and the parties leave all other items open to be resolved in another court proceeding. So if the court order or the stipulation of settlement doesn't resolve the issues of back rent claimed due or the return of the security deposit, you'll both be back in court in a few months to settle these issues.

Recovering the cost of repairs

If you're a landlord withholding a security deposit because of damages caused to the premises by the tenant, be able to produce photographs of the apartment when it was rented and when it was surrendered. Photographs should be of the entire apartment — not just the damaged areas. The damages have to go beyond reasonable wear and tear.

A landlord can't recover for reasonable wear and tear resulting from the expected and normal use by a tenant. So, if the landlord didn't paint the apartment during the five years a tenant lived there, the cost of repainting for a new tenant is generally not considered damages.

Damage caused by pets and children — stained carpet, crayoned walls — is usually considered beyond reasonable wear and tear, and the tenant has to pay to correct those conditions.

Landlords generally have problems proving their damages. The landlord has to bring receipts, paid bills, or estimates from the people who did the repair work. Often the landlord submits receipts that are not admissible into evidence because they don't establish any relationship to the landlord or the property in question. The receipt should have the landlord's name on it as well as a reference to the leased premises. Some states have by statute set out certain procedures to be followed if the landlord wants to keep the security deposit because of damage to the apartment. Check out the local laws in that regard before you decide to keep the tenant's money.

Proving where repair work was done is especially important for a landlord who owns several rental properties because the materials purchased or the labor performed must be linked to the property in question. Because the landlord is asserting it was for the apartment where the landlord is refusing to return the security, the burden of proof is on the landlord to establish that it is for that apartment. Bringing in receipts from a big-box national hardware chain without something linking it to the apartment in question is a non-starter. You can make the notations on the receipt, but make sure they are clear and relate to the point you want to prove.

Also, trying to convince the judge that your purchase of enough paint to paint a center line down Route 66 and back was necessary to cover the tenant's damage to the apartment won't be favorably received. Neither will replacing builders' fixtures with ones by a world-renowned designer suitable for the high-roller suites in Vegas.

If your local regulations require repair contractors to be licensed, it's a good idea to have the work done by a licensed person if you're a landlord. Some courts deny recovery by the landlord if the work is done by unlicensed contractors on public policy grounds. That is, the law wants such people to be licensed to protect the public, so you won't be reimbursed if you use unlicensed people, no matter how high the quality of their work.

Landlords can't redo the entire apartment and charge the tenant when the tenant only damaged one part. For example, if a pet stains the wood floor of the family room, the landlord can't redo all the floors in the apartment and bill the tenant. The tenant is only responsible for damage she caused — not for reasonable wear and tear.

Some landlords do the repairs themselves then try to make a claim for the cost of their labor. In general, a claim for your own labor is not recoverable. How is the court supposed to evaluate that charge? Do you get the labor cost that a local painter charges because you did the painting yourself? If yes, then how are you going to establish what that is? You'd have to bring in a painter to prove what the going rate is in your community. If you're a brain surgeon and the landlord, can you charge what your time is worth as a brain surgeon for the hours spent painting? Of course not.

The importance of a current lease

An agreement between an tenant and a landlord is only valid if it's spelled out in the most current lease. Sometimes when a tenant stays in a place for more than a year or so, landlords get lazy and fail to update the lease. As the years go by, the rent probably goes up and maybe the tenant adds some money to the security deposit so it matches the rent, but no one ever makes a new lease or records the added security deposit. So if either party produces the lease at a trial, it doesn't have the correct amount of the security deposit. The tenant then has to try to prove additional monies were given because she's the one saying that the amount set forth in the lease isn't correct.

Generally, if a written lease expires and you don't enter into a new written lease, the relationship becomes a month-to-month tenancy rather than a second term matching the original written lease. However, all of the other provisions of the original lease remain in full force and effect. This means the rent at the end of the original term remains the same for now, but can be changed on a monthly basis by the parties with all the other clauses of the lease still in effect. For example, the landlord asks to you pay an additional $100 a month, you agree and start paying the new amount. That's now the rent going forward.

Say you have a written lease that ran from January 1, 2005, to December 31, 2005. Monthly rent was $1,000 and you paid a security deposit of $1,000. The landlord pays heat and hot water according to the terms of the lease. In 2008, the rent is increased to $1,200 a month. Everyone is happy. No new lease is ever made. In 2012, the landlord tells you that the cost of heating oil is so high that she wants you to pay it. You refuse.

If the landlord sues for the cost of the heat and hot water in 2012, you can refuse because the original lease made that the landlord's obligation. The only changes to the lease were the monthly rent, which even though not done in writing, was billed and paid, and the term, which changed to a month-to-month tenancy when the original year ran out. If the parties change the heating obligation in writing, that would be an amendment, but the other terms of the original lease would stay in effect.

Evicting tenants for non-payment

In general, most states do not permit eviction cases to be brought in small claims court, but in some cases they are permitted. My best advice is to ask the court clerk or local bar association whether you can bring an eviction proceeding for non-payment. Also, before you become a landlord, think ahead and prepare for the day you'll be heading for court to evict a tenant. Knowing which court to go to is something to think about at the start.

In many cases eligible for small claims court, the landlord claims that the tenant has not paid rent for a particular month or months. These cases result only in a money judgment issued against the tenant. As a landlord, you don't just want to get a promise from the tenant to pay the back rent, you want that promise reduced to a judgment — meaning that you can have the court enforce the promise if the tenant doesn't pay.

After winning a money judgment against a non-paying tenant, the landlord then has to undertake steps to collect. The judgment does not give the landlord the right to regain possession of the apartment and evict the tenant.

Some small claims courts allow an action to not only recover the money owed but also to recover possession of the apartment if the money judgment isn't paid, so check with the clerk before you file.

If you want a money judgment and possession of the premises if the tenant does not pay the judgment quickly, then you may have to bring the case in different part of the regular civil court. In these cases, if the landlord establishes that the tenant owes rent, the tenant will be given a short period of time to pay, such as five days. If the tenant does not pay the judgment, then the landlord can evict the tenant and recover possession of the rental property.

In a non-payment proceeding, the tenant may offer as a defense that the rent is being withheld because of the landlord's failure to properly maintain the premises or provide a safe and habitable apartment. Lack of heat, lack of hot water, vermin infestation, and unrepaired leaks are all common grounds raised by tenants to withhold rent.

If you live in a place where a municipal agency inspects apartments when tenants complain, as a landlord you may receive notice of violations that can result not only in fines being assessed against you but in a reduction, called an abatement, of the tenant's rent. You have to make the repairs and are prevented from collecting the rent you claim is due. It is a good idea to properly maintain rental properties to avoid these problems.

One major no-no in most states is taking things into your own hands and changing the locks to lock out a non-paying tenant. Such action is considered a *wrongful eviction* and can lead to a court not only restoring the tenant's right to possession but assessing both compensatory and punitive damages against you.

Suing for recovery of possession

Sometimes, a tenant isn't necessarily a bad tenant, and, in fact, may be a good tenant who pays the rent on time and takes care of the place. The landlord, however, may want the apartment returned to her for any one of a number of reasons, including:

- ✔ For her own use or the use of a family member.
- ✔ She's planning to sell the building and wants to renovate.
- ✔ The lease has ended and she doesn't want to renew with the current tenant.
- ✔ The tenant *breached the lease* in some way, that is failed to live up to a material term of the agreement — such as not providing proof of insurance.
- ✔ She's selling the building and the new owner wants the building delivered free of all tenants.

In these situations, the landlord can terminate the lease and seek to recover possession. If the lease is up, the landlord can recover possession of the apartment any time after the end date because the tenancy under the lease term has ended. The landlord may have to give some sort of notice under the local law. If the tenant refuses to vacate, the landlord may be able to bring a lawsuit to recover possession without any preliminary notice of her desire to take back the apartment. She can do this even if the tenant has just been awarded tenant of the year from the National Landlord's Association.

If the lease isn't up, in order to recover possession, the landlord has to establish that the tenant breached a material term of the lease, was given notice of the breach — usually in writing — and had a reasonable opportunity to make good on whatever she did wrong. The breach must be *material,* which means it has to be important and adversely affect the landlord's interest. If the tenant fails to meet her obligations under the terms of the lease, the landlord can start legal action to recover possession and get an order of eviction. A couple examples illustrate material and non-material breaches:

- ✔ **Material breach:** Under the lease, the tenant is supposed to provide the landlord with proof of insurance, but doesn't do it. The landlord sends the tenant a notice reminding her to provide the proof. The tenant refuses. Most courts would consider this a breach of a material term of the lease and allow the landlord to terminate the tenancy and evict the tenant before the end of the lease term for noncompliance.

- ✔ **Non-material breach:** The lease requires the tenant to maintain 60-watt bulbs on all hall and outside lights. Instead, the tenant uses 30-watt, low-energy bulbs that give the same amount of light. In all likelihood a court would deny a request to evict the tenant on these grounds because, although a technical breach of the lease, the tenant's actions don't adversely affect the landlord's interest.

If the landlord has a legal right to recover possession and isn't using eviction to retaliate against the tenant for reporting her to the courts or a municipal agency about the lack of services or some other issue, the tenant generally has no legal recourse. The most the tenant can get from the court is some time to find a new apartment and move.

A landlord cannot successfully evict a tenant because the tenant legitimately complains to the authorities about the conditions of the rental property. However, if the complaints turn out to be baseless, then the landlord may be successful in an eviction because the tenant is filing false claims.

If the conditions in a rented home are so bad as to be unsafe, the municipal agency may issue a vacate order requiring the tenant to move immediately, which creates other problems and a probable lawsuit by the tenant against the landlord for the cost of having to move.

Most small claims courts do not deal with recovery of possession cases. Landlord-tenant cases often have to follow special rules and procedures that make them unsuitable for small claims courts.

If you're a landlord trying to evict a perfect tenant solely to recover possession, retain an attorney familiar with landlord-tenant matters. Courts tend to be sympathetic to tenants in these situations because you're trying to force someone to move from her home. This is not to say that the landlord doesn't have the legal right to do so, it's to note that many courts may be willing to cut the tenant some slack in finding a new place to live provided she continues to pay the rent while she's looking.

On the other hand, if you're a tenant and the court gives you some time to look for a new apartment, so long as you pay rent — or as it's called in some states, *use and occupancy* — don't abuse the privilege. If the court gives you 60 days, don't wait until day 59 to start looking and think you'll just go back to court and ask for an extension of time. Many courts cease being sympathetic at this point, and you may be making two calls: one to the movers and the other to Uncle Fudd and Aunt Clarabelle asking if you can crash at their place for a while.

Because evictions disrupt people's lives, many courts strictly enforce the law and evidentiary requirements in eviction cases and require the landlord to dot every *i* and cross every *t* in order to get an order of eviction.

In some states, the failure of the tenant to pay rent is not a ground to bring an action to recover possession even though it's a breach of the terms of the lease. The proper action is to sue for non-payment of rent. If the tenant habitually fails to pay rent, requiring the landlord to bring her to court every few months, the courts may permit the landlord to terminate the tenancy and recover possession.

On the other hand, courts are also aware that if you live in one side of a two-family house and your tenant isn't paying rent, you may not be able to pay your mortgage. If you default on your mortgage, both you and your tenant will be out on the street after a foreclosure. It's in everyone's best interest to resolve these cases quickly to avoid foreclosure and two families losing their homes.

If you're buying a house currently occupied by a tenant and don't want a tenant, make sure you have your lawyer or whomever prepares real estate contracts in your part of the world put responsibility for delivering the place empty on the seller-landlord. Leases generally survive the sale of the building.

Getting a tenant out of a place you're buying may delay your closing, but if the seller doesn't evict the tenant, you'll have to do it, and you'll not only have bought a house, but you'll have bought a lawsuit as well. You'll have to prove the terms of the lease agreement between the seller and the tenant — something you know nothing about — and you have to hope the seller provided you with accurate records as to the length of the tenancy, the rental history, and the security deposit. You don't want to find out that the month-to-month tenant at $1,000 a month has an enforceable lease for two years at $500 a month.

Going to Court with the Condominium or Homeowner's Association

Condominium boards and homeowners' associations often end up in small claims court with members who haven't paid their dues, fees, or assessments annual charges or special charges to pay for the upkeep of the common areas.

As a unit owner, you generally have no defense to the failure to pay these charges. They're obligations you're required to pay either by the state law or by the agreement you entered into with the other owners when you bought your unit. The amounts owed are clearly spelled out in the condominium or homeowner's association bylaws and covenants.

A homeowner can't successfully claim she didn't know about the obligation even if she never physically received a copy of the offering plan, declaration, and bylaws. The obligations are recorded with the county clerk or other proper county official, which gives every owner notice of her obligation.

Yes, you read that correctly. If the condominium documents are recorded, you're charged with knowing their contents. The recorded agreement is considered *constructive notice,* meaning it's there for you to find if you look. *Actual notice* is receiving the documents when you buy your unit. The fact that you're using that stack of papers to hold up the broken leg on the couch and never bothered to read them isn't a defense. After you receive a copy, the law says you have actual notice.

What this means is that even if you have a legitimate dispute with the board of the condominium association or homeowners' association over services not provided, problems over parking spaces, or use of the pool or common areas, you still have to pay the dues and assessments. You may have a right to bring your own lawsuit over those issues, but the existence of the dispute does not relieve you of the obligation to pay the charges.

This makes perfect sense because if every homeowner upset about something could stop paying dues, pretty soon no one would be paying, and the organization wouldn't have the money to properly run and maintain the association. The conditions at the property would eventually deteriorate and destroy the condominium or the homeowners' association. You have to pay these obligations and bring your own lawsuit seeking relief for the problems you allege the board of directors is failing to deal with.

Also, often there are assessments made beyond the monthly dues charges, which you're also legally obligated to pay. For example, the board of directors votes to repave the parking lot, or redo the roofs on all the units, or improve the pool. Rather than increase the dues, they may levy an assessment against each unit. The assessment may be due in one lump sum or payable monthly over a specified period of time. You're responsible for these charges as well, even if you personally voted against them. So long as they are assessed by the management after following the rules for doing so, you're responsible.

If you're sued for non-payment of dues or fees by a homeowners' association or other residents' board, you have two defenses:

- **Show you made the payment:** If you establish that you paid the obligation each month, that's a defense to the lawsuit. The legal documents that created the condominium or homeowners' association may permit late fees, interest, or collection costs to be added on to your obligation, so if you paid the monthly charge late a few times, you could still owe these penalties.

- **Claim that your unit is not a member of the condominium or the homeowners' association:** This defense is valid when the initial filings creating the condominium or homeowners' association are incorrect and for some reason don't include a few units in the filed documents. It may look as if your house belongs in the development, and people may think you belong, but you don't. Of course, if you're not a member, you don't have to pay dues, but you also don't have any benefits such as use of the common areas, pool, and club house. So you may want to think twice about raising this defense.

Even though you may have a legal obligation to pay the dues and assessment, the board of directors still has to prove its case by:

- Establishing that it has the authority to assess the dues.

- Showing that resolutions were passed fixing the dues and assessments and sometimes authorizing the start of the lawsuit and that the action taken complied with the bylaws and rules. For instance, notice may have had to have been given to all homeowners in a certain manner. If the notice was not proper, that may negate the action of the board in passing the resolution.

- ✔ Producing a ledger or account statement showing what amount was billed, that you were sent a bill, and what amount you paid, if any.

- ✔ Proving that it has authority to assess any late charges, interest charges, or legal fees it's trying to collect and that the amounts assessed are correct.

A common error in billing for late charges is that the board charges an amount different from that set forth in the bylaws and has no explanation for it or documentation to show that the bylaws were properly amended to permit the charge. For example, the board may assess a flat fee as a late charge, yet the bylaws require the late charge be a percentage of the monthly dues.

If you have a claim against the condominium or the homeowners' association, you may have to establish that you complied with the requirements in the bylaws for bringing your problem to the board of directors and any procedures set forth for resolving disputes before going to court. Also you may not be able to go to court initially. You may be required to file a complaint with the state agency that governs condominium activities before you can sue.

Say you buy a condominium at a 100-unit ski resort. An avalanche damages 10 of the units to such a degree that the town says those 10 units are unsafe to occupy. You decide not only not to pay your mortgage because you can't use the unit but also not to pay your condominium charges. Guess what? You're probably stuck and could wind up with a money judgment against you for the condominium charges.

Although most homeowners' associations sue to obtain money judgments against non-paying unit owners, most association agreements state that failure to pay the charges creates a lien on the property which can be enforced by seeking foreclosure and gaining ownership of the unit, similar to what happens if a mortgage is foreclosed. This type of action is generally not permitted in small claims court.

Disagreements over Down Payments

It's not uncommon for a person to put a down payment on a house and then have the deal fall through. If the seller is the one who calls off the deal, she usually authorizes the return of the deposit to the would-be buyer. Because she changed her mind, she can't keep the money. The buyer may have a separate lawsuit for damages for the expenses incurred as a result of the seller changing her mind, but that has nothing to do with the return of the down payment.

When the buyer is the one who changes her mind due to buyer's remorse, or a bad home inspection, or some other reason, she still usually wants the down payment refunded. Cases end up in small claims court when the seller refuses to give it back.

The buyer has to sue the seller to compel her to give back the money if she has it, or for her to authorize the escrow agent to return the money if it was put into an escrow account.

Using an *escrow agent* — a third party other than the seller or the buyer to hold the down payment money — is a good practice. An escrow agent is a *fiduciary* — a person with certain legal obligations and restriction on her actions who can't act unless the parties agree or she's ordered to do so by a court. The escrow agent can't unilaterally decide who gets the money. The escrow agent may be a lawyer, a title company, an escrow company, or a real estate broker, depending on the practice in your state.

Even though the escrow agent is not the person preventing the release of the money, if you're suing for return of a down payment, you have to name the agent as a defendant *stakeholder* — a person holding money for the benefit of others without an ownership interest in the money — so that she will be bound by the court order directing the release of the money.

Don't be surprised if the escrow agent as the stakeholder brings a lawsuit saying "Hey judge, I have these two guys who can't agree what I should do with the paltry sum of money I'm holding. Judge, please tell me what to do or let me pay it into the court so I can get on with my life." This *stakeholder action* is designed to relieve the stakeholder of responsibility for the money. This may or may not be brought in small claims court. In all likelihood, as either the buyer or the seller in the dispute over the money, you'll be named as a defendant. This lawsuit will result in an order telling the stakeholder whom to pay, so it may save you the cost of bringing your own lawsuit over the issue.

In order to keep the money, the seller has to establish that she was ready, willing, and able to perform the contract and sell the property. If the seller can't do so, then she can't keep the deposit. In order for the buyer to get the money back, she has to establish either:

✔ That the seller is in default of her contractual obligations and can't or won't sell the house.

✔ That the buyer was ready, willing, and able to close, or if she isn't able to close, it's not her fault. If you're the would-be buyer, you have to have a valid reason for not living up to the terms of the contract. You need to cite some unforeseen event that makes it impossible for you to fulfill the terms of the contract. Merely claiming, "I couldn't get a mortgage" doesn't necessarily entitle you to get the deposit released. Why you couldn't get a mortgage will become the key issue at the trial.

A couple of examples show a faulty reason and a low-fault one:

- ✔ A buyer has 60 days to get a mortgage commitment from a bank. She decided she doesn't want the house and waits until day 59 to apply. On day 61 she asks for her money back because she didn't get a mortgage commitment. The buyer would certainly have a hard time claiming she deserves her money back in this situation.

- ✔ The buyer has 60 days to get a mortgage commitment from a bank, applies on day 1 and by day 10 has a commitment subject to providing proof of employment and sufficient income until closing of title. On day 50, the buyer finds out that she has been laid off because her employer, MouseMobileMotors, a company that designs cars powered by rodents chasing cheese around a wheel, has been shut down by animal rights groups and the American Cheese Association because only French-produced cheeses were being used.

  This is a situation beyond the buyer's control, and in all likelihood, she would be able to recover her deposit. The would-be buyer has a legal obligation to notify the lender of her employment status. The failure to notify the lender may be considered fraud against the lender.

If you're the buyer, before you bring a suit to get your down payment returned, make sure you read the contract to see whether you complied with all of the terms of the agreement, especially any terms requiring that you give notice to the other side of your desire to cancel the contract and recover the deposit.

Chapter 17

Getting the Business: Suing over Business Transactions

. . . .

In This Chapter

▶ Suing licensed businesses

▶ Proving your business is licensed

▶ Bringing specific industries to court

. . . .

*B*ecause most people interact with a number of different businesses every day, the potential for small claims lawsuits involving a commercial transaction is high. From the dry cleaners to the car dealership, business transactions of every kind can go sour if the customer — that's probably you — thinks he's been treated unfairly or cheated in some way. If business owners remembered that the customer is always right, this chapter would be rather short; unfortunately, that often isn't the case.

Nearly every business is fair game for a small claims lawsuit, as long as the amount you're suing for falls below the court's limits. If you want a large amount of money — for a new car, for instance — small claims court probably isn't the place for you. But for many of the everyday transactions that go wrong, small claims court provides the perfect arena to air your differences and get justice.

License to Sue: Cases Involving Unlicensed Businesses

Business lawsuits are one of the biggest areas that both plaintiffs and defendants make mistakes about in their case preparation. The most glaring mistake involves unlicensed businesses. If the business is properly licensed or is one that doesn't need to be licensed, then the case will proceed as any breach of contract case would. If an unlicensed business is involved it creates procedural and proof problems both for the consumer and the business.

If you live in a place like New York City, there's a very good chance that the business you're having problems with in your case is licensed by somebody.

The licensing status of the business is an essential element of any case involving that entity, whether the business is the plaintiff or the defendant. However, if that business isn't properly licensed, you can use that fact to defeat a claim brought against you by that business or to prevent the business from defending an action you bring against it. Governments pass two types of licensing statutes:

- ✔ **Revenue raising:** These generate money for the state or local government. Revenue-raising statutes rarely generate any small claims cases as most disputes will be between the business and the government agency collecting the money — commonly called *revenuers* by those of you who live in flyover country.

- ✔ **Regulatory:** These protect the public by ensuring that the person running a business is properly trained. They also regulate the number of people holding a license.

Many licensing statutes designed to raise revenue are also regulatory to some degree. An example of a revenue-raising statute is a fee to get a fishing license. Anyone can just come in file an application, pay a fee, and get the license. Even if you don't know the difference between a fishing pole and a telephone pole, you can still get the license. But it's also regulatory if there's a limit on the number of licenses that can be issued to prevent everyone in the state from getting licensed, going fishing at the same time, catching all of the large-mouth bass in the state, and wiping out the species.

Some licenses start out regulatory and become revenue-raising. For instance, to run a barbershop, you need to prove you've been trained and have a license. Let's say the license is good for three years; after that you can renew it for additional three-year periods by just paying a fee. This starts regulatory but becomes revenue-raising, because there's no new training needed to keep the license.

A business that doesn't have a current revenue-raising license usually can sue someone or defend itself against a lawsuit in court as the license in this situation is irrelevant to the skill and expertise of the business operator. A business that doesn't have a required regulatory license cannot. When it goes to court, in most states, the business automatically loses. This is because a precondition to operating the business legally is showing that you have complied with the licensing law that protects the public.

Proving your business is licensed

If you're the owner of business that is involved in a lawsuit, either as the plaintiff or defendant, proving you're licensed becomes part of your burden of proof. When you come to court, make sure that:

✔ You bring some documentation from the licensing agency showing the license is current. Just bringing in your bill head or contract with a license number on it isn't sufficient.

✔ The name of the licensed person and the business name match. If the license is issued to Grumpy Dwarf individually, but you're bringing or defending a suit as The Seven Dwarf Home Improvement and Mining Corp., your license won't pass muster in court.

If you're being sued by a business that must be licensed in your locale, that business must prove — at a minimum — that it was licensed when the work was done. In some places, it must also prove it's licensed when the lawsuit is brought.

Common regulatory licensed businesses are home improvement contractors and automobile repair shops. Also, most professionals such as lawyers and doctors must be separately licensed in each state. So, if on the night of your small claims trial in New York, your lawyer cousin from Alaska happens to be in town and wants to represent you, he may not be permitted to do so because he's not licensed in New York, although he could make a request to the judge to allow him to appear.

If you're sued by a business, check that the person bringing the suit is properly filed as a corporation or a d/b/a —doing business as. (See Chapter 6 for more on finding out the real name of a business.) Why? Because many states prohibit an improperly formed or registered business from using the court system to bring a lawsuit.

Sometimes by checking with the corporate registration office of your state, you find out that the corporation has had its charter suspended or been dissolved because it failed to pay taxes or file the proper forms to continue its corporate existence. These failures may prevent the business from suing, and you're off the hook. Much of this information is now available in your state or county.

If the plaintiff is supposed to be licensed, but can't prove it, you can ask to have the case dismissed. But don't be surprised if the judge grants an adjournment for the business to produce its license, especially if it's out in the car or in the office around the corner. Small claims courts are designed to decide cases on the merits and not on a technicality.

For example, your neighbor is a home improvement contractor who also works a day job. Under your town laws, home improvement contractors are required to be licensed. Your neighbor is suing you for the last $1,000 you owe for the deck he built for your house. If the contractor doesn't have a license, he can't use the courts to recover this money. It doesn't matter that the deck is built exactly as you wanted it, that it conforms to the building code, and is so beautiful that it's going to be on some cable television program as the world's most beautiful deck. No license, no recovery.

Quantum meruit is the Latin term for the legal principal that allows a plaintiff to recover money for the reasonable value of the services rendered and received. The idea is to prevent someone from being unjustly enriched, in this case, getting a benefit — the new deck — without having to pay for it. However, most states don't permit an unlicensed person to recover even on this basis.

Most people would say that you got the deck, so you should pay for it. But the rule preventing the contractor from collecting is there for a reason: If an unlicensed worker can collect in court, then why bother to get licensed? The only way to protect the public and force contractors to become licensed is to deny them the right to sue, even if they did everything exactly the way you wanted it.

Buyer Beware: The Downside to Hiring Unlicensed Businesses

The law works both ways, so if you use an unlicensed business, generally you can't sue it. If you're the homeowner and sue the unlicensed worker because your deck was not built properly, most courts don't allow you to recover monies paid to the unlicensed contractor on the theory that the underlying agreement was illegal. Under old common law, the courts won't enforce an illegal agreement, so you're out of luck.

You have to absorb the cost of correcting the improperly done work or completing the work if the defendant did not fulfill the terms of the contract. Because in this situation the contractor has to be licensed, the law presumes that you had the ability to check with the local licensing authority to see if the contractor was properly licensed before you hired him and not as an afterthought to get out of paying.

Many locales have licensing information online so you can check before you enter into a contract with someone who is supposed to be licensed.

Checking your contract twice: Required language and clauses

In many places where licensing is required, the local authorities have rules on what clauses and language a legal contract must contain. The licensing authority may include local, county, or state agencies, and regulations may be enacted by law or part of a regulatory agency's administrative code, so you may need to do some detective work. When you find the required language, review all the documents you received from the business and make notes about where the business is not following the rules.

The written estimate, for example, should contain a license number or other information required by law. If the estimate doesn't contain this information, a court could prevent the contractor from recovering on the claim, even if he has a license. The license and the disclosures are designed to protect the public and they must be complied with to recover on a contract claim.

For example, you hire Cool Fool Pools to install an in-ground pool in your yard. You check and find out Cool Fool Pools is properly licensed and the contract even has all of the proper identifying information on the top. Looks like everything is fine. However, it turns out that of the 60 paragraphs on the back of the contract, 58 of them don't comply with or directly contradict the recommended terms for such contracts established by the licensing agency. It won't matter that Cool Fool Pools is licensed; the contract itself violates the rules, making it unenforceable.

Make sure you flip the contract over and read the back. Or if the front says page one, look for a page two. In an actual case, one well-established local car dealer had apparently copied a form that another dealer had used as its contract. Page one worked just fine. Unfortunately, no one except me, apparently, bothered to read the back where the entire agreement referred to another car dealer by name in another state.

In the absence of a local licensing statute, the best way to check on the reliability of the business is to check some local professional organization such as the Better Business Bureau or the chamber of commerce. You can also check the Internet, but remember — many sites have postings only from dissatisfied customers and don't filter who's making the complaint. Also, it takes a lot more effort to fill out a complaint form with a recognized organization than rant on your computer.

In many places, to add a deck or a pool requires that you get a permit from some local agency. Many homeowners are convinced by the contractor that to save some money, they should just let them install the deck or pool and worry about legalizing it later. After all, you're going to live here a long time, aren't you?

Guess what happens when you go to sell the house. You now either have to legalize or remove your illegal deck/pool, which will at a minimum delay the sale and may in fact lead to violations being placed against the property, which may impede your ability to sell the property and to fines from the municipality. Not only that — you'll probably be paying more money to comply years down the road. The best advice is to do it right the first time, even if you have to hire an architect or engineer.

Also, if you now decide to sue the deck/pool installer for the fines and expenses incurred to legalize the pool — guess what. The statute of limitations will most likely have run, barring your suit.

As a practical matter, making renovations without a permit may not be a problem in a small community because everyone in town knows about the improvement. In fact, the municipality may send someone to your house when the work starts so the city can raise your property taxes because your house is now worth more.

Bringing a Case over a Car

Car issues are another common source of litigation in small claims court. Being a mechanical object with numerous moving parts, cars don't always behave as they should, even if they've been properly repaired. Car repairs and issues that arise after buying a car are the most common automotive reasons for driving to court.

Making lemonade: Using lemon laws

If your new or "previously owned" — a fancy term for *used* — car breaks down the minute you drive away, and the seller refuses to fix it, or if your new or pre-owned vehicle keeps breaking even after being repaired, you can often take advantage of so-called lemon laws to resolve your case outside of court.

Lemon laws require the dealer to take the vehicle back and refund the purchase price of the vehicle if the car cannot be repaired after a certain number of attempts by the dealer. In effect, these laws establish a warranty process if certain problems with the vehicle arise that the dealer is supposed to correct and can't — or won't. Many people are unaware of this process. They don't utilize it and instead come to court with the dispute. But if you buy a 1967 Chevy Nova with 300,000 miles on it held together by baling wire and duct tape, don't expect the law to protect you.

Your state's lemon law may not only give you redress outside the court system, but may also allow you to recover reasonable attorney's fees if you're successful, making legal representation more attractive to your cause than small clams court.

New cars sold by a registered car dealer, as well as used cars with less than a certain amount of mileage sold by a dealer, are covered by lemon laws in many states.

Seeking redress on repairs

An even more common case filed in court occurs when you claim the repair shop didn't fix your car properly.

These cases aren't always easy to prove, especially if you're dealing with an older car. These cases usually arise on vehicles that are about ten years old or have mileage of over 100,000 miles. Proving the defendant did something wrong on vehicles of that age and mileage is a difficult task. You may need an expert, such as another mechanic, to testify that the defendant either failed to diagnose the problem or improperly treated the problem.

Repair shops are often licensed by the state or the county, so check them out before taking your baby in.

In order to prevail, you must establish that the current problem is the same one for which you brought the car in for repairs earlier. So, if the initial problem was the transmission, and the repair shop repairs the transmission, you have to establish that the reason the car is not functioning properly is that the defendant failed to properly repair the transmission. If the problem now is that the alternator is not working, it doesn't mean that the defendant either failed to repair the transmission properly or that the transmission was not the problem at the time the repair was made. Your burden is to prove that the defendant failed to do the repair you contracted with him to fix.

You have to prove the defendant didn't do the repair as agreed in order to get money back. Finding someone who would have charged less for the repairs after the fact doesn't entitle you to a refund. If you overpay, that's not something that law will remedy. After all, why didn't you find the cheaper guy sooner? And even more important, is the second guy doing the same repairs with the same parts as the first?

Another common car repair problem occurs if, after the fact, you go to court because you never authorized a particular repair on your car but the shop did it anyway and is now charging you for it. Many states require that automobile repair shops get written authorization for the repair or that, if the repair is authorized on the telephone, that a notation is made on the estimate listing of who they spoke to get the authorization and when that occurred. Not that that actually proves that this was done, but it's difficult to prove you didn't authorize the repairs when the defendant produces a computer-generated estimate with your signature or the notation "authorized on the phone."

To be sure you authorize only the repairs you want, either don't sign anything that's blank as to the cost and extent of the repairs, or don't authorize repairs to be done over the phone. Have the estimate faxed to you, sign it, and send it back. This way you and the repair shop each have a copy.

Many shops assess storage charges for the days that the car sits on their property waiting for you to authorize the repair or remains at the repair shop after the repairs are completed.

In many states, if you don't pick up your car, the repair shop has what is called a lien for the money you owe. (A *lien* is a pledge of real or personal property along with the right to sell the property to pay or satisfy an obligation to the person holding the property. Mortgages are common liens.) By following the applicable law, the repair shop can have your car sold by the sheriff or some other third party at auction to get the shop's lien paid.

Suing an Airline over Lost Luggage

Lost or damaged luggage is one of the major headaches of travel. Most often, the luggage isn't lost, it's merely misplaced, having gone to Sheboygan rather than accompanying you to Chicago. Why your luggage would want to do that is another issue entirely. If you've never had your luggage go astray, you probably know someone who has. But bags can also disappear forever into the night or can be mashed to pieces when a truck accidentally backs over them.

Lost, broken, or misplaced luggage cases (no pun intended) are often brought in small claims court because the value of the property lost fits under the small-claims limit. Unfortunately, unless you declare the value of the property ahead of time and notify the airline, and then purchase insurance, the monetary recovery for lost luggage is limited.

International flights are covered by the Warsaw Convention and the more recent Montreal Protocols — two documents that you didn't even know exist, but I assure you, the airlines are very familiar with.

These documents cover all international travel within the countries that signed the agreements, which is pretty much every country, and limit your rights concerning lost luggage.

If you didn't buy additional insurance, your monetary loss is determined by the weight of the checked baggage. So if you packed your rock collection in your suitcase, you're in luck. If your suitcase was filled with paper money, which doesn't weigh a lot, you're not so lucky. If you're shuttling the cousin of the Hope Diamond and the long-lost sister of the Mona Lisa for an around-the-world tour, buy insurance or carry your precious items in your carry-on bag.

Similar rules apply to flights within the United States. These restrictions are referred to as *tariffs* and the details and the limitations are set forth on your ticket. Because these rules are designed to cover all passengers, they will restrict your rights to the terms and conditions set forth on your ticket. Make sure you keep a copy of your ticket so you know how to properly file a claim.

You may never have taken the time to read your airline ticket, but if you're transporting something incredibly valuable in checked luggage, you really should. After all, if you don't declare the items and pay the insurance, how are you going to prove you even had them with you?

Here's a true story: A plaintiff was flying overseas to attend a family wedding. She claimed that she had packed her jewelry in a carry-on bag to take with her on the plane. When she got to the plane toward the end of the boarding time, all of the overhead racks were full. The airline required her to check her baggage at the gate for storage in cargo. When she arrived at her destination, the jewelry was gone. The airline denied any liability, because she couldn't prove she had the jewelry with her. She never declared the contents. Another snag was in determining where the jewelry disappeared — in the United States or in another country. The moral of the story is always keep small valuables with you, arrive at the gate early, and buy insurance.

Making the Moving Company Make Good

Moving companies are not regulated by state or local government; they're regulated by the federal government through the Interstate Commerce Commission. This means that local law will not be applied to your claim, and that any common law contract or state statutory contract rights you have will be secondary to those of the Interstate Commerce Commission.

You can still sue in your local court — it's just that the agreement is subject to the federal rule. After all, you don't think that a federal judge really wants to deal with your damaged furniture claim, do you?

In order to avoid some of the more common moving-company problems, deal with recognized and established moving companies and not four guys with a truck who posted a notice at the supermarket. It will cost you more, but you generally won't have as many problems getting a claim resolved. A reputable company probably has insurance to cover claims made against it so you won't have to try to figure out who really owned the moving truck.

Dealing with damages

As with airlines, if you don't pay for additional insurance coverage, the amount of damages you can recover is limited to the weight of the items. As with lost luggage, if the mover loses an item, the burden of proof of the value of the item is on you. These restrictions on recovery are also referred to as *tariffs*.

Moving is a pain in the neck, and you may be so eager to get the movers out of your new house and life that you just scribble your signature on the document that says everything was delivered in "good condition" without taking a close look. Oh, you may have taken a cursory look to make sure that none of the boxes were dented and the furniture still had all its legs, but not much else. It's not until you unpack grandma's priceless china that you find that most of it is smashed to smithereens or start looking for box 714 a week later and it's not between boxes 713 and 715.

Notify the mover as soon as you discover any damage. The issue of whether the items were damaged by the mover then becomes one of credibility at trial. Taking pictures of the furniture before and after the move may be time-consuming but will assist you in proving your claim.

In all likelihood, you probably initialed the invoice waiving the option to purchase insurance, which automatically binds you valuing items based on their weight. Obviously, you shouldn't do this, especially if you have priceless household goods. Or you should transport those items in your car, if they aren't too big.

To help make sure that your most precious belongings aren't damaged or that you can seek compensation if they are:

  ✔ Don't waive your option to purchase insurance. If you initial the invoice where it binds you to a value tied to the weight of an item, you can lose out if your collection of rare origami animals get flattened.

  ✔ Transport truly priceless and very fragile items in your car, if they fit.

  ✔ If there is an extra charge for special packing and handling, pay it.

The amount the mover will pay by the pound is nowhere near the real value of the item. It's sort of like getting reimbursed the sale price of store-brand bologna when you bought imported truffles, but at least you get more money for big items, such as couches and beds.

Unfortunately, the couch will probably still cost more than its weight in mover money. For instance, a dining room cabinet weighing 100 pounds may be reimbursed at 60 cents a pound. For 60 bucks you can't even buy one of those self-assembling cabinets from a Nordic furniture store.

When have you ever weighed your personal property? For that matter, when have you seen a mover produce a scale? If you are planning to bring a lawsuit, you have to prove the weight of the item — the moving company doesn't have that obligation.

If the item is in pieces, obviously it can be weighed, but if the item is taking a detour across the United States you'll have to settle for the standard weight of a similar piece of furniture.

It's a good idea to keep documentation of big furniture purchases for this reason. It can make a world of difference if your dining room set is made of ironwood or balsawood.

Escaping extra charges

Broken goods aren't the only hassles you can have with a moving company. A more challenging situation arises when you have a contract with the mover, but when they get to your new house, the movers tell you there are extra charges involved and threaten to take one or more equally undesirable actions unless you pay the added charges:

- ✔ They refuse to unload the truck.
- ✔ They say they will take the truck back to the old house and unload.
- ✔ They tell you that they will take your goods to storage and charge you extra moving and storage fees.

This is known as extortion, and you should call the police. Make sure you have a copy of the contract to establish the terms of the agreement. Unfortunately, the police at times will say it is a civil matter and not a crime and that you need to sue in court to resolve the dispute. So there you are, back to small claims court, if the dollar amount is less than small claims court limits. This is why you should try to deal with recognized movers who have a long-existing business in your community.

Suing a Store for a Refund

Many people sue stores, claiming they returned purchased items and were not given a proper credit or refund. Check to see whether your state has a law governing return policies of merchants. For instance, the state law may require the policy of the store to be "conspicuously" posted at the cash register or some other visible spot in the store.

If the merchant doesn't comply with the statute but has the policy on the receipt, you may still get your money back because having the policy on a receipt isn't a substitute for posting it, according to many statutes.

If your state has a statute regarding returning items for refund, the law may contain a requirement that you act to get a refund within a certain period of time — perhaps as short as ten days. So even if the store lacks a posted refund policy, if you wait too long to act, the law may prohibit any recovery.

If the item you purchased is defective, there may be a breach of one of the *warranties* — promises as to certain conditions and uses — set forth in a law called the Uniform Commercial Code (UCC). Because just about every state has adopted the UCC in some form, there's a good chance you can make a viable claim under this statute even if the merchant refuses a refund, citing the store policy.

Some of these warranties can't be waived by the merchant, but you must raise them in a timely fashion, so don't delay. These rules are found in Article Two of the UCC, which, if you're allergic to wool and can't count sheep to get to sleep, makes a perfect sleep inducer.

Getting Your Just Deserts: Collecting Your Wages

A recurring issue in small claims court is cases for wage claims. These claims are usually brought by day laborers or other unskilled workers hired off a street corner or without any paperwork. Many employers feel they can get away with not paying these persons at all or giving them less than the promised amount because as a group they're reluctant to use the court system.

Of course, in these situations there's nothing in writing, so you claim you were supposed to be paid $X and the employer says he promised to pay $Y. The case then becomes a credibility issue.

Check the court records in places where the employer does business and see if he has been sued by other people for unpaid wages, as this information can help the judge decide the credibility issue. Or check with your state labor department, as they're often interested in employers who aren't following the rules.

Fortunately, many advocacy groups now bring cases to court for these workers. If they prevail on the claim, in some states statues may make the employer liable to pay punitive damages in addition to the wages owed and subject the employer to other penalties if the employer is licensed business.

You shouldn't let your inability to speak English fluently or some other problem deprive you of money due you. There are agencies both governmental and private that will assist you.

Understanding Bailments

Bailment has nothing to do with going to jail. It also shouldn't be confused with a breath freshener given you when you are released from police custody — that's a bail mint.

A *bailment* is a temporary transfer of possession of personal property from one person — the *bailor* — to another — the *bailee* — such as giving the dry cleaner your clothes to clean. It's not a transfer of ownership. It's the understanding of both parties that the property will be returned by the bailee to the bailor when the purpose of the bailment is complete. It differs from a sale or gift situation where ownership is transferred as well as possession.

Numerous situations in everyday life create bailments. What makes bailments interesting, from a legal standpoint at least, is that a bailment is a contract relationship but it uses a negligence standard in regard to the care the bailee has to use while in possession of the property.

However, I understand if that doesn't interest you all that much; you probably just want your money without the legal jargon.

Types of bailment

The law recognizes three categories of bailment:

- Bailment for the sole benefit of the bailor.
- Bailment for the sole benefit of the bailee.
- Bailment for the mutual benefit of both the bailor and bailee.

Why do you care about this? Because depending on the nature of the bailment, the rights and obligations of the parties — which includes you —differ.

The bailment situation is one in which you may see exculpatory clauses, which are used by the bailee to limit its liability. (Exculpatory clauses are dealt with in Chapter 4.)

Benefiting the bailor

A bailment for the sole benefit of the bailor is sometimes called a *gratuitous bailment.* In this situation, the bailee does something solely for the benefit of the bailor. Essentially, the bailee is doing a favor for the bailor, so the bailee owes the bailor only a duty of slight care and is responsible only for gross negligence.

Ordinary negligence uses a reasonable person standard and a reasonable care standard; gross negligence is acting in a manner that is far below how a reasonable person would act in a similar circumstance.

Say your neighbor's employer is temporarily assigned to an office in another state. He asks if he can store his 1928 Duesenberg in your garage while he's away. You agree to do it as a favor. That is, you'll receive no money for the storage and you can't use the car.

While the car is in your garage, the San Francisco earthquake startles Mrs. O'Leary's cow, who kicks over a lantern starting a fire, and a spark from the fire is caught in a tornado and is dropped on your garage in Kansas along with some ruby red slippers, causing your garage to burn to the ground with the Duesenberg inside. Because this is a bailment for the sole benefit of the bailor, and you did nothing wrong, and you have no liability.

Benefiting the bailee

A bailment for the sole benefit of the bailee occurs when the bailor delivers the property to the bailee only for the benefit or convenience of the bailee. In this case the standard of duty is *slight negligence,* which means that any damage suffered, aside from an *act of God* (legalese for a natural disaster or an occurrence beyond human control), is the bailee's responsibility.

For example, you ask to borrow your neighbor's Duesenberg to use at your daughter's wedding. While opening the door for the bridal party, your walking stick inadvertently breaks the window. You're liable to your neighbor for the damage and the repair costs. Because the standard is slight negligence, just about any fault on your part makes you liable.

Benefiting both bailor and bailee

The most common bailment, and one you're probably familiar with, is the mutual benefit bailment. The bailor delivers the personal property to the bailee for a particular purpose, the bailee is expected to perform some service involving the property and expects to be compensated for that service when the property is returned to the bailor. The standard of care is *ordinary negligence* — how a reasonable person would act in the same circumstances.

Using the example of a fender bender, taking your car to the repair shop is a mutual benefit bailment. You, the bailor, expect to get the car back repaired, and the bailee shop owner expects to get paid for the repairs. There is a mutual benefit to both parties.

At the car rental business you, the bailee, want the use of the vehicle while the bailor car rental company wants to be paid for the time you use the car and wants it returned in one piece. Again, there's a mutual benefit in the transaction.

Because so many everyday transactions are bailments, some of them are covered by statutes. Some of these statutes may allow you to seek punitive damages in situations where the defendant business failed to act properly. This is something to check out when you're preparing your case.

In some states you may have to assert the punitive damage claim as part of your complaint, but in others the judge may award it to you if you prove the defendant failed to act in the required manner.

When bailments occur

A bailment occurs when a bailor delivers some type of goods to another person, the bailee. As the bailor, you want the goods back when you request them or want them disposed of according to your instructions.

Here's an example: You take your clothes to the dry cleaners. You're surrendering possession of the clothes with the intent that they will be returned to you when you pay for the services.

Here's another example: You're in a fender bender. This often creates two bailments: One when you take your car to be repaired, and the second when you borrow a car from your neighbor to use until your car is repaired. When you deliver your car to the repair shop, you're the bailor and the repair shop is the bailee. When you borrow your neighbor's car, you're the bailee and your neighbor is the bailor.

The problem with litigation based on a bailment is not necessarily proving that you're the original owner and that you deserve to have the item given back, it's proving that you suffered damages and how much they should be. *Damages* are the value of the item on the day it was damaged; unless you had a prior agreement (preferably in writing), you don't get replacement value or the cost of the item when it was new.

Say you take a business suit to the cleaner. When you pick it up, it no longer fits you because it's shrunk or has turned from a lovely navy blue to a hideous shade of purple. Your problem is to establish the value of a two-year-old suit. Further, if you're a man, and the pants are ruined, the defendant may argue that you can still wear the jacket, so you may not get the full value of the suit. For a woman, if the skirt is ruined, there's a better chance that she can recover the value of the entire outfit. This is probably some sort of vestige of sexism.

By the way, a good merchant knows that the customer is always right and will attempt to make good in these situations, especially if you're a regular customer. If he doesn't, you should probably find a new dry cleaner.

Although most bailments are *voluntary,* that is, both parties intend to enter into the agreement, the law recognizes involuntary bailments as well, such as finding lost or mislaid property (as opposed to abandoned property). For example, you have a meeting in your office. After everyone leaves, you notice one of your co-workers left his computer.

Yelling "finder's keepers, loser's weepers" doesn't give you ownership of the computer. The law creates a bailment in which you're the bailee of the co-worker's computer and must return it to him.

Chapter 18

Getting Personal: Suing Those Closest to You

*A*ny time you're involved with people, there's a potential for conflict leading to a lawsuit — after all, where's the challenge in suing an inanimate object? Even when dealing with your nearest and dearest, personal issues in the form of broken promises and unpaid loans can send you to court.

Suing someone with whom you have a personal or business history can be tricky business. The emotional stakes are higher, and you want to be sure court is the right course of action for you.

In this chapter, I review the types of contract disputes that can arise with acquaintances as well as businesses you use. However, the emphasis of this chapter is on areas with more of a personal twist, such as loaning people money, reining in problems with pets, and dealing with engagement and wedding issues.

Neither a Borrower nor a Lender Be

Polonius from Shakespeare's *Hamlet* advised, "Neither a borrower or a lender be." I hope that sound I just heard is not the book closing. I promise not to make any other Shakespeare references, but, for a guy who may or may not have lived 400 years ago, he had some pithy advice that still holds true today.

Unfortunately, not enough people heed his words and find themselves in small claims court trying to collect on money they loaned a friend or a relative.

When a friend or relative asks for a loan, the first thing to ask yourself is, "Why me and not a bank?" The reason the person with her hand out isn't going to a lending institution is probably because she has bad credit or lacks the ability to make timely payments. So she turns to the Bank of Mom and Dad or Good Friend Financial Service, which you're the poster child for.

The first question to ask the potential borrower is, "How and when will I get paid back?" Because the person is either a relative or a close, personal friend, you may be embarrassed to ask this question. Especially when those puppy dog eyes say, "Why, don't you trust me?" Stick to your guns and get a commitment in writing. A response like, "Of course I trust you, but the last person I helped out got captured by aliens, and in the process they erased her memory so I was never able to get repaid, which will put my family at a disadvantage in case a meteor hits me in the head."

Obviously, when these types of money transactions occur between parents and kids, it may be years before you ever see your money. Most parents forget about loans made to kids, rather than hauling them into court. But if a friend or more distant relative — who actually can afford to pay you back — defaults on the loan, then you have issues.

One reason to get your kid to acknowledge a loan in writing is to forestall issues with your other children. If you intend all your children to share equally in your estate, giving one some bucks puts your other children at a disadvantage if you don't get the money back before it's time to settle your estate. The favored child may come in for a little — or a lot of —resentment. Better to have your kids not putting flowers on your grave rather than not talking to each other over money or personal objects after you're gone.

Proving your case in court isn't easy unless you take steps to actually treat your loan like a loan — writing up a legal document or promissory note and having it signed and witnessed. Without anything in writing, the issue becomes one of credibility. The judge has to decide which story sounds more plausible — yours or the defendant's. If you did do things properly, good for you — this will be much easier to prove in court and may actually inspire your friend or relative to pay you back sometime so you don't have to go to court.

But alas, because the money is usually loaned to a family member or friend, people are reluctant to ask for a written document acknowledging the debt — after all, you wouldn't want to reduce your personal relationship to some sort of business transaction, right? If she doesn't pay you back, however, and you have no paperwork stating the amount or the terms, you're in trouble, for a number of reasons:

✔ You may have waited a long time to sue, in the vain hope that your friend would pay you back. If you wait too long, the defendant can claim that the statute of limitations has run, making the debt uncollectible in the court system.

✔ If the defendant doesn't admit the loan, proving the terms becomes difficult. Because you have the burden of proof, you have to prove your case. It's amazing how many defendants get amnesia about the transaction or claim the money was a gift.

✔ If you gave someone cash, you have to establish where you got the cash. Preferably, you took it from a bank account and not from under the mattress, so you can show the withdrawal of funds. If the money was given by check, then the issue is, why was it given?

✔ You claim the money was a loan, but the defendant alleges it was a gift, presumably tied to the fact that both of you celebrate National Cupcake Week or the anniversary of the laying of the first transatlantic cable.

✔ The defendant alleges she is being paid back for moneys she previously lent you, which of course there is an equal lack of documentation to prove. Or she uses the old reliable excuse that she's being paid for odd jobs she did for you.

You can't expect any interest on the loan unless those terms are included in the written agreement. If you didn't specify any interest in your documents, the court may not grant you any or grant *statutory interest*. However, if you win and the judge awards interest back to the time of the loan, rather than the date of the judgment, you may actually get more than you would have designated in a promissory note. For instance, in New York, statutory interest is nine percent, which is more than most people charge in these days of low interest rates.

If you're loaning money by check, making a notation on the check such as "loan" is helpful. This also prevents your warm, close, personal friend from filling in the blank notation line with "gift," or "repayment of loan," or "for yard work." I know, this never happens; I made it up . . . want to buy a bridge?

If you gave the defendant the money by check, make sure you have a copy of the check in hand before you file your case. You don't want to show up in court and have to ask for an adjournment to get the evidence you need. The judge doesn't have to grant an adjournment and then you have to try to prove your case without the necessary documents. This often results in what's called a "loss."

Because most banks don't return the actual checks anymore, and some don't even produce copies, getting a copy of the check is something to address early on. The best time to do this is when you first make the loan — request the check from the bank in anticipation that in a year or so you'll be in court and need proof.

And remember that if the bank isn't cooperative, you may need to get a subpoena from the court to have the bank records produced, causing further delay in your quest for justice.

Don't let the bank tell you they can't get that information. If you believe that, I have another bridge to sell you.

Get a copy of the front and the back of the check. This helps prove the borrower received the money and cashed the check. This is especially true if you stupidly made the check out to "cash."

Breaking Up — and Sometimes Getting Together — Is Expensive to Do

A special problem arises when people live together and then break up. Suddenly all money spent while living together becomes a "loan," or, on the other side, a "gift." Claims for the dinner you paid for when you took her mother out for her birthday are not converted into a "loan" merely because the relationship is over.

Invariably one party, usually the plaintiff, kept exact records of every transaction the parties entered into during the relationship, with the receipts kept in date order in a shoebox. The other person, however, has the record-keeping method of a guy who jumped on a boxcar in a 1930s Depression Era film.

One of the more difficult types of small claims cases in which to assess damages are the ones arising out of weddings and all of their attendant — no pun intended — expenses.

Buying or borrowing together

If you gave a deposit to a car dealer directly or guaranteed a loan so the defendant could buy a car, and the defendant has the car, you probably can recover any money related to that. The problem, of course, is proving your case and establishing the expectations of the parties when they entered into the transaction and the relationship. This is a ripe area for the gift defense without some documentation.

If you co-sign a loan, and your ex stops paying, the lender can still collect from you. You may have a claim against your ex for the money you now have to pay, but neither the lender nor the court will relieve you of your debt obligation. The bank isn't going to care that she said she would pay it back and she has the car and you don't.

This is known in the law as your problem and not the bank's. The bank had you co-sign for precisely this reason: The loan officer knew you would be around to get some money from if the car and "Ms Wonderful" drive down the highway of life without you in the passenger seat.

Dealing with wedding-related lawsuits

What makes these cases difficult is that the problem arises at a once in a life-time event. Even if you get married more than once, this particular wedding is still a unique one-time occurrence. The next sections deal with the woes that often accompany weddings, from returning the ring in a broken engagement to fighting with the caterer.

Breaking off the engagement — and keeping the ring

Just as there are many who slip between cup and lip, there also are many who falter between ring and altar. The issue in these cases is that when the engagement is broken, the potential groom wants either the ring or its value back. Other than to torture the guy, why would you want to keep it?

Under the common law, courts often look to see which one of the parties was at fault. So if your future spouse was caught at the No-Tell Motel, as the inno-cent party, you can either keep the ring or get it back. Finding out there was a stripper at the bachelor/bachelorette party is one of those cases that could go either way.

These days, many courts look to see if the ring was a gift in contemplation of marriage or just a gift. If a gift in contemplation of marriage and the marriage doesn't take place, the person giving the ring can get it back. And in many states this is irrespective of the issue of fault. If it is just a gift, then the recipi-ent can keep it.

Lawyers always advise not giving an engagement ring on your future spouse's birthday, Christmas, or some other holiday or event when it can be argued that it was given simply as a gift unrelated to any marriage plans.

Invariably, if the future bride refuses to return the ring or claims it was lost, then the issue becomes the value of the ring. Suddenly the ring, which was pur-chased at a discount jeweler on a side street in the diamond district, now has appraisals from guys who are so high-end they refuse to appear on *Antiques Roadshow.* In most cases, you can only recover what you paid for the ring.

Throwing out the ring with the (monkey's) diaper

This is a true story from my court: The engagement was broken. The couple, while living together had adopted a pet monkey. The future bride, when sued for the return of the ring by her former intended, swore it was lost when she was changing the monkey's diaper and it got thrown out.

I remember this case vividly, but no one else I worked with does, and I can't find the decision because it was before we stored stuff on the computer so I can't do a search. As there's no proof that memory can be affected by too many contact highs experienced during the late shows at the Fillmore East in the '60s, let's assume it's true.

Another problem arises if the ring is a family heirloom given as an engagement ring. In these cases, courts are more inclined to order the ring be returned because it has sentimental value to the person giving it, and this fact can cause it to be worth more than its market value because it's a unique item.

Another problem with engagement rings and jewelry in general is that the seller gives an appraisal and then the buyer has someone else look at it and guess what — it appraises for less than you paid.

An appraisal is only someone's opinion. So if there are two competing appraisals, and you want to prove your point, go get a third appraisal. And try to use legitimate appraisers and not some guy who hung a tear-off sign at the local supermarket.

Also, don't be surprised if you get stuck with a ring of dubious quality if you bought from the guy with the moveable jewelry store on the corner, with the appraisal from his brother-in-law. If a bargain seems too good to be true, it probably is.

Getting refunds when wedding plans go wrong

Lawsuits arise when the bridal party doesn't get exactly what it bargained for. In most cases, the defendant — the caterer, the bridal dress seller, the photographer, the disc jockey (DJ), the reception site — has partially performed or delivered what it believes it agreed to but you're dissatisfied with the outcome.

Obviously, if you were supposed to have filet mignon as the main course and got chicken, an adjustment of the bill should be made. But if you order 100 pictures and for some reason there only are 90, and certain shots were never taken, a 10 percent reduction in the bill won't make you happy.

Some redo's just aren't possible. You can't recapture the moment of getting the cake pushed in your face if the photographer missed it. The fact that in this day and age everyone at the reception captured the moment on their cellphones doesn't relieve the professional photographer from having to perform.

If there was partial performance by the defendant, in most cases you won't get all of your money back. So be prepared to compromise when you get to court and the judge asks if you can resolve the matter. My advice is:

- Carefully read the contract over and understand what it says before you sign. If you want something added, make sure you put it in writing and don't rely on the word of the person you're dealing with. What happens if your day turns out to be that person's day off?

- Check whether the business is supposed to be licensed. If it's supposed to be licensed and isn't and is suing you for payment, then of course it can't collect any money due no matter how well it performed.

- Make sure you know whom you're dealing with. Some businesses are middlemen who contract with third parties to provide services such as the limousine, the photographer, or the musicians/DJ.

- Be prepared to bring in an expert to establish the diminished value of what you received.

Examples of ways wedding arrangements can lead to lawsuits include:

- You contract to have a white 1940 Rolls Royce as the bridal vehicle. The defendant even shows you pictures of the car. On your wedding day, a yellow Checker Cab shows up. You're furious and want your money back. But you read the small print of the contract that says that the defendant has the right to substitute another vehicle based on availability. If she says the Rolls had mechanical problems, how are you going to prove it didn't?

If you want a particular vehicle, flowers, photographer, or ballroom, specify it in the agreement and make sure that the defendant agrees to it in writing. You probably still won't get all of your money back if you don't get what you want. You still received some benefit , albeit not what you planned on, so it still has some value to you.

- You sue the photographer to get money back because certain guests at the wedding aren't in the photo album. The photographer's defense is that was the group of people who got into a fight with the people from the other wedding and they were taken to jail and/or the hospital, making it impossible for her to perform the contract through no fault of hers. An offer to photo-shop the police line-up mug shots and the emergency room pictures into the album probably isn't acceptable, so settling this case sounds like a good idea.

Another method to insure getting what you want: At my son's bar mitzvah, I told the DJ that if he said, "let's put our hands together" more than once, I wouldn't pay him. It seemed to work.

Another technique used in thousands of movies is to tear the $100 bills in half and only give the vendor half the bills at contract and the rest at completion of the hit . . . I mean job.

Looking at Pet Lemon Laws

How much is that doggie in the window? The one with the waggily tail, worms, fleas, and a host of other horrible problems?

Because of our collective love of pets and the fact that emotion rather than common sense often governs transactions involving them, many states have passed laws protecting consumers who buy pets from pet shops.

These *pet lemon laws* give you, the purchaser, a right to return the animal if the animal is sick, to have your own veterinarian examine the animal, and other protections. In some places, the animal is not referred to as a pet; you're its human companion or caregiver.

The problem is that if you have children, they quickly become attached to the pet, and even though you have a right to return it, this may not be a practical solution. You soon find yourself paying veterinary bills that far exceed the value of the pet.

To get the company you bought the pet from to fork over any money toward its unending medical bills, you must establish that the animal had the condition while in the possession of the pet store and didn't catch it from your other pets or pick it up in the car on the ride home.

Some breeds are prone to certain health conditions and may be exempt from the law's protection, assuming you were given notice that this was a possibility. You quickly learn the difference between hereditary and congenital conditions and which are covered.

The law still views animals as personal property, so if the animal dies, you only get the value of the animal. So if you spend several thousands of dollars for an *all-American dog* (the politically correct term for *mutt*), don't expect to recover what you laid out. If however, the pet is being bought for breeding purposes and is going to be used to generate income for you, you have to establish that so you can get additional damages such as the inability to breed. If not, you get the value of the dog. Some states have passed laws allowing pet owners to recover additional damages for the emotional harm suffered with the loss of the pet.

The pet seller may have tried to reduce your rights by the terms of the contract of sale or some exculpatory clauses in which the seller tries to eliminate her liability for her own wrongful acts. One of the more common ones is to refer you to a veterinarian the pet shop recommends rather than encouraging you to select your own vet. This may be expedient, but it may or may not be the best course of action.

I hope you read this before you take a pet home, but with your excited children hopping around and fighting over who gets to carry the puppy or kitty, you probably didn't.

Even if the seller had you sign a restrictive contract, check to see if your state has a pet lemon law, because that probably negates any such attempts by the seller. In other words, just don't rely on the terms of the contract. Also, be aware that not all types of pets are covered by the laws. Often birds and fish, small rodents, and more exotic animals are excluded.

Because laws regarding pets vary from state to state, check with local animal rights groups to find out the obligations of pet stores when an animal they sold requires veterinary treatments after purchase.

Hassling with the Health Club

You join a health club and things are going along fine, except that you aren't losing any weight and continue to look like the before picture in every body-building ad, even though you work out an hour every day. It can't possibly be the fact that after you're working out you go to your local fast-food chain and order a quadruple burger with all the fixings, supersized, and an extra-large chocolate shake.

It must be the health club's fault. Getting out of the health club contract, however, may prove much harder than they made it sound when you signed up. For example:

- You want to quit, but when you signed the contract, you checked off the box approving automatic monthly payments against your credit card. You sent a letter stating you want to quit, yet the charges keep on coming, like endless waves on the beach or campaign commercials in a swing state.

- You sustain an injury in an accident or develop a medical condition, which prevents you from using the health club for an extended period of time. You ask to be relieved from the contract. You even send a doctor's note to verify the injury, yet the charges keep on coming, like a herd of wildebeests.

- The health club within walking distance of your home closes so you join another local health club, yet the charges from the old one keep on coming, like a light brigade into the valley of death, because the contract stated that you're still a member so long as there was another location within 25 miles of the old one and there's one 24.5 miles away as the crow flies.

The simplest solution is not to authorize automatic payments from any bank account or against a credit card. If you do, you may be checking out federal or state electronic fund transfer laws in order to terminate the contract and recover monies deducted after you canceled your membership. Although it may take some time to check out these laws, this can be a fruitful endeavor, especially if you show that the health club didn't follow the rules for automatic withdrawal.

Many states have laws that prohibit fees in excess of a certain amount each year, give you a right to cancel for a period of time after you join and get your money back, require the club to refund your payments if you have a medical condition that prevents you from using the club for an extended period of time (such as more than six months), or if you move a certain distance from the nearest club or the club closes. In some states, if the health club violates the law, you, the consumer, can get punitive damages from the club.

Paying for Professional Services

When I ask defendants being sued by people who rendered professional services to them if they should get paid when they do work, they generally agree that they should. But for some reason, many don't have that same attitude for professional services they received from a doctor, lawyer, or an accountant.

In many cases that end up in small claims court, after the clients received the services, they decide that they really didn't get what they paid for, or their great-grandpa, who hasn't left the nursing home since 1999, told them that the price they were charged was outrageous, so they aren't going to pay the balance of the bill due and owing.

The fact that you may not have gotten the result that you wanted does not necessarily mean that the professional didn't perform the service in a competent manner and as they agreed to do it.

Lawyers and accountants

Lawyers and accountants generally have retainer agreements or letters of engagement signed by the client, which spell out the services to be rendered, the hourly rate being charged, and other terms of the understanding. Many states require these professionals to have a written agreement with all clients.

If there's no state rule, look for a code of conduct issued by the professional association such as a bar association or accountant's organization. Your court case will likely hang on whether or not the professional suing you has documentation:

- ✔ If the professional produces the written agreement and her billing records and work product records, it's extremely likely the professional will prevail and collect what is due her. After all, how are you going to establish that she didn't do what the documents show she did?

- ✔ If the person suing you doesn't have a written agreement, hourly records, and work product, in all likelihood she'll have a tough time collecting, because courts tend to believe that professionals have an obligation to inform their clients as to the nature, the extent, and the cost of the services rendered. And if the professional had kept these records, there would be no basis for dispute.

  If you're the professional suing for a fee and don't have the required documents, don't expect a court to be too sympathetic. After all, you're the professional and should be the one taking steps to insure the client knows what services you intend to perform and how much it's going to cost. You should take steps to protect your fee.

In many states, if you owe a lawyer money, the lawyer has to offer you the option of having the matter resolved through *fee dispute arbitration* or *mediation*. Arbitration and mediation are attempts to resolve the matter outside the court system. If the issue isn't resolved, or if either side wants to challenge the finding from that process, generally you're provided the right to have the dispute heard in court.

In the computer age, there is no excuse not to put all agreements in writing and keep billing records. I know that in small, one-or-two-person firms, the professional is usually so consumed with keeping up with the work, that having retainers and billing records diverts you from that work, but you're the professional and the client isn't, so it's up to you to protect yourself.

Doctors

Doctor bills present a different issue. Did you have insurance? If you did, why wasn't your claim paid? Did the doctor agree to accept whatever she received from your insurance or did you agree to pay the difference? Sometimes the issue is one of who failed to provide the carrier with all the information to process the claim. In any case, check to see if you agreed to be responsible for the bill and the doctor only consented to assist you in processing the claim.

Unless the doctor agreed to accept only the insurance reimbursement, you may be stuck with the bill. However, if the doctor agreed to accept the insurance amount and wasn't paid and is now looking to collect the over-the-counter rate from you, you probably can convince the court you should only have to pay what the insurance carrier would have paid. In other words, the doctor agrees to accept the insurance rate of $100 but when she wasn't paid, she charges you $150. She's going to have to justify why there's a difference.

If children are involved, as the parent you're responsible for the bill, in almost all cases — courts don't make minors pay.

Courts also don't like to find out that dad isn't paying because mom has custody and didn't tell him that junior needed medical treatment before she sued him for nonpayment. Small claims court isn't for matrimonial disputes, and professionals don't particularly want to be dragged into your family drama.

Another quirk of human nature, which as a judge I never totally understand, is the refusal of people to provide additional copies of documents to the doctor to process the bill. "I sent it to them once" or "I gave them that information" really isn't a good excuse for having everybody use up a few hours of their lives to hear a judge say, "Obviously they didn't get the information or it was lost, so just give it to the doctor again so she can get paid by the carrier and not by you."

Chapter 19

Pardon My French: Understanding Tort Cases

*T*ort is the French word for *wrong,* and in American law a *tort* in essence means just that: a wrong. If you're involved in a tort case, it means someone has done another person a civil wrong that doesn't involve a breach of contract. (Not to be confused with *torte,* which is a French cake.)

A civil wrong isn't necessarily illegal — although it may be — but it still results in someone being harmed or damaged in some way. Tort cases are common in courts, because many people appear to feel themselves wronged by someone in some way every day.

In this chapter, I try to help you right the wrong done to you or help you if someone thinks you wronged them.

Battling with the Neighbors

Taking your neighbors to court may sound like a good way to get uninvited to the neighborhood block party, but neighbors are good candidates for tort cases.

You probably see your neighbors every day, at least in passing. And because your houses are next to one another, multitude opportunities for torts can occur. Trees fall down and damage property, cars back over prize rose-bushes, carelessly thrown balls break windows, pets do unspeakable things, and countless other careless acts or random accidents can occur.

In the next sections, I look at all the ways you and your neighbor can come to blows — or at least to court — over torts.

Tangling over trees

Maybe Joyce Kilmer never saw a poem as lovely as a tree, but if so, he obviously never had one of his neighbor's big pines fall on his roof. They may be pretty, majestic, and offer cool shade in summer, but trees are the source of numerous lawsuits between neighbors.

Trees can lead you to court in several ways. The following sections describe a few.

Trimming trees

As a general rule, you can trim branches that hang over your property so long as you don't kill your neighbor's tree. Likewise, your neighbor can enter your yard to trim the tree so as to prevent it from causing damage to you or a third party. If he does so without your permission, technically he commits the tort of trespass to real property and you'd be entitled to damages. As a practical matter, the court would think you're crazy if you brought suit, especially if there was no actual damage to your property, and if, in fact, the trimming was done to prevent a limb from falling on your property.

If you sued for mere trespass, it would be one of those situations where you'd only get nominal damages. You would have proven your legal point but had no compensable injury.

Now, if in the process of trimming the tree, your neighbor managed to cause the branch to fall onto the statue of Elvis you have in your garden, causing the King to look like one of Henry VIII's ex-wives rather than your idol, your neighbor can expect a legal notice suing him for damages to Elvis's cranium.

Falling trees

A different situation exists when a branch from a neighbor's tree, or in some cases the entire tree, falls onto your property. The first thing to do is call your homeowner's insurance company and file a claim. This is why you have insurance. Many insurance companies supply an attorney as part of the coverage they provide, or at a minimum gather the evidence you need to go it alone in small claims court.

If the cause of the tree falling was extreme weather conditions, the event may be labeled an *act of God,* which means that what occurred was beyond the control of any person. Unless you have insurance to cover your loss, it's unlikely that you can get any money from your neighbor. The general rule is that you can't recover damages to property resulting from an act of God.

If the falling branch is not an act of God — it just fell down all by itself — then you have to prove that your neighbor was negligent in maintaining the tree. You have to establish that there was a problem with the tree; that your neighbor knew about the problem; that the neighbor failed to address the problem; and that as a result of your neighbor's failure to act, your property was damaged. Even if it turns out the tree was diseased, you still have to prove that the defect in the tree was either obvious to see or reasonably discoverable if the tree was properly being maintained.

If you notice a problem with your neighbor's tree, tell him about it. Common courtesy says you do this orally; an attorney would probably tell you to do it in writing so that there's a paper trail as to when you gave notice to your neighbor and whether or not he had a reasonable amount of time to take steps to deal with the problem.

If you're reluctant to send a written notice to your neighbor but tell him about the problem orally, it's a good idea to keep a written record of your conversation with the date, time, place, and name of anyone who was present when you told him about the tree.

To prove your case, you may have to hire a tree expert to determine that there was a problem with the tree your neighbor should have addressed, or that if he did address it and your property still suffered damage, that he didn't treat the problem properly. In this and any other situation where you may need an expert, it's always a good idea to talk to the expert before you file your suit. You may discover that there was no way for your neighbor to have known about the condition before the event or nothing he could have done about it had he known. Better to find this out before you go to court rather than have the expert say it on the witness stand.

If you ask your neighbor to address the problem and he doesn't do so, you can always ask permission to remove the tree and either split the cost, or if it's really hazardous, do it at your own expense.

You can bet that if you do cut down your neighbor's tree without getting permission, it will turn out to be his favorite tree which had great sentimental value because it was planted by great-grandma when great-grandpa went to meet his maker. And if great-grandpa is actually buried under the tree, you may have opened a real hornet's nest.

Some places have local laws to preserve trees, such as in hillside districts, woodland, or wetland areas. This may mean that, absent an emergency, you just can't take a tree down — you have to get permission. And if you do get permission, you may have to plant a new tree of equal width.

Falling leaves

Your neighbor may decide to sue you because leaves from your tree are falling into his backyard pool. This falls into the category of what the law calls, "you've got to be kidding me" cases. Another example is "smoke from your barbecue is wafting into my yard" lawsuits. Technically, these are classified as *nuisances* and certain nuisances can be stopped. The people bringing these lawsuits usually have moved to the suburbs from the city where they lived in a 100-story apartment building and don't know the difference between silk and real flowers and a pool cue from a barbecue.

Courts generally take judicial notice of such occurrences, noting that leaves tend to fall from trees and the wind blows them and barbecue smoke to places willy-nilly. This means that the court without being asked can take notice of common events and occurrences that are governed by natural law, the law of gravity, and not man-made law. In other words, you don't need to resurrect Sir Isaac Newton to testify that an apple falling from a tree may hit you in the head.

As a practical matter, if you regularly take your neighbor to court over falling leaves or barbeque smoke, on which side of the property line the rosebush is, who parked too close to whose driveway, and such, eventually one of you will have to move.

As with any suit based on a nuisance theory, small claims court may not be appropriate because small claims court generally only gives money damages and not equitable relief, such as stopping the nuisance.

Border wars and proving property lines

Any time you go to court over disputes with your neighbor, one of the key elements of proof is who owns the tree or fence you're talking about. One necessary element of proof is to establish the property line between the parcels of land. This is done by a survey.

Both you and your neighbor should have had a survey done when you purchased your respective houses. A survey is a picture of your property. It shows where the boundary lines are; where on the property your house, garage, and other structures are located; and it should show fences, walls, and maybe trees. It should be done by a licensed surveyor, and dated and certified to you, the prior owner of your property, a bank, or a title company.

When the judge compares your survey and that of your neighbor, the two surveys should show the same boundary line. The fun starts when they don't. You may need an expert such as a surveyor or title insurance agent to come in and explain the discrepancy. This is especially true if the judge has no idea how to read a survey, which is a possibility if the judge never did real estate law before going on the bench.

You can't assume that where your fence is located is your boundary line. Fences are often not on property lines, and many states permit them to be up to one foot beyond the property line without creating any legal rights for the encroached-upon party. This is another reason why you need a survey and not just some photographs.

Surveys cost money, so see if you can find the one from when you bought your property. If you can't there's a good chance that either the lawyer who represented you, the bank holding your mortgage, or the title company that insured your property has a copy.

Get a survey done or get a copy of a previous survey before you start your lawsuit. Trying to get a copy of a survey may be time-consuming and will delay your case if you do it at trial time.

Fighting over fences

Good fences may make good neighbors, according to a Robert Frost neighbor, but they also produce a lot of lawsuits. As noted in the section, "Border wars and proving property lines," just because there's a fence between your property and your neighbor's doesn't mean it's on the property line. And if it is on your property, that doesn't make it your fence. When larger pieces of property are subdivided, developers sometimes leave old fences where they are to save the cost of removing them and so as not to bother the old neighbors. Some fences are so old, no one knows who installed them.

But if a fence is on your property more than a few inches off the mapped property line, you probably can remove it. If you don't care, the better practice is to send your neighbor a letter letting him know the fence is on your property but you'll let it stay just to be neighborly.

Disputing over driveways

Another area of neighborly conflict arises in urban areas where there are common driveways. That is, there's one driveway between the two houses that leads to separate garages in the backyard. The driveway is barely navigable by a subcompact car, yet it's there for both parties to use.

What this means is that neither you nor your neighbor in a fit of pique can put a fence down the middle of the driveway. As a matter of fact, you may not even be able to put a fence between the corner of your house and the corner of your garage to enclose your yard, if it would make it impossible for your neighbor to maneuver his '59 Caddy into the garage.

If you seek to have the fence removed, small claims court may not be the place to go. Why? Because small claims court doesn't deal with equitable claims like ordering the fence to be removed. A small claims court can award money for the intrusion onto your land, so you may have to bring a damage claim seeking money damages for trespass — the money damages being the value of the fence trespassing on your property.

If you're dealing with a surveyor, decide whether you want a new survey showing your property line or whether you want to pay for the property to be staked. If the property has staked-markers placed by the surveyor in the ground to show the location of the corners of your property, it may be helpful to you, but it is useless to the judge in determining where the fence is located. Staking is an additional and expensive cost and may not be what you need. Also by the time you get to court, gremlins or some other mysterious force may have removed the stakes.

Wrangling with Rover: Pet Disputes

If you're bitten by a dog, there's a good chance your case will be in regular civil court and not small claims court because the potential recovery would exceed the monetary jurisdiction of small claims court. The dog-bite cases that end up in small claims court are when your neighbor's Maltese gets loose and bites your Irish wolfhound and you sue for the veterinary bills you incurred.

One way to prevail in a dog-bite case is to determine whether your state or locality has a *leash law* that states that if a dog is off the owner's property, it must be on a leash, and if it's on the property, the property has to be fenced to prevent the unleashed dog from running loose. If your locale has such a law, the defendant then has to justify why his dog was running loose. You don't have to prove why it was. The burden of proof shifts to the defendant. In some places the law may be in the local health code.

Dogs are considered personal property, and you are compensated for their value in that regard. In other words, if the value of the pet is less than the veterinary expenses, you may only recover the value of the animal. That may not seem fair when you know in your heart that your pet is worth two of any person you know, including your neighbor. But the law isn't always fair when it comes to matters of the heart.

If you have a dog-bite claim against you, contact your homeowner's insurance company; the claim may be a covered event and the carrier may provide legal services to you as part of your coverage.

Making a Case for Malpractice

When a professional fails to perform up to community standards for that profession, he may be sued for malpractice. *Malpractice* is a type of negligence. The most common types of malpractice cases are medical, dental, veterinary, and legal. However, cases can be brought against any professional including architects and accountants.

If you're bringing a medical malpractice case in small claims court, there's a major problem with your case. Medical malpractice cases are very complicated and require the skill and expertise of an experienced attorney to succeed. They also require expert testimony and production of medical records — both of which are expensive propositions.

If you're in small claims court with a medical malpractice case, the odds are you lack a provable case; otherwise, an attorney would have leaped on it. Or, you are what's known as a difficult client, meaning no attorney will touch your case with a ten-foot pole. But even difficult clients with provable cases get attorneys for malpractice claims.

Medical malpractice cases usually take years to get to trial and require the expenditure of a lot of money getting ready for trial. Lawyers typically take them on a contingency basis, meaning they only collect a fee if they win. It also means that they only take them if they're confident that they can get a settlement or a victory at trial.

The most common malpractice cases in small claims court are dental malpractice and veterinary malpractice, where the stakes aren't quite as high.

Open wide! Dental malpractice

Dental malpractice can cover anything that goes wrong in your mouth, and often includes false teeth and bridges not being done properly, a root canal that has to be redone, teeth whitening that doesn't meet the patient's standards, or the like. There may not be any big claim for pain and suffering in dental malpractice — although there could be — but the plaintiff is seeking to get back the money paid for the unsatisfactory dental procedure.

The key thing to remember when you go to small claims court is that you're bringing a malpractice action. And malpractice cases require expert testimony to establish the community standard for a dentist performing that procedure and that the dentist deviated from that procedure. Unless the malpractice is so blatant that an average person would conclude the dentist acted improperly, such as removing the wrong tooth, an expert is mandatory to prove malpractice.

Just because there's a bad result doesn't mean there was malpractice. You have no guarantee that a dental or medical procedure will be successful even if everything is done properly. Malpractice requires that the professional did not perform the procedure properly and that caused the injury to the plaintiff.

Also, in all likelihood a professional being sued for malpractice will retain an attorney, which in some states will automatically move the case out of small claims court.

Taking the vet to court on Fido's behalf

The same rules that apply to malpractice committed against humans apply to malpractice involving animals. Expert testimony is needed to establish that the veterinarian violated the standard of practice expected of veterinarians in the community where he practices.

An added problem with veterinary malpractice claims is proving the amount of damages. Because people become emotionally attached to their pets, they often spend more on treatment than the pet is worth. Pets and animals are property, so their value is calculated using that standard.

Generally, if you spend more for veterinary treatment than the animal is worth, you can only recover the value of the animal. In most states, the emotional toll on a pet owner is not recoverable as damages, even assuming that you can prove malpractice. However, some states have passed legislation in that regard, so check your state's law or speak to a pet rights advocacy group to see what the current status of the law is in your state.

Turning the tables: Suing your lawyer

Usually legal malpractice claims are raised when an attorney sues to collect a fee and the defendant raises the malpractice of the lawyer as a defense. It also can arise when a client sues to get a fee back, claiming the lawyer didn't provide the services as agreed.

Again, because this is a case involving professional malpractice, expert testimony is needed to recover a fee if you claim the lawyer did not do what he agreed to do. You also need expert testimony if you're raising legal malpractice as a defense to a suit by the lawyer for an unpaid fee. A professional suing for a fee can become his own expert; he doesn't have to call another professional to establish that the community standard was followed.

The legal profession and, in some states, the judiciary has created its own set of rules for dealing with legal malpractice claims arising in the context of legal fee litigation, including the following:

- Many state and local bar associations have fee arbitration or mediation programs, where the dispute over legal fees can be resolved without resorting to the court system. Most states that have these programs require the lawyer to give the client notice of the existence of the program and the process to be followed if the client elects to participate in it.

  This is an inexpensive way of resolving the dispute without going to court. Don't ignore this avenue just because it may be managed by the local bar association.

- To prevail on a claim for legal fees, the lawyer should have a written retainer which sets forth the work he engages to perform and how the legal fee is to be calculated, whether by a flat fee, an hourly rate, or on a *contingency basis,* in which you pay no fee unless the lawyer recovers money for you.

- The lawyer should also keep time records setting forth the work done, the amount of time spent doing the task, and the fee incurred. No matter what type of fee arrangement is agreed to between the client and the attorney, if the client terminates the relationship, the lawyer is entitled to be paid for services rendered on an hourly basis.

One big problem with lawsuits alleging legal malpractice is that in order to hold the lawyer liable, the client has to prove he would have prevailed on the underlying lawsuit if the lawyer hadn't committed the malpractice. In other words, there is no malpractice even if the lawyer did something wrong during the case if the client can't prove he would have won the litigation but for the negligence of the lawyer.

To prove you would have prevailed on the underlying case means you need expert testimony. Yes, everything comes back to that with malpractice cases. So if the lawyer never filed your case and the statute of limitations has run barring another lawyer from picking up the pieces and running with it, to win the malpractice case you have to show you would have won the underlying litigation.

With all professional malpractice claims, the law does not hold that the professional guaranteed a result unless he specifically promised to do so. They only have to perform up to the standard of a professional in their community with the same expertise.

What this means is that a cardiac surgeon in New York City may be held to a higher standard than a cardiac surgeon in Point Barrow, Alaska, which doesn't seem fair if you live in Point Barrow, but there it is.

Suing over Property Damage

One of the most difficult kinds of cases for a plaintiff to prove is property damage claims arising from a flooded basement. Obviously it's easy enough to prove there was a flood; that's not the problem. The difficulty arises from establishing what caused the flood and putting a price tag on the amount of damages.

Damage from some types of flooding are recoverable in court, but others aren't. It may all look like water over the dam to you, but the court sees it differently.

Causes of floods: Water mains and sewer backups

The two most common causes of basement flooding other than ground water after rainstorms are water main breaks and sewer backups. These both have a similar proof problem — where is the break or backup? If it's on your property before your line hooks into the municipal water or sewer system, you're responsible for repairs and damages. You usually won't know this until after you've undergone the expense of digging up your lawn to locate and replace the break. This is when you call your homeowner's insurance carrier to see whether you have coverage.

If the problem is in the municipal system, you still have a difficult case to prove because the law requires that the municipality have some prior notice of a problem with the system. If this is the first time it's happened, then there's a good chance that the municipality won't be held responsible, and you'll have to absorb not only the water in the basement but also the financial loss.

To prove your case in this situation, subpoena the records of the local water or sewer authority to see whether there have been complaints or repair orders in your neighborhood. You may also be able to do this with a Freedom of Information Law (FOIL) or Act (FOIA) request, depending on how your state labels it.

The problem with a FOIA request is that you may not get the information you seek before the time limit to file a claim expires. You may have to sue first and get the information later with a subpoena.

Remember, because you're going after a government agency, there may be special rules to follow before you can bring a lawsuit, including whom you have to notify as well as delineated time limits for making such a claim. If you fail to meet these requirements, you may never get to court on the merits of your claim.

This points out why it is important to file complaints about water and sewer backups; complaints put the municipality on notice of a defective condition and may permit you or your neighbor to successfully bring a suit the next time there's a problem.

Another reason to get the records is to establish that even if the municipality did not have *actual notice* of a defective condition and knew about it because someone told them about it or because they created the problem, they should have *constructive notice* — meaning that had they been properly maintaining and inspecting the system in question, they would have known about the condition. You can argue that had the municipality done even routine maintenance and inspection, they would have discovered the problem and corrected the condition. Records can help prove previous notice or a lack of maintenance and inspection.

With sewers, you may also need to determine whether it's a storm sewer or a sanitary sewer. In theory, a *sanitary sewer* is a closed system subject to backups only if it isn't properly maintained. In other words, the likelihood that your neighbor flushed a mattress down the toilet and caused a backup is pretty slim. Of course, an alligator flushed down the toilet in its youth and now living large in the sewer system is a whole other problem. Therefore, after you get past the notice requirement, the fact that the municipal sewer line is clogged gets to be an easier case.

With storm sewers, the problem often is related to the fact that they're not closed systems. They can include drainage ditches and conduits to streams and brooks. This means that the system is not under the exclusive control of the municipality. Neighbors can throw mattresses and debris into the system at various places causing a backup a great distance away. In these cases, you need the municipal records showing how often the system is cleaned and inspected.

Finally, if the flooding occurs after particularly heavy rain or unusual snow melting, the municipality will claim the event was an act of God that they had no control over and could not have prevented. If an act of God is established, you can't recover.

Damages: Proving the value of property

After you establish that the municipality is responsible for the flooding condition, you still have to prove the monetary value of the personal property you lost.

The measure of damages is the value of the property on the date of loss. It's not:

- ✔ Replacement value
- ✔ The cost to buy a new object at current market price
- ✔ The price you initially paid for the item

For recovery purposes, you get the value of the property when it was destroyed. A ten-year-old rug is valued as a ten-year-old rug and not a new rug. If you notify your homeowner's insurance company, they can send out someone who's an expert at valuing property in casualty loss situations. If you don't have insurance or can't file a claim, you may have to hire a *public adjuster* — someone who can value the property loss and prepare an estimate for use in court for a fee.

Chapter 20

Looking at Legal Issues in the Internet Age

In This Chapter

▶ Making legally binding agreements online

▶ Providing electronic evidence to prove your case

*I*t's obvious that the Internet has changed the world in a number of ways. Whether this is good or bad depends on your perspective. From a legal perspective, the Internet has opened up a whole new source of potential lawsuits from contracts gone bad and unfulfilled promises.

The trouble with the law is that it doesn't move as fast as technology does. Because of this, the legal system often finds itself trying to apply common law rules or existing statutes to fit cases that arise out of the changes in technology.

In this chapter, I explain some of the more common problems that arise when you conduct business over the Internet and help you deal with some of the problems you may encounter, both in determining your contract rights and in trying to prove your case.

Making Agreements on the Internet

Not too long ago, you would have purchased this book by going to your local neighborhood bookstore, and having them order if for you if they didn't have it in stock. Now, I dare say, most of you either bought the book at a national bookselling chain or ordered it from a national distributor online. In fact, you may not even have a paper copy of the book; you may be reading it on an electronic device.

You can now buy goods from any place in the world through the Internet. In the vast majority of cases, the online ordering system works flawlessly. If there are problems, they're often resolved amicably. But if you have a problem with someone halfway around the world or even halfway across the country, things become complicated.

When you buy something from someone, there's an implied contract between you. To determine when you've been wronged in a legal sense and what to do about it, you need to know:

- ✔ Was there a contract between you and the seller?
- ✔ What are its terms?
- ✔ What are your rights under the terms of the contract?
- ✔ Where was the contract made?
- ✔ Where can you sue to enforce the terms of the agreement?
- ✔ What state's law applies to the contract?

If you're like most people, you have no idea how to answer these questions, even though the information is generally available at the time you order goods online.

In the next sections, I look at the differences between Internet transactions and those between you and a local merchant, how location determines your actions, and what type of recourse you have when an Internet business doesn't keep its end of a bargain.

Determining the contract terms

When you buy something or enter into some type of transaction on the Internet, the question of whether you've entered into a binding contract probably never crosses your mind. In most cases, you do have a contact, although you may not think of it that way. But if you're dealing with a business that regularly engages in Internet commerce, someplace in your online order you probably were asked to "accept" or "decline" the terms or to click that you "agree" to the terms. This language is often referred to as a *click-through* or *click-wrap agreement* and actually constitutes a contract.

It's likely you've never bothered to read what you agreed to. Almost certainly, it never occurred to you to print it out so you have a copy of the terms of the agreement and not just a receipt for the item you ordered. If you actually did, raise your hand. I don't see too many of you having to put this book down so you can raise your hand. As with traditional purchase agreements with the small print on the back, most people don't read the terms. This is because in the overwhelming majority of transactions, everyone does what they agreed to do, or if there is a discrepancy, it gets resolved without going to court. In most cases, you really don't have to read the fine print.

The difference between traditional and Internet purchases is that in the traditional contract setting, you have a paper copy issued when you enter into the transaction. It shows your rights and obligations on the date of the agreement.

With the Internet sale, if you don't print out or in some manner preserve the terms of what you agreed to when you entered into the transaction, you may have a problem producing the agreement for your trial, if things go sour.

The reason you want to keep a copy from the date of the agreement is because the terms and conditions attached to any Internet offer can be changed by the seller at any time. So if you don't print out a copy on the date you purchased the product, you may be printing one out when you're looking to start your lawsuit and the terms may not be the same. How will you know that without printing out or somehow preserving a copy on your computer? Do you really want to show up in court and have the defendant producing a copy of the agreement and you standing there without any documentation as to what were the terms of the contract?

If you download the agreement at a later date, that agreement may not contain the same terms as existed when you entered into your agreement.

You may get another chance to save a copy of the agreement when the product you ordered arrives. It may contain the terms of the contract in a separate box or envelope shipped with the item. But you, like most people, want to see your new toy and probably never read the enclosure. Hopefully you don't throw it out with the shipping material, although it's a fair bet that most of you do, even though you shouldn't.

There's a good chance that the contract in the shipping container says something to the effect that if you open the box, you agree to all the terms of the contract. If it's not that restrictive, it will say that if you use the item shipped, you agree to the contract terms.

If you're negotiating directly with a seller over goods you purchased over the Internet, proving the terms of your contract becomes even more difficult.

You can produce e-mails between you and the seller, but you have to produce all the e-mails sent — the entire history of all communications between you and the seller.

What's covered in online contracts?

If you enter into an online agreement as a seller, include certain clauses in your sales material. If you're the buyer, actually read the contract and see if the online offer has these clauses:

- A clause establishing how you'll be paid for the goods when you're the seller or how you'll pay for it if you're the buyer.

- A clause indicating which state's sales tax is to be applied and who pays it.

- A clause listing the refund policy and return policy, if any. This clause must conform with the refund policy, if any, set by the state whose law applies to the contract or the state where the contract is enforced. In other words, if the seller sets the jurisdiction for all disputes to be settled by Iowa law, the refund policy must match the Iowa statute.

- A clause advising you what recourse you have if the goods are defective or not what you ordered.

- A clause indicating how you can accept or agree to the contract terms.

- A clause with disclaimers of liability for certain uses of the goods.

- A clause establishing the dispute resolution policy.

- A clause listing where litigation would take place in the case of unresolved disputes.

You can't just submit the e-mails that support your position. Well, you can, but if the seller produces her set of e-mails and they're different than yours, then what? The court can decide none of the e-mails can serve as evidence because the court can't determine whether yours or the seller's are accurate. Or, if the seller's turn out to be the complete set, guess whose credibility will sink like the Titanic?

E-mails only create a legal agreement when they address the terms of the contract. To be valid evidence in court, they have to spell out what was offered and the terms for return or recourse if you weren't happy with your purchase.

Check out a couple examples of typical online issues:

- You're a collector of memorabilia from a certain company that produces animated features and runs amusements parks around the world. You find someone on the Internet selling a highly sought-after item at a really low price. You e-mail the seller an offer and she accepts. You even pay for overnight shipping because you're so excited about your pending acquisition that you want it in your hot little hands as soon as possible.

The item arrives and you're dissatisfied with the condition, which the seller indicated was "VG." You took this to mean "very good," but the seller says it meant "virtually garbage." You want to go to court, and now have to prove exactly what you and the seller agreed to. Based on these facts, the agreement may be nothing other than the sale "as is," because you never clarified what you believed "VG" to mean or what your rights would be if you were dissatisfied. Without those things, the common law rule of *caveat emptor,* let the buyer beware, kicks in and you have no case.

✔ A different problem exists when you purchase goods through a third-party website where individual sellers post items for sale. If the transaction was facilitated by the third-party website, there's a good chance that you agreed to be bound by the terms of the listing and sale agreement established by that third party and not by you and the seller. This agreement lists your rights and obligations in regard to claims involving the third-party website and may also provide for some settlement process for disputes between sellers and buyers.

Entering an e-signature

Because you can't reach into the Internet and physically sign papers (there's probably a blond joke here but I'll refrain from taking a cheap shot), the Internet has developed the concept of *electronic* or *e-signatures.* The law recognizes them as being as valid as a handwritten signature would be under the common law.

By statute, an e-signature can be an electronic sound, symbol, or process used by a person to indicate intent to sign the electronic record. The term *record* refers to information stored in an electronic medium and retrievable in a perceivable form.

Although lawmakers are trying to make e-transaction regulations more consistent, some states don't allow e-signing for certain transactions. Because this isn't consistent between states, you'll have to check out your own state rules to make sure you have a valid e-contract. So even though you agreed to the contract by e-signing, the court of your state may not permit e-signing to be used for that type of transaction. If your state doesn't allow e-signatures for what you sold or bought, you'll be trying to prove the terms of the contract in other ways such as through e-mails, a course of conduct between you and the seller, or a standard of practice used by other businesses in that industry.

In regard to credit card agreements, whether entered into online or in a conventional manner, some states hold that the card issuer doesn't need anything signed by you in order to have a binding contract. If you're sent a credit card in the mail and you use it, you're bound by the terms of the credit card agreement whether you signed one or not. In fact, in some states, even if you don't receive the card agreement, if you use the credit card, you're bound to the terms of the card issuer's standard agreement in effect when the card is used.

Understanding arbitration clauses

You have a problem with an item you purchased online, and were smart enough to save the click-wrap agreement. You read through to see what you need to do to bring the matter to the court's attention. To your surprise and possible dismay, you find that the contract says you agree to go to arbitration before a private arbitration association and forfeit your right to bring an action in small claims court — or any other court for that matter.

Because the arbitration clause is included in the agreement, most courts recognize that as the avenue you must follow to resolve the dispute. This is the case even if the arbitration may be conducted some distance from where you live. This means incurring the expenses not only of filing for arbitration, which in many states exceeds the small claims court filing fees, but also of traveling to the arbitration site if you want to be there personally to see justice done.

Some arbitration forums conduct the hearing by mail, meaning that you send in your evidence and written arguments supporting your position. This may or may not be an advantage to you, depending on your particular situation.

Actually you may find yourself in court over the transaction but not because of the breach of the sales contract but because you're now part of a class action suit challenging the constitutionality or the fairness of the arbitration process. Some courts have found some of these mandatory arbitration processes so unfair that they are deemed unconscionable and unenforceable. The better course is to read the agreement in advance so you know what you're getting into.

If there's an arbitration clause in the agreement, the arbitration is one of three types:

✔ **Binding arbitration:** Neither side can appeal the arbitrator's decision to a court of law.

✔ **Binding arbitration with a right of the parties to go to court to enforce the arbitrator's award:** The arbitrator's award is considered binding. If the arbitrator rules in your favor and says you're entitled to money, and the defendant fails to pay, you can go to court to enforce the award. The court won't conduct a trial on the merits of the claim because the arbitrator already found your claim worthy. The court converts the arbitrator's award to a court-issued judgment, which you can then seek to enforce against the defendant. (Chapter 21 discusses enforcement of judgments.)

The defendant can go to court to seek to overturn the arbitrator's decision. But this is difficult to do and the ability to go to court is limited to certain fact situations, such as fraud or bias on the part of the arbitrator.

✔ **Non-binding arbitration:** If either party is dissatisfied with the arbitrator's decision each has a right to go to court and start all over with a new action in the court of law. This is called a *trial de novo*. (*De novo* means "over again.")

If you do have a right to a *trial de novo*, check the rules in your state; the time to bring such an action may be severely limited to as short as thirty days, and the lawsuit may have to be brought in a regular civil part of the court and not small claims court.

If there's an arbitration clause in the contract, you have to use that avenue to resolve the dispute. Courts almost uniformly enforce arbitration clauses for two reasons:

✔ You agreed to it in the contract.

✔ It takes a lot of litigation out of the court system.

Determining where the contract was performed

In normal transactions, it's easy to figure out where the contract was made — it's where the parties were when they made the agreement. The same question isn't as easy to answer when you're dealing with online contracts. You may know where you are, but you often have no idea where the seller is or where she conducts business. The Internet makes it possible to instantly enter into an agreement with anyone in the world.

The reason it's important to know where the contract was made or performed is that you can only bring a lawsuit in a state that has jurisdiction (a word often heard in small claims court) over the out-of-state defendant, especially if there's no clause in the contract listing where cases can be tried.

If the contract doesn't state that any case must be heard in a particular predetermined location or venue, one of the factors determining where you can bring your lawsuit may be whether the seller has an active or passive website:

✔ **An active website** allows you not only to get information about the seller and the product but also to complete the transaction online. A commercial business has an active website, in most cases.

✔ **A passive website** basically provides information only. In order to complete the transaction, you must contact the seller by some other means, such as a telephone call, facsimile (fax) transmission, letter, or some other traditional method of communication.

Courts in cases involving passive websites have almost uniformly not permitted buyers to sue in the state where they live. Because of the unlimited number of potential purchasers, it's deemed unfair to hold the seller open to suits anywhere in the world. So in all likelihood, you'll have to sue where the seller is.

In cases involving active websites, courts haven't given the seller that protection. Because the seller created the website and knowingly invited you to buy, and you can be anywhere in the world, the courts expect the seller to take steps to protect herself and clarify issues such as where lawsuits should be filed.

An active website likely provides a click agreement which gives details on where the contract is deemed to be made or performed for jurisdictional purposes. If the seller neglected to protect her rights in regard to where she can be sued, a court may be more favorable to a suit where you are. Also, because the active website sets all the rules for completing the transaction, the seller can, as part of the agreement, designate where all claims must be brought. Unless you're very lucky, that isn't likely to be a court near you.

Determining whether you can sue

Just because you've established the terms of the agreement doesn't necessarily mean you can bring a case against the defendant in small claims court. Ask yourself the following questions:

✔ Are you limited by the contract to arbitrating disputes or to using some other out-of-court dispute resolution process?

✔ If you can use the court system, is the defendant subject to the jurisdiction of your state? In other words, does the defendant have enough purposeful contacts with your state so that it's fair to have her come from wherever she's located to your state for a trial? How much business does the seller transact in your state? Does she have an office or warehouse? Does she ship a lot of orders into your state or is yours it? Does she advertise and solicit transactions in your state? All of these and other regular, consistent activities may be enough to constitute purposeful activities for jurisdictional purposes.

✔ If the seller has enough contacts with your state, can you use small claims court to resolve your claim?

On this point, you have to consider what relief you're seeking. If it's money damages, then small claims court is the proper jurisdiction. If you're seeking something that qualifies as equity relief, then small claims isn't available in most states. For example, the seller never sent you the item you successfully bid for and you want the object. You're probably not going to settle this in small claims court because this is really a suit for specific performance, an equitable remedy. (I discuss types of relief in Chapter 2.)

In some states, to get a defendant into small claims court, she must live, have a place of employment, or have a business office in the county. If your small claims court has these restrictions, then there's no way to bring the Internet defendant seller into your local small claims court. This just means you will have to sue the defendant in a regular part of the civil court and not small claims.

Finally, if there was a contract between you and the defendant, you may have agreed to bring your suit in the court system designated in that agreement. It won't matter where you or the defendant are located. The contract may state that you agree to a particular court to hear any dispute.

Finding out what state's laws apply

Even if you can get the Internet out-of-state defendant into your state's court, the next issue to figure out is which state's law apply. What this means is that if you have an enforceable contract with the Internet seller, you may have agreed in the contract to apply the law of a particular state. For instance, you're in Maine and the defendant is in Hawaii. Yet you or the seller designate in the contract that any lawsuits are to be heard in the courts of Minnesota and that the law of the state of Louisiana will be applied.

As crazy as this seems, this would be a valid clause if the parties agreed to these terms. A court isn't going to be too thrilled with this type of an agreement because if neither you nor the defendant has a lawyer, who is going to tell the court what the applicable Louisiana law is? The best advice is to READ the agreement as soon as possible so you know what you're getting into.

Providing E-Evidence

Proving your case in the Internet age has created problems for litigants and the courts system. Often judges who are not computer savvy have trouble understanding the technical aspects of electronic transactions. This puts a burden on you as a litigant to know what you're talking about and to be able to explain to the judge how the contract was made and how your electronic evidence was produced.

All states now permit the use of electronic, or *e-evidence.* However, before the e-evidence can be used in court, you may have to prove you complied with your state's statute for the gathering, storage, and retrieval of electronic documents. You may also need someone to certify that there was a security system in place to prevent the doctoring or removal of evidence. In some cases, you need an expert to verify the reliability of the process.

E-records are subject to being subpoenaed, just like any other documentary evidence. But there always is the problem of establishing the completeness and authenticity of the e-records. This can become an expensive proposition. As always, if you're in small claims court, substantial justice is the standard and a failure to comply with strict evidentiary rules are generally relaxed. Some of this information may be in your state's evidence code. Other states may set out the procedure in a technology law or some other statute devoted to electronic transactions.

At a judicial training seminar a few years ago, a digital expert from the FBI made a presentation on the use of something as common now as digital photographs. He showed how someone could take a picture of an intersection and add or remove a stop sign. Or take a photo of a sidewalk on a summer day and have the sidewalk covered with ice and snow. To the naked eye, you couldn't tell the photograph had been doctored. In a serious case, if this were an issue, you would need a pixel expert to point out the alterations. This is why compliance with the state electronic security law has to be established to insure the authenticity of any electronically made records.

Two major statutes are applied to Internet transactions:

- ✔ **The Uniform Electronic Transactions Act (UETA),** which is an attempt to have each state adopt as a state law the same laws to govern electronic transactions. It has been adopted in almost all states in some form.

- ✔ **The Electronic Signatures in Global and National Commerce Act (E-Sign Act).** This federal law applies in all states, but will defer to the state law if the state has adopted UETA.

Part V
Handling Post-Trial Issues

Tips for making an appealing appeal

- ✔ **Keep it on the record.** Without a record of what went down in court, you can't make an appeal.

- ✔ **The best things in life are not always free.** Be sure an appeal is a cost-effective move for you — it may not be.

- ✔ **Judgment is not the same as payment.** You can win a judgment without receiving a cash award.

- ✔ **This is not a do-it-yourself job.** Do not argue your own appeal — seek help from a lawyer.

In this part . . .

✔ Know what to expect after your judgment is delivered and ways in which you can collect what you've been rewarded if your claim is successful.

✔ Look at considerations to keep in mind when deciding whether to appeal a decision, and understand the procedures for making an appeal if you choose to.

✔ Check out Dummies.com for free articles on a variety of topics, legal and beyond.

Chapter 21

Getting the Verdict and Collecting Your Judgment

*Y*our small claims court case will end in one of two ways: You'll win or you'll lose. But winning often isn't the end of the story. Winning on paper is nice, but collecting your money can be something else altogether. Not surprisingly, losers don't always want to pay their judgment and look for ways to avoid it. In this chapter, I discuss the different ways of making sure that you get what's coming to you if the defendant doesn't hand over your money immediately.

Waiting for the Decision

If you're looking for immediate gratification in terms of knowing the outcome of your case , prepare to be disappointed. Sometimes it takes time just to find out whether you won or lost, and it always takes time to get money from the defendant.

In a small claims courts with a light calendar, the judge may let you know from the bench as soon as all your evidence is presented. In places like New York City, where there are more than a hundred cases on the calendar each small claims court session, you get a decision in the mail.

Sending notification of a decision by mail is often the preferred way to go for a few very good reasons:

✔ The judge doesn't have to stop hearing cases in order to complete the paperwork necessary for the court records. He can get to another case and keep the calendar moving.

✔ The person who loses probably won't be too happy and may even be antagonistic and hostile, threatening the safety of you, court personnel, and more importantly, me — the judge. The court system doesn't want to have the case being resolved by taking the argument outside.

✔ Reaching a decision later gives the judge the opportunity to look at the evidence quietly without the time constraints of the courtroom, check out applicable statutes because it's a pretty sure bet that the parties didn't (although having read this book you may have at least tried), and come to a reasoned decision.

As a supervising judge, one of the most common complaints I receive from litigants is that they felt that the judge or the arbitrator really didn't spend any time looking at their evidence. Or, if they get a written decision from the court, it just says who won and lost but not why. My practice is to write a decision on every trial I hear and explain why someone won or lost. It may mean you may not know the result for several weeks, but at least you'll know why I decided the case the way I did.

Counting the Ways You Can Collect

After the judge renders a decision declaring you the winner, you're faced with the problem of collecting on your judgment. Vince Lombardi, the legendary football coach, is the one who said, "Winning isn't everything: It's the only thing." If he had been a lawyer, he would have added: "Collecting; That's another story." Just because you won at trial is no guarantee you're going to get paid.

The best scenario is that the defendant gets the judge's decision and immediately mails you a check for the full amount of the judgment. It would be nice if that happened. It would also be nice to win the lottery. You can bet your bottom dollar that collecting your judgment won't be easy. The following sections describe some of the likely scenarios of getting what you're owed.

Check with the clerk of the court whether the judgment is automatically *docketed* — entered into the court records — when the judge renders his decision or whether you have to complete some paperwork in that regard.

The sooner the judgment is entered, the sooner you can take steps to try to collect on it, and the less time the defendant has to *make himself judgment proof,* that is, hide his assets so you can't collect. However, for the most part the amount of a small claims judgment is so small that most defendants won't be hiding assets.

Entering into a payment plan

If you won a substantial amount of money, chances are that the defendant won't have the financial resources to send it to you in a lump sum. Rather than engaging in the risky business of chasing him down and collecting through one of the methods I explain in the upcoming section, "Enforcing your judgment," you may want to enter into a payment plan with the defendant.

In some states, having a payment plan for defendants is part of the court rules. With a payment plan, the defendant pays the money to the court and the court then sends it on to you.

If you agree to a payment plan, make sure to

- ✔ Put the agreement in writing and have both you and the defendant sign it.

- ✔ Agree to a payment plan the defendant can fulfill. It makes no sense to set up a payment schedule the defendant can't meet. If you do, you're just asking for problems. You may as well just have the marshal or some other approved entity try to collect.

- ✔ Decide whether the payment plan will include interest to you. In theory, if you had the money in a lump sum, you could put it in the bank and earn interest on it. (However, with the interest rates so low currently, this probably isn't a big issue. It may be better to skip the interest in exchange for timely payment.)

- ✔ Include a clause that says if a payment is skipped, interest will be assessed back to the date of judgment as well as providing for the addition of collection costs if you have to go to the marshal.

- ✔ Set forth some *default notice* to the defendant in case he misses a payment. If you don't get a scheduled payment, before you go running off to the marshal or back to court to enforce the judgment, you send the defendant a *notice to cure,* which says, basically, "Hey defendant, you missed the payment due January 1. If I don't have it by January 15, the settlement agreement is null and void, and I'll take other steps to enforce my judgment." You'd be surprised how many checks still get lost in the mail.

✔ Provide a clause that says that after all the payments have been made as agreed, you'll issue a satisfaction of the judgment or notify the court that the judgment has been satisfied . A *satisfaction of judgment* is a document in which the judgment creditor —meaning you, the winner of the case — acknowledges that the defendant has in fact paid all of the money due to you.

Most people don't do this, which results in the defendant having to chase you down years later to get the satisfaction to clear up his credit. Fair is fair. If the defendant pays up, give him the satisfaction of acknowledging it.

In some states, you're required to register a satisfaction of judgment. If you don't, you may become liable for the costs the defendant incurs in chasing you down to get one or in returning to court to prove the payments were made. Remember the judgment is a legal record and can adversely affect the defendant's credit, and the failure to issue a satisfaction of judgment when you have an obligation to do so may expose you to a lawsuit for *impairment of credit* by the defendant.

In many small claims courts, if you as the plaintiff notify the clerk that the judgment has been satisfied, the court record will be marked to reflect that. In other states you may actually have to file a specific form to accomplish this. Again, check with the clerk as to what is the procedure in your small claims court.

Some small claims courts permit creditors to sue individual defendants, although they aren't permitted to do so in every locale. In consumer credit transactions, especially credit card debt cases, I'm always amazed when the defendant, who has been out of work for two years, admits owing the money and wants to pay it off, and the creditor says something like, "Your honor, the defendant owes $5,000. My client is willing to accept a payment plan of $500 a month for ten months." At which point I'll say something to the effect of, "Counselor, if the defendant could pay you $500 a month, do you think we'd be here today?" At which point the matter either goes to trial or gets resolved some other way.

If you, the plaintiff, agree to accept less money than the judgment amount because you're going to get paid sooner rather than later, include a clause that says if the payments aren't made by the defendant as agreed, you can enforce the full amount of the judgment, plus interest, costs, disbursements, and attorney's fees if permitted, less a credit for any money he paid. A clause like this hopefully motivates the defendant to pay on time.

Enforcing your judgment

Suppose that as soon as the defendant finds out you won the case, he calls you on the phone and informs you that you can expect to be paid either when hell freezes over or when a certain baseball team from the Windy City whose symbol is a baby bear wins the World Series — whichever comes first. Weighing the possibility of the choices, you wisely conclude that option one won't happen any time soon and neither, come to think of it, will option two.

You're now left with using the legal system to try to enforce your judgment. As your victory was rendered by a judge, you can use the marshal, the sheriff, or some other local official to collect the judgment. But to do so, you must first locate an asset of the defendant's that the marshal can *execute on.* That is, you have to find an asset such as a bank account, wages, or rent the defendant collects from a tenant that the marshal can seize to pay your judgment.

If you prepare your case from day one with your eye on the end game — winning and collecting on your judgment — you can effectively attempt to get paid.

In Chapter 6 I point out that it's important to have the correct name for the defendant. The marshal generally won't execute on the defendant's property if there's a discrepancy between the defendant's name on the judgment and the ownership of the asset you're trying to attach — get money from. So if you sued the defendant in the name of the business and it turns out to be a corporation, you're out of luck.

For example, say you sued and got a judgment against "Klown Kollege Corp. doing business as Bozo's Klown Emporium & Kar Repair." You ask the marshal to execute on the judgment by going after the defendant's bank account, which is in the name of Klown Kollege Corp. only. Because of the difference in name — that is, no "doing business as Bozo's Klown Emporium & Kar Repair" — on the bank account, the marshal may not be willing to execute on your judgment.

You may have to return to court and have the name on the judgment amended. If the account happened to be in the name of Clown College Corp., it would be considered a different legal entity because it doesn't have the same name and you would be out of luck. You would have to start a new action against that corporation. On the other hand if you sued the Klown Kollege Corp. and the correct name was the Klown Kollege Inc. and there was no registered entity as the Klown Kollege Corp., the likelihood is you could apply to the court and get an order changing the defendant's name to the correct one without having to start a new lawsuit.

Of course, you don't have this problem because you have a copy of the check or credit card statement with the defendant's correct name on it, right? Remember I advised you to get a copy of any check you used to pay the defendant so you would have a record of where he banked and the name on the account at the bank. You may get similar information from your credit card statement.

You have several different and rather simple ways to enforce a judgment:

- ✔ Garnishment of wages
- ✔ Attachment of bank accounts
- ✔ Seizure of personal property
- ✔ Lien on real property

Notice that debtor's prison is not on the list. Even if some states still have laws on the books saying that failure to pay a debt is cause for incarceration, it's unlikely that anyone is going to go to jail because of a failure to pay a judgment. If the defendant is ordered to provide information to you about his assets and doesn't do so, it may be possible to obtain a contempt order against the debtor and have him arrested and brought to court to *cure his contempt* — failure to comply with your enforcement procedures.

In some states, the defendant may have to complete a financial disclosure form setting forth his assets and liabilities so you can identity assets to collect your judgment from. In other states, you may have to serve an *information subpoena* on the defendant in which he has to answer certain questions about his assets and liabilities. In either situation, the failure of the defendant to comply may lead to him being before the court to explain why he didn't do it. After a court order is involved, the failure of the defendant to provide the information may be considered contempt of court with penalties such as fines or imprisonment.

Garnishing wages

One of the easiest ways to get paid when the defendant isn't doing it voluntarily is to garnish his wages. Garnishing doesn't mean putting a sprig of parsley into his pay envelope on payday. *Garnishing* means that the marshal notifies his employer with a wage garnishment execution, which instructs the employer to take money out of the defendant's wages each paycheck to pay you.

If you're owed a substantial amount of money, most states are not going to permit you to take the defendant's entire paycheck to pay your judgment. The law isn't going to make the defendant destitute so that he pays you and then becomes a public charge.

Generally, if there are no other garnishments in place, the marshal can take ten percent of the defendant's net wages — not his gross wages. This means that taxes, medical benefits, pension monies, and the like are paid first. Also, if the defendant is having his wages garnished for child support or spousal support, you're after those deductions in the pecking order. The percentage you'll be paid may be reduced so that the defendant, in theory, takes home enough money to live on.

If you use the marshal for the garnishment, the marshal collects a fee for his services, which comes out of the amount collected each check. For instance, if the defendant is having $100 taken from each of his paychecks to satisfy your judgment, you may receive $90 or some other amount because the marshal gets his fee paid first.

One advantage of a wage garnishment, especially if the defendant works for a small private business, is that the employer may not be too happy having to incur the bookkeeping nightmare and expense to comply with the garnishment each paycheck. The employer may suggest to the defendant that he either locate some money and pay off your judgment, take out a loan to do so, or enter into a voluntary payment plan.

Because each state has its own rules for garnishing wages, you should check with the clerk of the court or the marshal as to what is the proper way to proceed.

One thing you don't want to do is improperly execute on the defendant's wages. If you haven't followed the proper procedure, you can have a problem if you wrongfully attach the defendant's wages or other property.

Attaching bank accounts

Grabbing the money in a defendant's bank account has decided advantages over wage garnishment. You ask the marshal to issue a restraining notice on the defendant's bank account. This means all of the money in the account is frozen, and the defendant cannot access his money.

The advantages of attaching a bank account include:

- ✔ If there's enough money in the account, you may get paid in full in one shot and don't have to wait for the drips and drabs you'd get each payday.

- ✔ This method insures payment even if the defendant gets fired or quits his job.

- ✔ It causes the defendant major inconvenience. You may think an Olympic sprinter moves fast, but watch how quickly a defendant moves when his bank accounts are restrained. The defendant will often run to court to file an order to stop the bank from paying out the money and to cancel the restraining notice. You may need to make another court appearance for this, but often you get the defendant's consent to a payment plan in exchange for getting access to his account. Judges aren't very inclined to release bank accounts if the defendant isn't going to pay you. In fact, you can sometimes get the defendant to pay you a sizeable portion of the money he owes you from the bank account so that the balance is released for his use.

Of course, nothing in life is perfect. Restraining bank accounts can cause some problems:

✔ You have to know where a bank account is located. You can't just tell the marshal to send an execution to every bank in town. You need to have at least a good faith belief that the defendant has an account at a particular bank. The marshal usually doesn't work for free and the more executions he issues, the more money it costs. If you're looking for the defendant's assets, you'll be footing the bill initially.

This is when having foresight can really pay off. If you had any monetary transactions with the defendant, having copies of checks or other documents that show where he has an account makes all the difference now.

✔ Many states allow banks to ignore restraining notices if the amount of money in the account is less than a certain figure. For instance, a state law may say that any account containing less than $1,500 is exempt from an execution. If there's only $1,400 in the account, you as the judgment creditor can't touch it.

In the states that have this restriction, consumer advocates aren't the ones who got the legislation through, although they supported it. A lot of the impetus came from the banking industry, because the paperwork and labor to restrain these small accounts is costly for them.

✔ By law, certain monies can't be taken. These include social security payments, disability checks, pension funds, public assistance monies, and the like. You can still get a valid judgment, you just can't execute against these particular monies. But if there are funds in the account over and above these restricted payment sources, you can get that money.

The defendant has to prove the money is exempt. You don't have to prove you can attach it.

I'm always amazed by how many defendants say they're holding money in their account for their dear old Aunt Suzie or some other relative whose assets can't be touched. Unless the defendant can prove it, this generally is not a successful tactic. The defendant has the burden of proving that the money in the account is not his and is his relative's; this means bringing in deposit slips and the like.

✔ Money in a joint account with a spouse or a relative may be untouchable. The law presumes that the money is that of the defendant, but the defendant is given a chance to prove it's not his money. For instance, the account is in the name of the defendant and his granny and is used solely to pay granny's expenses. If the defendant can establish that none of the money in the account is his and all of it is granny's, you can't touch it.

Levying on personal property

It's not easy to find personal property of the defendant to levy on. *Levying on* property means attaching the property to satisfy the judgment. You have to identify the property, and the defendant has to own it free and clear. So if you want the marshal to take the defendant's car, you better be sure that the car isn't leased or financed, because even if you can get the property sold, the finance company gets paid first and there may not be any money left for you.

Likewise, trying to grab office equipment at the defendant's business may be a problem for the same reason: It may be leased or financed. The marshal generally isn't going to want to get into the middle of a dispute over ownership of the property, particularly because if he seizes something that isn't owned by the defendant, the marshal may be opening himself up to being sued.

If you want to take property from the defendant's house and have it sold, you have a similar problem. First, if the property is jointly owned with the spouse and your judgment isn't against the spouse, it's unlikely that you can get it sold. Also state laws may prohibit the sale of certain necessary items such as a stove or refrigerator.

Hopefully, you can find some piece of personal property the defendant owns — such as his baseball collectibles — and the marshal can sell the items at auction for you. The defendant may also own stocks and bonds or other personal property readily convertible to cash to pay you with.

Levying on real property

If the defendant owns real estate, you have an excellent way to get paid at some time in the future. First, you must realize that just because you have a judgment against the defendant doesn't necessarily mean you have encumbered any real estate he owns. When property is *encumbered,* it means that the person doesn't own it free and clear —liens on the property have to be paid before the property can be sold.

The most common encumbrance is a mortgage or real estate taxes. You may have to go to the county clerk and ask to have your judgment recorded against all real property the defendant owns. Because this entails additional paperwork, the small claims court may charge an additional fee to issue a certification or transcript of the judgment, which is a document to take to the county clerk to record against the real property in the defendant's name.

You probably have to pay a fee to get a certification or transcript of the judgment from the clerk of the small claims court. You then take the certification to the county clerk and pay another fee to record your judgment against any real property the defendant owns. Someday the defendant will go to sell his land, and voilà, your judgment will turn up as a lien against the property.

You have to be paid the judgment amount and any statutory interest accrued on it to clear the lien and give the property a clear title. Statutory interest is probably at a higher rate than you would earn if the money was in the bank.

How do you find out what real property the defendant owns? Well you can go to the county clerk and search the land records to see if any real property is registered in the defendant's name or you can hire a title abstractor, someone who checks out real property records for a living and will be able to locate property owned by the defendant.

A title abstractor is insured against malpractice if he makes a mistake. You won't have such protection, and if you improperly place a lien against the wrong property, you can be sued for impairing title to the property — sometimes called *slander of title*.

For instance, you want to place a lien on the property of the defendant John Smith; however, there's a good chance there's more than one John Smith in your county. If you tie up the wrong one's property, you have a problem.

If the defendant is a landlord, you can levy on the rent payments he receives from his tenants. Payment of the monthly rent would go to the marshal first and the balance, after deducting his fee, goes to you each month, similar to a wage garnishment.

Locating Assets

You're probably saying to yourself, all of this stuff is great, but I don't have any idea what assets, if any, the defendant has. You may have trouble even finding out the defendant's real name. Don't fret. You can ferret out this information, and in the next sections, I tell you how.

Tracking down information

In order to find the defendant's assets, in some states you can

- ✔ Send an information subpoena to the defendant's employer, his bank, his landlord, or anyone else having some knowledge of the defendant's assets. (The next section talks about information subpoenas.)
- ✔ Contact the state Department of Motor Vehicles to see if the defendant owns a car.
- ✔ Check the county clerk's office to search land records to see if the defendant owns any real estate.

✔ Contact the licensing agency if the defendant is engaged in a business licensed by the city, county, or state. As part of the licensing requirement, the defendant may have had to post a bond or some other measure of financial security to serve as a fund if he fails to pay judgments arising from his conduct as a licensed business.

If you were in a car accident in the movie theater parking lot with the defendant, and it has nothing to do with his livelihood, you can't collect from the agency fund. If however, he failed to fulfill the terms of a contract for work you hired him to do because he was licensed, the agency fund may be fair game.

If the litigation arose out of the conduct of the licensed business, the agency may bring him in to explain why his conduct shouldn't warrant suspension, revocation, or non-renewal of his license. Sometimes the agency can prevail upon the license holder to resolve the dispute with you rather than lose his license.

I'm often amazed at how many people don't pursue relief through the licensing agency process. There's a good chance that if you had a problem with the defendant, so did other customers. The agency's policy may be to not go after license holders unless there are a certain number of complaints. Maybe yours is the one more that they need to rein in someone not fulfilling his obligations.

Getting an information subpoena

Your state may require you to ask the clerk to issue an information subpoena. An *information subpoena* asks the defendant to answer certain questions under oath as to what assets he has and then to send the answers to you.

In some states you can do an information subpoena yourself or ask a lawyer to assist you with this task. But generally, it's just a form you can get any place that sells legal forms. This document is then served on the defendant. It may be served in the same manner as a summons and complaint is served, or the law in your state may prescribe some other method of service.

Check with the clerk of the court as to how to properly serve the information subpoena on the defendant. If it's served wrong, it won't be effective and the defendant may be able to ignore the request.

If the defendant doesn't respond at all, or sends it back with incomplete information, you can bring an application before the judge to compel the defendant to answer the questions. To ask the court to intervene, however, you must establish that you followed the procedure on how to serve an information subpoena in your state. To do this:

> ✔ Start with the clerk first. (Chapter 7 explains the importance of getting on the clerk's good side from the beginning of your case.)
>
> ✔ If your small claims court has a Help Center, talk to the staff person there.
>
> ✔ Consult with a lawyer to make sure you serve the information subpoena properly or hire a professional process server familiar with the procedure to serve the information subpoena.

After you establish that you properly served the information subpoena and that the defendant failed to respond, you can ask the court to issue an order to the defendant to respond or be held in contempt of the court.

This order to hold the defendant in contempt has to be served on the defendant. If it is and the defendant doesn't respond, he will be in contempt of court. Another order may be issued and served to give the defendant an opportunity to appear in court and cure his contempt. If he doesn't respond to this notice, it's not unusual for a judge to order some arm of law enforcement to visit the defendant and bring him to court to explain his failure to act, because at that point he is in contempt of court.

When the defendant files for bankruptcy

If the defendant files for bankruptcy, all attempts on collecting your judgment are stopped or stayed until either the defendant is discharged by the bankruptcy court or the defendant withdraws his bankruptcy petition. (See Chapter 2 for more on how the defendant's bankruptcy affects you.) If the defendant is in bankruptcy, keep track of the status of his bankruptcy for the following reasons:

✔ If the bankruptcy is withdrawn, any stay will be lifted and you can try to collect through the small claims court enforcement process.

✔ If the bankrupt defendant is issued a discharge and your debt was not listed in his petition, you can start chasing him again because you weren't included in the discharge order.

✔ If you're included and there is a discharge and you're not paid, you may be out of luck unless you took your judgment and made it a lien on the defendant's real property.

Most people who file for bankruptcy and receive a discharge in the bankruptcy court fail to ask for the additional relief of having any judgment liens also discharged. This means the original debt and judgment can't be enforced through the small claims process, but your judgment remains a lien of the defendant's real property and you will someday be paid. In any case, if you're aware that the defendant is in bankruptcy don't go blindly ahead thinking you can still collect on your judgment without the approval of the bankruptcy court. Bankruptcy judges are not very tolerant of people who ignore their orders.

Chapter 22

Appealing a Decision

- -

In This Chapter

▶ Deciding whether to appeal

▶ Following proper procedures

▶ Using a lawyer for the appeal

- -

*I*f you're not satisfied by the outcome of your court case, you have the right to appeal. In the context of legal proceedings, an appeal means that someone, in most cases the losing party, is asking a higher-level court to change the decision of the trial court.

Generally speaking, you don't want to be the person making an appeal, because this generally means you lost your case, although in rare circumstances you may appeal even if you won. When you appeal, you ask for a new court to review the evidence and the transcript of the trial and either outright reverse the small claims judge or send the case back for a new trial.

The rules involved in appealing a case generally have to be strictly followed. The common practice of easing procedural rules in small claims court in order to do substantial justice doesn't apply to appeals. In this chapter, I explain the rules for when and how to appeal your case.

You also have to consider the cost of an appeal. Most states charge an additional fee when you appeal your case.

I touch on some of the factors to consider in determining the economics of appealing and the possible outcome, which may influence your decision about whether to go forward.

The last part of the chapter deals with some of the procedural technicalities you should be familiar with as you're in the appeals process.

Deciding to Appeal

How and when you find out who won in small claims court is a key element in the appeal process. (See Chapter 21 for more on how you get the good — or bad — news.) It's important because your time to appeal starts to run when each side gets notice of the small claims decision. The three common events that trigger your time to appeal are

- ✔ If the judge renders a decision from the bench, the time may start running from that event.

- ✔ If the judge reserves decision at the trial, that is, doesn't rule from the bench, you'll receive a copy of the decision in the mail. Your time to run may start either when the decision is mailed or when you receive (or should have received) the decision in the mail.

- ✔ The judge reserves decision, but the court rules that the time to appeal runs from the date the judgment is entered in the court records, irrespective of when you got a copy of it. After the judgment is entered, you have *constructive notice* of its existence, which means that if you have the opportunity to check the court records yourself and can find out the result, the fact that you don't check them doesn't mean your time to appeal isn't running.

When you get a copy of the judgment from the court, it should inform you of your right to appeal and how long you have to file.

Beating the time clock: Appealing on time

Your window of time to appeal is very short. In most states it's 30 days, but it can be shorter. Don't make assumptions about the time frame; find out before you leave the courthouse after your trial.

If you miss the time frame to appeal, you're generally out of luck. Unless you have some really good excuse, you won't get an extension of time.

Just because you haven't received a decision from the court, don't assume that the case hasn't been decided and a judgment entered. Check frequently. In some states you may be able to monitor the status of your case online. If you do, you can't assume that the information is accurate or that you'll be given extra time if there's a mistake. The best way to protect yourself is to personally check the court records. Most judgments are entered within a few days of the trial.

The most efficient way of doing this is to physically go to court and check for yourself.

In Chapter 7 I warn you to keep on the good side of the courthouse staff. This is another occasion where having acted like a jerk can hurt you. Obviously if you show up at the court to check, you'll get the information. However, if you opt for some other method like phoning every 15 minutes you'll not be to successful.

Having your call unanswered or being put on hold so long you noticeably age are not uncommon when dealing with really busy clerk offices. Also, phone contact can always lead to a misunderstanding of your request — if either you or the clerk inverts your docket number or checks a case with similar names, you may receive incorrect information. It's better to show up in person.

Before you leave the courthouse after your trial, make sure the address the clerk has for you is correct. If you move anytime while you're dealing with the court, make sure you change your address in the court records. You really don't want to be making an application to have your case restored to the calendar or to get an extension of time to appeal because you never got a notice sent to your old address. It's my understanding that the staff psychic in most small claims courts was the first person let go in the recent budget cuts.

Determining if you have the right to appeal

In many states, you have a right to an appeal only if your case was heard by a judge. If your case was decided by a non-judge authorized to hear cases in your state, you may not be able to appeal.

For example, in New York City, you can only appeal a decision made by a judge. You can't appeal a decision made by an arbitrator because there's no record kept in these cases. This means that even if the arbitrator was wrong on the law applicable to your case and completely misinterpreted the facts, you still can't appeal her decision except in extraordinary circumstances such as fraud or bias.

Litigants are told they have the choice of the judge or an arbitrator when the calendar is called and that there is no appeal from an arbitrator's decision. Then when they appear before the arbitrator, the parties sign a statement acknowledging there is no appeal. In spite of all of these warnings, the court gets motions to vacate the arbitrator's award or applications to permit an appeal. All of these are usually denied.

The key issue determining whether you can appeal is this: Was there a record made of the trial? A *record* is any type of court documentation of the testimony and evidence used by the court to make the decision. (Your sister's videotape of the procedure on her cellphone doesn't count.) A record may be made by a stenographer who takes down the testimony of the witnesses or by some electronic recording device.

If there's no record, there's nothing for the appellate court to review. There's no way to determine what went on at trial — who said what, what evidence was submitted, and what rulings were made by the judge. It's the record that the appellate court looks at to determine whether the trial was properly conducted. Just because you appeal it doesn't mean you get a whole new trial.

The standard in small claims court is *substantial justice*. So as long as the judge gave the parties substantial justice, her decision will generally be upheld. The very concept that was helpful to you in bringing and proving your case can actually work against you on appeal because the small claims court is not bound by the strict rules of evidence and procedure. (I discuss substantial justice in Chapter 2.)

In some states, only the defendant can appeal; the plaintiff is prohibited from appealing. The theory behind this is that, as the plaintiff, you chose the small claims court as the forum for your dispute, and you didn't prove your case, so you don't get another chance.

Check with the clerk of the small claims court for your state's rules before you start planning your appeal.

Weighing the cost of an appeal

If you determined that you have a right to an appeal and that the benefits outweigh the downside of not appealing the small claims court decision, the next factor to consider is the cost. Most states charge a fee to appeal. This serves at least two purposes:

- ✔ It covers part of the expenses the court system must incur in processing an appeal.

- ✔ It discourages people from making frivolous appeals. If it were free, the appellate courts would be hearing just about every case over again.

In addition to the filing fee, in some states you have to pay to have a transcript prepared so that the appellate court has a written record to review. Generally, the cost of a transcript depends on the number of pages produced for review. As technology improves, some courts are permitting recordings or videotaping to be submitted instead of a transcript.

Whatever method is accepted, you can be sure there will be a fee involved. If your appeal is heard in a different county, you may incur additional expenses commuting to that location. You may also have to pay for a judgment bond (see the upcoming section, "Posting a bond or the judgment amount").

If you have limited financial resources, most court systems have a procedure to have fees waived. You'll have to make an application to the court for a waiver. Whether to grant it or not is within the judge's discretion. You'll have to provide some proof of your financial situation such as establishing that you receive public assistance or perhaps something showing your monthly income and expenses.

The law doesn't want to deny any person access to the court system or to an appeal if they legitimately lack the financial resources to pay filing fees. On the other hand, the courts don't want to open the floodgates to free appeals. Remember in most states when you make an application for financial hardship relief you'll be signing an affidavit as to your status, and filing a false affidavit is not only a fraud on the court but is a crime in most states.

Appealing Even if You Win

Why would you want to appeal if you won the case? Most people who win are satisfied and don't want to appeal, but in a few possible scenarios you may consider it:

- ✔ The court didn't award you all the money you asked for.
- ✔ The court gave you only nominal damages and didn't find you to be entitled to any compensatory damages.

Appealing a case you won can open up a can of worms better left unopened. For example, if you appeal even though you won, you face a variety of possible outcomes:

- ✔ The appellate court may review the small claims court record and decide that the judge was wrong to decide the case in your favor. This may result in your case being reversed, with the appellate court making its own binding findings based on the trial record or a new trial being ordered. If this happens, you can only hope there's an even higher court you can appeal to if you go from being a winner to being a loser.
- ✔ The defendant may also decide to appeal (sometimes called a cross-appeal) because you've opened the door, even if she already decided to abide by the decision of the small claims court judge. She has nothing to lose by filing a cross-appeal and gets a second chance to possibly reverse the decision at your expense, because you'll be paying the costs of the appeal.
- ✔ The appeals court may decide that there were mistakes at the trial level, but decide not to completely reverse the small claims judge. Instead, the appeals court *remands* the case, meaning it's sent back for a new trial.

> ✔ The appeals court can decide you're right and entitled to more money. But the amount you're seeking had better be worth the time involved and the downside risks.

If you're the plaintiff and the defendant appeals the case, you don't have to stop trying to enforce the judgment until after the appeal is heard. You won, so go and enforce your rights against the defendant. Most courts don't automatically prevent you from collecting your money just because the defendant is appealing the decision.

The defendant may ask the small claims court to stay, or temporarily hold up, your enforcement pending the appeal, but most states require that the stay be obtained in the court hearing the appeal. This is because after the notice of appeal is filed, the case is technically in the appellate court, and the lower level small claims court can't tell the appellate court what to do. This means you have to find out where the appellate court is located. It may be in the county seat or some other place not in your locality.

Having Your Case Heard

You can't just sit back and rest after you decide to appeal. You have decisions to make and actions to take. The next sections describe the processes involved with going forward with your appeal if you're the defendant.

Generally, small claims court appeals are decided on the written submissions and the record. You probably won't have to go to the appeals court and argue your case in front of the judges. (If you do have to appear and argue your appeal, read Chapter 11 to increase your likeability factor.)

When there's an appeal, the order of the parties' names may or may not be changed on the papers. If the defendant is appealing, her name may now be first in the appellate court record and yours second. The person appealing is called the *appellant* or *petitioner*. The person responding to the appeal is called the *appellee* or *respondent*.

Posting a bond or the judgment amount

Many small claims courts require the defendant to either post the amount of the judgment with the court pending an appeal or to purchase and submit an appeal bond. This is to insure that while the appeal is going on, the defendant doesn't make herself *judgment proof* by disposing of all of her assets so that you can't collect should the appeal either be denied or never completed.

The advantage of the bond for the defendant is that she doesn't have to pay the entire judgment amount to bring the suit. She can delay paying and gamble that the appellate court will either reverse the lower court entirely or order a new trial.

If a party doesn't go through with the appeal, the common term is to say the appeal was dismissed because the person appealing "failed to perfect the appeal."

Monitoring the status of an appeal

No matter which side of the fence you're on in the appeal process, the status of your appeal may be something you want to monitor yourself, for a couple of reasons:

- The appellate court may not notify you right away if the appeal is dismissed.

- The person appealing may fail to act within the prescribed time, but the appellate court may wait before it issues an order dismissing the appeal. If you're monitoring the process and see that the appellant missed the deadline to act, you can make an application to the appellate court asking that the appeal be dismissed. If you do, wait until the allotted time has passed or the person appealing may give the court a good excuse why she was late and get an extension of time.

You should be aware that the appellate court can take months and sometimes as much as a year or more to decide an appeal. If you start getting antsy about the time, it's generally not a good idea to put the clerk of the appellate court and the appellate judges on speed-dial so you can monitor the case. This can have two possible results, neither one of which is going to enhance your appeal. First, your case can find itself on the bottom of a very high pile because in reviewing it the court determined that there are important issues that will take a long time to research. Second, you are perceived as a really difficult litigant who doesn't have legal representation for a good reason and the merits of your case are weak.

Choosing to use a lawyer

Even though you may have been barred from having a lawyer for your small claims court trial or decided to go it alone initially, you can have lawyer represent you for your appeal. You still have to factor in whether the expense of a lawyer outweighs the cost involved. This applies whether you won or lost the case. (I discuss the pros and cons of lawyers in Chapter 3.)

If the defendant files an appeal and you feel you need a lawyer for the appeal, it may make sense to take less money in full payment of the small claims judgment rather than pay for the lawyer. There's also the possibility that you can lose the appeal and wind up with nothing other than the expense of hiring the lawyer. On the other hand, if there are some real legal issues involved, such as interpretation of a statute and how it applies to the facts of your case, a lawyer may be worth the money to prepare papers that are clear and to persuasively argue the legal points.

Also some states have extremely technical rules for filing appeals including what font to use, page layout, how pages are numbered, and the like. In order to make an appeal a "less appealing" option, many states don't relieve self-represented persons of these requirements. You'll be held to the same standards as an experienced appellate lawyer. On the other hand, many states aren't so strict and do eliminate entirely or overlook defects in the formal format requirements they'd expect from lawyers.

Some of these filing requirements are so technical and regarded as archaic in this day and age that lawyers use legal-services companies to format, prepare, and print the papers they submit on appeals. If your state doesn't have less stringent rules for small claims court appeals or appeals when you're self-represented, the cost of this service can be an important factor in determining whether you even want to embark on an appeal.

Looking at the possible results

The appeals court can render several different decisions:

- ✔ It can *affirm,* or uphold, the small claims court finding.

- ✔ It can modify the decision of the small claims court. For example, it may increase or decrease the money you were awarded.

- ✔ It can reverse the small claims court and make its own decision after reviewing the record.

- ✔ It can reverse and remand for a new trial back in small claims court. This means both parties are put back to square one.

Part VI
The Part of Tens

Brush up on the basics of law at www.dummies.com/extras/filingand
winningsmallclaims.

In this part . . .

- ✔ Avoiding major blunders that can make you a loser in court.

- ✔ Preparing your facts, evidence, and story before appearing in court.

- ✔ Doing your homework — reviewing legislation related to your case.

- ✔ Establishing and justifying the dollar amount you are seeking in court.

Chapter 23

Ten Ways to Improve Your Odds of Winning in Court

In This Chapter
▶ Looking at ways to come out on top in court
▶ Keeping yourself on track throughout the process

Winning in small claims court isn't always about whether you're right. The way you present your case — and yourself — in court can also be a factor in determining whether or not you walk out the door with the winner's ticket. To ensure that you have your best shot at winning your case, this chapter provides a quick overview of ways to improve your odds.

Remembering That Substantial Justice Is the Goal

If you want to win in court, remember that the standard of proof in small claims court is "substantial justice." This means you don't have to be Perry Mason (a fictional but top-notch trial lawyer) and you don't have to take a cram course on evidence and trial techniques. It means that you have to be prepared and ready to present your case in an organized manner. It also means that the court can give you some leeway and ignore the strict application of the procedural law in the interest of reaching a just result.

Creating the Right Message

Going to court gives you the chance to tell a story. Every story needs a beginning, middle, and end. And, to hold people's attention and make them relate to it, a story must have a relatable message. So, before you go to court, compose the message you want to present.

Coming in without thinking about what you want to prove and how you're going to prove it won't help you, and in fact can guarantee you a loss in some cases.

Sometimes the person who's best prepared wins. That isn't necessarily the person with the best set of facts or the one with the law on his side. It may be with one with the best message and the best method to present that message.

Preparing to Appeal

Never assume, before going to court, that you're going to win. The facts may be undeniable in your eyes, and maybe all your friends and family have said you can't possibly lose, but the fact is that you can lose.

Prepare your case before you start assuming that you may not win and have to appeal. This doesn't mean going in with a defeatist attitude, but it means being prepared with your case and anticipating the defendant's response. This may mean:

- ✔ Having the judge hear your case and not a non-judge. (Chapter 11 discusses both processes.)

- ✔ Making a record so you have information to review in an appeal. (Chapter 22 lays out the appeals process.)

- ✔ Organizing your evidence so you can present it in a logical manner, so that an appellate court reviewing what went on can understand what you wanted to prove and how you tried to prove it. (Chapter 6 has tips on making the most of your evidence; Chapter 22 deals with appeals.)

Choosing the Right Location

Location, location, location. It's as important in small claims court as it is in buying real estate. Finding out where to file your case and where it should be heard is an important part of giving yourself a head start in court. Bringing your case in the wrong court or the wrong county leads to an immediate dismissal.

Locating the correct court means checking the small claims rules of your local courthouse first and making sure you have the type of case it can hear. It also means you've located the defendant and have made sure your local court has jurisdiction over him. (I discuss filing in Chapter 7 and how to notify a defendant in Chapter 8.)

Reviewing Legislation

If you're suing a business or you are a business bringing a lawsuit, check and see if there's any legislation that regulates that business.

Legislation may require the business to be licensed or to have certain terms in contracts, and if the business you're suing doesn't, you may have an automatic win on your hands. But you won't know this until you check out the applicable laws and then see how the business stacks up. Legislation may also give you the right to ask for punitive damages if you prove your case. In Chapter 17, I focus on the special problems of suing businesses.

Treating the Clerk Kindly

Sometimes it may seem as if the clerk is deliberately standing between you and your goal of getting to court. Nothing can be farther from the truth. The clerk is there to help you, and he'll go further for you if you treat him as your friend and not your enemy.

The clerk can save you a lot of headaches by directing you to forms, making sure you're in the right place, finding resources to assist you in preparing your case, and telling you of mistakes in your forms before the judge sees them and tosses your case out of court.

For more working effectively with your clerk, see Chapter 7.

Making Lists, Checking Them Twice

Lists can be a big help when you need to organize information logically and ensure that you don't leave out any important details. Make lists for all of the following:

- ✔ The events that happened that convinced you to go to small claims court.
- ✔ The evidence you need to win your case, including witnesses and documents.
- ✔ What you want to prove at trial, including your desired outcome.
- ✔ Questions you want to ask the defendant and witnesses.

Looking Good in Court

You only have one chance to make a first impression on the clerk and on the judge. This means don't have a confrontational attitude with everyone — or anyone. It means to dress for court like it's an important event for you. This means no sneakers, no pants hanging down around your knees, and if you're female, no excessive cleavage. Ask your mom if she thinks your cleavage is excessive; if she says it is, change your outfit. Comb your hair and get enough sleep the night before court so you sound coherent.

How you look and act can convince the judge that you're the more serious and believable person when the sole issue in the case is the credibility of you and the defendant.

Investigating the Facts

Part of preparation is investigating the various aspects of the case. The only person who is going to do this for your case is you, so don't do it halfway. Spend time and get all the information you need, because you won't get a second chance in most cases.

Make sure you investigate:

✔ Who is the proper defendant. I tell you how to find out who you're really suing and how to use their proper title in Chapter 6.

✔ All the applicable laws that apply to the facts of the case or to the business you're suing.

✔ How to hire an expert or how to get copies of documents currently in the hands of third parties. See Chapters 12 and 13 for more.

Establishing a Dollar Amount

Small claims court is generally about money. If you're looking for monetary damages, figure out how much you're really entitled to. This means knowing what classification of damages you suffered and how you're going to prove them. Asking for too much money or too little money means you didn't prepare properly. For more on monetary matters, see Chapter 5.

If you don't want money from the small claims court, then make sure you're not asking for a type of relief you have to get in another court.

Chapter 24

Ten Blunders to Avoid

In This Chapter

▶ Making smart moves to help win your case

▶ Avoiding pitfalls that can lose your case

*E*veryone who goes to small claims court goes with one objective in mind: to win. One way to win is to not sabotage your own case by making mistakes that will cost you points in the courtroom.

I've witnessed thousands of cases in my career, and I have seen the same blunders made over and over. In this chapter, I share with you the ten most common and most damaging mistakes that can cost you on court day.

Heading for Court Before Thinking about Alternatives

Too many people immediately run to court without checking out other options, like trying to resolve the problem directly by talking to your potential future opponent or through mediation or similar out-of-court settlement services.

Do as Goldilocks would do and consider all your options before going to court — bring your case to court only if you're sure it's the best way to resolve your dispute. Revenge may be a dish best served cold, but it's also a terrible litigation strategy.

Failing to Prepare Adequately

Never go to court without taking the time to properly prepare your case. The time to think about proving your case is before you file your case and not after you walk through the courtroom door for your trial.

Information is what often wins a case. Having the proper information before you file you lawsuit prevents you from having your case bounced. Show up knowing the correct names, addresses, dates, and other details to support your claim.

Know who is the responsible party you want to sue, know what you want to prove, know how to prove it, and know what to do if you win or lose. You should have answers to all these issues before you file your suit.

Assuming the Judge Understands What You're Talking About

Presumably, you know what happened to you and what made you think going to small claims court was the way to have justice served. You also know what you want to prove. But that isn't good enough. You have to be able to tell it to the judge in a way that helps her understand the situation and make a ruling supporting your position.

Rambling on without a focus is a sure way to confuse the judge as to why you're in court. As is telling the judge about your version of the Thirty Years War with your neighbor when the case is about one incident two months ago. Sharing the history may be therapeutic for you but is a sleep inducer for the court.

Deciding against Using a Lawyer

Lawyers counsel people for a living. So why not talk to someone who knows the ins and outs of court before you go there, possibly for the first time in your life? A lawyer can help you understand the issues and help prep you for trial.

Not consulting a lawyer may be a fatal mistake. Although many small claims courts don't allow you to be represented by counsel during the trial, nothing prevents you from speaking to one before you file your claim. Chapter 3 focuses on dealing with lawyers.

Refusing to Listen

Listening may be more important than speaking. Not listening — especially to court personnel — is a serious mistake. Listening to the clerk helps you properly file your papers. Listening to what is going on in the court with other cases will give you an idea on how things work in real courts. Listening to the judge keeps you on track during the trial.

Listening to what your opponent is saying during the trial rather than speaking over her can help you prevail.

Not Making Things Clear

Not being clear about what you want to prove and how to prove it can cause a good case to go down the tubes. Failing to properly classify your case can have you pursuing the wrong legal theory and presenting evidence that is not only irrelevant but that doesn't convince the judge your position is correct. In Chapter 4 I give you some tips on how to figure out what kind of case you have.

Lacking Vital Information about the Court

Always do your research and know the rules of the small claims court. Reading this book is a good first step, but be sure you know all you need to know about your own local court and what the rules are.

Check to see if they have any publications that explain what's goes on in the court. Contact your local bar association or state bar association, as they may have helpful information.

Not visiting the small claims court and seeing how the court is run and what everyone's function is before your trial are blunders that can be disastrous.

Having the Wrong Attitude

Attitude is important. Having a confrontational attitude with the clerk, the court personnel, the judge, and the defendant won't win you any points and can kill a case where credibility is the issue.

If you're in court, obviously you're upset and you may well have every reason to be. But losing your head in court won't win you any battles. Stick to the facts and keep calm.

Teddy Roosevelt's foreign policy advice to "speak softly and carry a big stick" applies equally well to your court appearance. Speak confidently and politely but have your evidence — your big stick — ready to go.

Underestimating Your Opponent

You may think the person you're suing is a first-class jerk — after all, you're right and she's wrong. But if you think she's not going to prepare as much, if not more, for the trial than you, you'll be the one wearing the dunce cap. Remember you brought the case, and you have to prove your claim. In theory the defendant can sit there and do nothing — in reality that never happens. She'll be ready to counter your claims.

Consider your case from the defendant's point of view and anticipate the defense she will make. Be prepared to respond intelligently and convincingly to your opponent's arguments. After all if she read this book too, she'll know what you have to do to prove your case and will be prepared to counter your evidence with her own.

Making the Wrong Monetary Decisions

Money is the root of all evil, and if all you focus on is the dollar signs rather than how to get the dollars by understanding the process and preparing your case, money can also be a fatal flaw in your case.

The judge is going to decide the amount of damages you're entitled to, if any, but you have to prove it to her. Don't assume the judge knows how to evaluate the monetary amount of your particular damages even if she's heard hundreds of similar cases. You have to give her proof. Overestimating or underestimating the amount of your loss will leave you less than satisfied.

The amount of money you think you are due cannot be based on how angry or resentful you are. It has to be rooted in facts that you can support and defend. If the judge thinks you're just out for vengeance or to score a big payday, she'll be unlikely to reward in your favor.

Glossary

Glossary is just a big word for a list of defined terms — in this case, legal terms you should know before you get involved in any litigation. I considered presenting them in the order that I thought of them, but the editor thought alphabetical order would make more sense.

The definitions here are general in nature and similar to those you would find in a legal dictionary, with the difference being that I've tried to put the meanings into plain language.

Sometimes local practice attaches a special meaning to a term. If you still don't understand something, you may have to consult with an attorney just to get a handle on your problem. In any event, you should always check your local court rules before you begin any case.

actual notice: In some cases the *plaintiff*, in order to win the case, must prove that the *defendant* had actual notice or knowledge of an existing physical condition or an event. For instance, if the plaintiff fell in a hole, and the law in your state requires the plaintiff to prove actual notice, the plaintiff would have to establish that the defendant knew about the hole and did nothing to correct the condition.

adhesion contract: A type of agreement often found in consumer transactions in which there is no real negotiation of the terms. The stronger *party*, such as a bank or credit card company, dictates the terms, and the weaker party must accept them as offered. Sometimes called a "take it or leave it contract."

adjournment: A postponement of a trial. It may be requested by either the *plaintiff* or the *defendant,* usually because he's not ready to proceed and wants the case postponed to another day. An adjournment may be ordered by the court.

actual damages: See *compensatory damages*

adjudication: The process by which evidence and arguments are presented to a neutral third party asked to resolve a dispute between the *parties.* A court proceeding is an example of adjudication, as is arbitration.

affidavit: A sworn written statement made before a person authorized to take such statements, or oaths, such as a notary public. Generally, affidavits are not admissible in court because the other side doesn't have the opportunity to cross-examine the person making the statement.

affirmative defense: A legal reason presented by the *defendant* as to why the *plaintiff's* claim should be dismissed.

allocution: The process in which a judge puts the *plaintiff* and *defendant* under oath and reviews the terms of any agreement entered into between them to make sure that both parties understand the terms and exactly what they are agreeing to do under its provisions.

alternate dispute resolution (ADR): An alternative to a trial before a judge. Two of the most common methods utilized in small claims courts are *arbitration* and *mediation*. See also ***award***

answer: The *defendant's* response to the *plaintiff's summons* and *complaint*. In small claims court it may be written and filed with the clerk before the trial date, or oral — made by the defendant in court on the trial date.

appeal: The process by which a dissatisfied *party* seeks a higher court's review of a lower court's decision.

appearance: A requirement to show up in court on the date set forth in the *summons* and *complaint*. A *default judgment* may be entered against a person who doesn't appear.

arbitration: A form of dispute resolution in which, instead of going to court, the parties present their respective claims and defenses to an independent third person called an arbitrator who decides the case.

assignment: The transfer to a different person of a *party's* rights or rights to enforce a judgment. The person making the transfer is called the assignor. The person to whom the transfer is made is called the assignee. The right to collect money from a debtor can always be assigned.

award: The ruling of an arbitrator.

bailment: The temporary transfer of personal property to a third party, usually for a particular purpose. The person delivering the personal property is called the bailor. The person receiving the personal property is called the bailee. Common bailments involve taking clothes to be dry-cleaned or an automobile to a shop to be repaired.

bait-and-switch: An illegal advertising gimmick whereby a store promotes a product at a low price, but when the customer gets to the store, the product is sold out or otherwise unavailable and a more expensive product is presented to the customer in its place.

bona fide purchaser: A purchaser acting in good faith.

browse-wrap terms: Terms and conditions presented to the Internet customer as a product is being downloaded. The user does not have to click a separate "I agree" message before installing or using the product.

burden of proof: The responsibility of a *party* to bring forth enough evidence and facts to support his claims and obtain a judgment in his favor.

by the court: When the cases are called in small claims court, the rules of the court may permit the *parties* to have the case heard either by a judge or by an arbitrator. If one of the parties wants the case heard by the judge, that party would yell "by the court" which will result in a trial before the judge. If neither party requests the judge an arbitrator would hear the case.

capacity: The legal ability of a person to enter into a contract.

chattel: See *personal property*

click-on agreement (click-wrap agreement): A type of agreement used in online purchases in which the customer accepts the terms and conditions being offered by clicking on an "I agree" message.

common law: Non-statutory law as developed from judicial decisions thereby establishing legal precedents.

comparative negligence: The idea that fault for an accident is allocated based on the percentage of responsibility of at least two parties.

compensatory damages: An award of money designed to put the *plaintiff* in the monetary position he would have been in had the *defendant* fully performed his end of the bargain.

complaint: The reason a *plaintiff* gives for suing a *defendant*. See also *summons*

confession of judgment: A tactic used to either avoid litigation or end litigation before trial in which the debtor admits he has no legal defense against a creditor's claim and acknowledges owing the creditor the monies claimed due.

consequential damages: Special damages that arise from a breach of contract or an accident not directly related to the event but reasonably foreseeable — the cost of renting a vehicle while a damaged car is repaired, for example.

constructive notice: Notice of a legal or factual condition the law determines a *defendant* has either because the issue in question is a matter of public record or in regard to real property because it's so long-standing or obvious that the law presumes the defendant knew or should have known about it.

consumer debt: Financial obligation undertaken by an individual to purchase *personal property* or household goods.

contract: An agreement enforceable in a court of law.

contributory negligence: The legal concept that if the *plaintiff* contributed even one percent to causing an accident, he is barred from recovering any damage.

cosign: The act of signing a document jointly with another person with the intent of assuming the responsibility of performing the obligation set forth in the document.

counterclaim: A claim a *defendant* asserts against a *plaintiff*.

cross-claim: A claim one *defendant* makes against another defendant. Also a claim one *plaintiff* has against another plaintiff.

cross-examination: Questioning of a witness called by the opposing *party* during a trial. See also ***direct examination***

damages: Monetary loss owing to the *defendant's* conduct. See also ***compensatory (actual) damages***, ***nominal damages***, and ***punitive damages***

default: The defendant either fails to appear for a court date or fails to answer the *complaint*. See also ***default judgment***

default judgment: A judgment entered against the defendant if he does not answer a *summons* and *complaint* or fails to appear for a scheduled court date. See also ***default***

defendant: The person being sued.

de minimis: Latin term for *small* or *minimal,* it refers to the situation in which the information or facts presented, although true, have no legal effect on the outcome of the case.

de novo: Latin term for *starting over,* it refers to beginning the case again as if there had not been a prior case.

deposition: A method of *discovery* in which a *party* or witness is put under oath and asked questions by the opposing party's lawyer, while a stenographer is present to record the questions and answers as sworn testimony. The person being questioned has the right to be represented by his own lawyer. The person who gave testimony is then given a printed transcript of the questions and answers to review and to swear to the truth of its contents before a notary public.

direct examination: Questioning of a witness by the *party* who called the witness to testify to help prove the questioning party's case. See also *cross-examination*

discontinued: The condition of a case the *plaintiff* has voluntarily agreed not to pursue or one in which the plaintiff enters into an agreement with the defendant not to go forward. A case may be discontinued with prejudice, which means that the plaintiff can no longer pursue it, or without prejudice, which means that the plaintiff can revive the litigation at some future time. See also *stipulation*

discovery: The process by which each *party* tries to find out more information about the other party's claims in regard to the facts of the case. In small claims cases, discovery generally isn't permitted without the prior consent of a judge.

e-commerce: Business transacted over the Internet.

e-contract: An agreement entered into over the Internet.

e-evidence: Information either electronically recorded or generated by a computer.

e-signature: As defined by the Uniform Electronic Transaction Act, an electronic sound, symbol, or process attached to or logically associated with a record executed or adopted by a person with the intent to sign the record.

equitable remedy: A remedy other than money damages. For the most part, small claims courts only grant money damages and cannot issue equitable remedies.

evidence: The information a *party* needs to prove his case.

exculpatory clause: A clause in a contract in which one *party* seeks to relieve itself of any liability for its own wrongful acts. Courts are reluctant to enforce such clauses.

execution: Process by which a creditor seeks to collect the *judgment* from a debtor.

exemplary damages: See *punitive damages*

fraud: The intentional misstatement of a material fact made with the intent to deceive.

fraud in the execution: A category of fraud in which a *party* thinks he is signing one type of document when in reality the document has a different purpose. Also called *fraud in the inception*.

fraud in the inducement: A type of fraud in which one person makes intentional false statements in order to get another person to sign a contract or buy or sell something.

garnishment: The process by which the *plaintiff* seeks to enforce a judgment against the defendant by having money deducted from the defendant's wages.

general jurisdiction: The power or authority of a court to hear every category of case brought to it.

guarantor: A person who agrees to pay the debt of another only after that person fails to pay. A guarantor cannot be sued until the original debtor fails to pay.

hearsay: A rule of evidence that restricts the type of testimony that can be used at trial.
An out-of-court statement, either written or oral, offered into evidence to prove the truth of a statement.

identity theft: A situation in which a person's personal information such as name, date of birth, and Social Security number are used without that person's consent to either get access to that person's financial resources or to obtain credit in the victim's name for use by the thief.

indemnification agreement: A contract in which one person agrees to compensate or reimburse another person for any losses suffered or expenses incurred.

information subpoena: A document issued by a *judgment creditor* to a *judgment debtor* or to someone who may owe the judgment debtor money in an effort to obtain information about the judgment debtor's assets.

injunction: An *equitable remedy* whereby the *plaintiff* seeks to stop the *defendant* from taking some action. In general, small claims courts can't grant this type of relief.

inquest: The procedure for having a case heard when the *defendant* does not appear for the scheduled trial of the case. The *plaintiff* still has to prove his case.

intentional tort: A civil wrong committed by the defendant against the plaintiff in which the defendant intended the act and either intended the harm or reasonably should have foreseen that harm would occur. Intentional tort cases are rarely brought in small claims court because the amount of money is usually beyond the monetary jurisdiction of the court.

interrogatories: A *discovery* method in which written questions are sent to a person to answer in writing. The recipient must swear to the truth and accuracy of the answers before returning them.

judgment: What the court awards the prevailing *party* in a case. A judgment in the *plaintiff's* favor generally is an award of money.

judgment creditor: The winner of a lawsuit who is owed the amount of money set forth in the judgment by the *judgment debtor.*

judgment debtor: The loser of a lawsuit who owes the *judgment creditor* the amount of money set forth in the *judgment.*

jurisdiction: Power or authority. See also ***general jurisdiction***, ***personal jurisdiction***, and ***subject matter jurisdiction***

laches: An *equitable defense* in which the *defendant* asserts that the *plaintiff* has waited for an unreasonable length of time to bring the lawsuit, thereby making it unfair for the case to be heard. See also ***statute of limitations***

leading question: A question that already contains the answer; the witness just has to answer "yes" or "no."

lease: A contract to transfer the right of possession and use to *real* or *personal property* for a period of time in exchange for rental payments.

legal remedy: A remedy other than an equitable remedy. The awarding of money is the most common legal remedy. Small claims courts deal almost exclusively with the legal remedy of money damages.

lessee: A person getting possession of a *leased* apartment or *personal property.* In real estate situations another term for tenant.

lessor: A person surrendering possession of an apartment or *personal property* in return for money or other consideration. In real estate situations another term for landlord.

liability: Responsibility for an accident or event or for breaching a contract.

lien: An interest created in either *real* or *personal property* that gives the lien holder the right to *foreclose* against the property in the event the debtor fails to pay the obligation. Small claims courts generally don't have the jurisdiction to foreclose a lien.

limited or special jurisdiction: Limitations a legislature sets restricting the type of cases that can be brought in a particular court. Small claims courts are courts of limited jurisdiction.

mediation: A form of *alternate dispute resolution* in which a third party sits down with the *plaintiff* and *defendant,* listens to their respective stories, and tries to get them to resolve their dispute by coming to a mutually acceptable agreement without going before a judge.

mitigation of damages: A *plaintiff's* obligation to take reasonable steps to reduce or minimize the damages caused by a *defendant's* breach of contract.

monetary jurisdiction: A restriction of the ability of certain courts to hear cases in which the amount of money being sued for exceeds a predetermined amount.

mortgage: The security interest — the pledge of the property — a person gives to a lender in order to protect the lender if the borrower fails to repay the money borrowed. It gives the holder of the mortgage the right to proceed against the property directly to have the obligation satisfied. Mortgages can be given in *real property* or in *personal property.* If it involves personal property it's called a chattel mortgage.

motion: A request to the court for some interim legal relief — to take some action at the moment of request rather than have the issue raised or decided at trial.

negligence: A civil wrong in which a person intends the action but doesn't intend or reasonably foresee the harm that results; the failure to act as a reasonable person would have acted in similar circumstances.

nominal damages: An award that acknowledges that harm was done by the *defendant* but that the *plaintiff* suffered no monetary loss or damages.

note: A written promise to pay money to another person on or before a certain date and with a specific amount of interest. It gives the person holding the note the right to seek money damages if the note is not paid.

parol evidence: Oral evidence of negotiations and dealings between the opposing parties during the period prior to entering into a written agreement. It's offered by one *party* to alter or vary the terms of what appears to be a complete written contract.

party: The person or persons on either side of a lawsuit. Generally called the *plaintiff* and the *defendant,* but may also be called the petitioner and respondent. In some small claims courts the party bringing the lawsuit is called the claimant.

personal jurisdiction: The power or authority of a court to require a particular *defendant* to be brought before that court and have that defendant's rights determined.

personal property: All property other than *real property.*

personal service: The act of giving notice to the defendant so the defendant knows why he's being sued. It includes personal delivery, substituted service, conspicuous service, and mail service. See also *service of process*

plaintiff: The person who brings a lawsuit. This person may be called the claimant or the petitioner.

pleadings: Legal papers including *summons* and *complaints,* answers, and replies. Pleadings may also include *motions, affidavits,* and other legal documentation submitted to the court.

power of attorney: A legal document by which one person appoints another to act in his place. The person designated in the power of attorney is called an "attorney-in-fact."

***prima facie* case:** The legal requirement that in order for the *plaintiff* to prevail, he must establish all of the legal elements of his case.

pro bono: Latin term meaning "for the good," a situation in which an attorney intentionally provides legal services without seeking compensation from the client.

pro se: Latin term meaning "for himself" or "in his own behalf," a situation in which a *party* to a lawsuit appears without counsel and represents himself or herself during legal proceedings. Small claims court is designed for *pro se* litigants. The term is being replaced by the phrase "self-represented."

punitive damages: Damages designed to punish the *defendant* because the law finds the defendant's conduct to be unacceptable, outrageous, and beyond certain legally acceptable standards.

quantum meruit: Latin term meaning "as much as he deserves," the concept that allows a person providing services without a contract to recover the fair and reasonable value of those services. Otherwise, the person receiving the services would get a benefit and be unjustly enriched.

real property: Land and everything attached to it including buildings, improvements, and plants.

recuse: The determination that a judge will not participate in the trial and decide a case, made either at the request of a litigant or by a voluntary withdrawal by the judge.

remedy: The relief given a *party* to compensate him for a violation of his rights by another.

replevin: The *remedy* in which the *plaintiff* is suing to compel the *defendant* to return some item of personal property. Because the plaintiff is not seeking money but the return of specific property it's considered an *equitable remedy* and not a *legal remedy*.

reply: A legal response to a *counterclaim* or *cross-claim*.

respondeat superior: Latin term meaning "let the master answer," it applies to a situation in which a *plaintiff* sues an employer when the plaintiff was injured by an employee acting within the course and the scope of the employee's employment. The law does not permit the employer to escape responsibility in that situation.

restraining notice: A method of enforcing a monetary *judgment,* it's a legal document issued by the court or by a sheriff or marshal to a bank where the *defendant* has money, seeking to have the money paid to the plaintiff to satisfy the judgment.

scienter: Latin word for "knowingly," it's the knowledge or intent necessary for a fraud claim. If the *defendant* lacks scienter, then the *plaintiff* may pursue only a *negligence* claim.

scope of employment: The standard applied to hold an employer responsible for the actions of an employee while on the job. See also ***respondeat superior***

service of process: The method used to give notice of a lawsuit to the *defendant.* See also ***complaint***, ***personal service***, and ***summons***

service by mail: A type of *service of process* in which the *summons* and *complaint* is mailed to the *defendant.* The defendant returns an acknowledgement of receipt. The most common method used in small claims court to give notice to a defendant.

shrink-wrap agreement: A *contract* inside the box in which goods are packaged.

so ordered stipulation: An agreement in which parties agree to resolve their dispute, with the added protection of having the agreement reviewed by a judge and made an order of the court.

sovereign immunity: A legal defense that prevents citizens from suing the government. In general, federal, state, and local governments cannot be sued unless they pass laws allowing themselves to be sued and thereby waive a defense of sovereign immunity.

standing to sue: The legal idea that an individual must have a sufficient stake (standing) in the controversy or dispute so that it is fair for them to bring a lawsuit.

statute of frauds: A classification referring to certain contracts that must be in writing to be enforceable. Each state has its own list of the kinds of agreements covered.

statute of limitations: A law that sets a time limit to bring a lawsuit. The statute of limitations to bring a particular type of lawsuit varies from state to state.

stipulation: A contract in which the *parties* resolve their dispute and reduce it to writing. If one of the parties fails to live up to the agreement, the non-defaulting *party* may enforce the terms of the stipulation.

subject matter jurisdiction: The power or authority of the court to hear a particular type of case. Not every court can hear every type of case.

subpoena: A document that compels a person to come in and testify or to bring certain documents and records to the court.

summons: The document that notifies a person that he is being sued. It contains the name of the *plaintiff(s)* and *defendant(s),* the court the case is being brought in, and when and where to physically appear and/or answer. See also ***complaint***

surety: A person who co-signs a note and agrees to be directly or primarily liable to pay the creditor.

tort: A civil wrong other than breach of contract. An action may be both a tort and a crime. See also ***intentional torts*** and ***negligence***

usury: Charging an excessive rate of interest. Each state has its own usury rate.

venue: The place a case may be brought. Venue usually can be set where the *defendant* resides or conducts business, where the plaintiff resides or conducts business, or where the transaction or incident arose. Small claims courts may have specific venue rules.

Index

● *Q* ●